THE THIRTEEN PRINCIPLES of FAITH

THE THIRTEEN PRINCIPLES of FAITH

A Chasidic Viewpoint

Noson Gurary

compiled and edited by
Moshe Miller

JASON ARONSON INC.
Northvale, New Jersey
London

This book was set in 12 pt. Berkeley Oldstyle.

Copyright © 1996 Noson Gurary

10 9 8 7 6 5 4 3 2 1

All rights reserved. Printed in the United States of America. No part of this book may be used or reproduced in any manner whatsoever without written permission from Jason Aronson Inc. except in the case of brief quotations in reviews for inclusion in a magazine, newspaper, or broadcast.

Library of Congress Cataloging-in-Publication Data
Gurary, Natan (Guraryeh)
    The thirteen principles of faith : a chasidic viewpoint / by Noson Gurary; compiled and edited by Moshe Miller.
       p. cm.
    Includes bibliographical references and index.
    ISBN 1-56821-532-0 (alk. paper)
    1. Thirteen articles of faith (Judaism)   2. Judaism—Doctrines.
3. Habad.   4. Hasidism.   I. Miller, Moshe.   II. Title.
BM607.G87   1996
296.3—dc20   95-36646

Manufactured in the United States of America. Jason Aronson Inc. offers books and cassettes. For information and catalog write to Jason Aronson Inc., 230 Livingston Street, Northvale, New Jersey 07647.

This book is dedicated to the Lubavitcher Rebbe, Rabbi Menachem M. Schneerson, whose willingness to share his extraordinary vision and achievements inspired this book, and whose personal example continues to motivate the attainment of all the goals and ideals contained within its pages.

TO
MRS. SARAH KOREIN

Rabbi Israel Bael Shem Tov teaches us that our Hebrew name is our true essence. The name Sarah is associated with the attributes of nobility, refinement, and kindness. The first Sarah was a role model exemplifying these attributes.

In your case, Sarah, you are a role model for this generation. Your friendship and your attributes are a true inspiration to me.

Contents

Introduction   xiii

FAITH   1

    A Matter of Faith, 1
    Faith and Experience, 1
    The Role of *Mitzvahs*, 4
    Faith and Self-Sacrifice, 5
    Faith and Reason, 9
    Faith as a Commandment, 10
    Reason and God's Will, 15
    Faith and Trust, 18
    Trust and Positive Thinking, 20
    Faith and Life, 21
    The Intellect Enhances Faith, 23

THE FIRST PRINCIPLE   27

    The Nature of His Existence, 27
    Continuous Creation, 29

Creation and the Sabbath, 33
Time, 36
Planes of Reality, 37
Why *This* World?, 39
The Role of Man, 42

THE SECOND PRINCIPLE 47

The Finite from the Infinite, 47
The Oneness of God, 50
Duality and Oneness, 52
Being and Nothingness, 54
Being and True Being, 58
The Human Ego and the Unity of God, 61
He Alone Is Our God, 62

THE THIRD PRINCIPLE 69

Human Terms for God, 69
A Deeper Explanation, 71
Time and Change, 72
Two Systems, 74

THE FOURTH PRINCIPLE 79

Time and Space, 80
Time in the Spiritual Worlds, 82
Above and Below, 83
The First Cause, 85
First and Last, 87

THE FIFTH PRINCIPLE 93

Prayer and Human Needs, 93
Prayer as Service of the Heart, 95

Meditation, 96
To God Alone, 98
Prayer as Bonding, 100
Revealing Divine Attributes, 102
Is Prayer a Commandment?, 104
Prayer and Blessing, 106
A Substitute for Sacrifices, 108

THE SIXTH PRINCIPLE 113

Belief in the Prophets Is Belief in God, 113
The Prophetic Experience, 115
Prophets and Sages, 117
Preconditions for Prophecy, 117

THE SEVENTH PRINCIPLE 121

Moshe (Moses) and the Other Prophets, 122
The Stature of Moshe's Prophecy, 122
Levels of Prophecy, 124
Moshe as the Mediator, 126

THE EIGHTH PRINCIPLE 131

God within the Torah, and
  the Torah within God, 132
Torah and the Jewish People, 136
Divergent Torah Views, 138
The Torah of Moses, 141
The Torah, 142

THE NINTH PRINCIPLE 145

Can God Change the Torah?, 145
The Immutability of Torah, 149

The Messianic Era and the World to Come, 150
Conclusion, 151

THE TENTH PRINCIPLE — 157

A Matter of Divine Providence, 157
Revealed and Hidden Providence, 159
Levels of Divine Providence, 161
Part of God Above, 163
Concealed Providence, 165
How Does God Know?, 166
God's Foreknowledge and Man's Free Choice, 168
Knowledge and Existence, 170
Two Realities, 172

THE ELEVENTH PRINCIPLE — 177

Man's Place in the Universe, 178
Two Types of Reward, 179
Paradise and the World to Come, 184
God's "Home," 186
Torah and *Mitzvahs*, 188
Punishments in the Torah, 189
The Physical World, 192
Revealing the Essence, 195

THE TWELFTH PRINCIPLE — 201

The Ultimate Goal, 202
Concealment and Revelation of Godliness, 205
Achieving Perfection, 207
The Soul of *Mashiach* (The Messiah), 208
"Self-Realization," 211

Contents

THE THIRTEENTH PRINCIPLE 215

A Matter of Life and Death, 216
The Purpose of Creation, 218
Reward and the Ultimate Purpose, 220
The Equality of Spiritual and Physical, 223
The Superiority of the Material World, 226
Body and Soul, 229
The Ultimate Reward, 231
Beyond the Torah?, 232
Conclusion, 233

Index 237

Introduction

MAIMONIDES

Maimonides, Rabbi Moshe ben Maimon, best known by the acronym Rambam, was born in the city of Cordoba, Spain, on a Sabbath afternoon on the day before Passover, 14 *Nissan* 4895 in the Jewish calendar, or March 30, 1135. Due to Islamic persecution, his family fled Cordoba when Maimonides was only thirteen years old, and after wandering from city to city in Spain, seeking a haven where Jews could remain faithful to their religion, they eventually moved to Fez, Morocco, in 1160. In the year 1158, during the years of exile and wandering, Maimonides began writing his *Commentary on the Mishnah*, one of his earliest major works. In an interesting autobiographical note at the end of his *Commentary on the Mishnah*, Maimonides informs us that he completed the task some seven years later, at the age of thirty, in Egypt.

THE THIRTEEN PRINCIPLES

The thirteen principles, which Maimonides described as the root and foundation of the Jewish religion, first appeared in his *Commentary on the Mishnah* as an introduction to the final chapter of the tractate *Sanhedrin*. They were subsequently abbreviated, possibly by the Rambam himself,[1] and were later appended to many versions of the daily prayer book. To this day, they constitute one of the clearest statements of Jewish belief ever written.

Why were only these thirteen principles chosen as expressing the fundamental creed of the Jewish religion? Surely there are many other matters that are essential, and yet these are not described as principles of the faith. One of the answers is that although there are many matters of faith to which a Jew ascribes, these thirteen define the essence of Judaism. In other words, if a person does not believe in one or more of these thirteen principles, even though he believes in everything else written in Scripture and rabbinical literature, he is considered an apostate. He may believe in God, and he may even wish to follow all of the commandments. But if he does not believe in even one of the thirteen principles, he is missing the foundation of Judaism.

Furthermore, the thirteen principles are not to be understood as a thirteen-point dogma but rather as matters pertaining to reason and knowledge. Indeed, this is the approach that Maimonides takes in his monumental *Mishneh Torah*; he identifies "the most fundamental of principles, and the pillar of all wisdom" as knowing that God exists.[2]

The first part of this work discusses why each of the thirteen principles, as found in most prayer books, begins with the words, "I believe with complete faith. . . ." What is meant by faith? And what part do reason and understanding play in the thirteen principles?

THE THIRTEEN PRINCIPLES IN *CHASIDUS*

After Maimonides completes his exposition of the thirteen principles, he instructs us to review them again and again, and to meditate upon them deeply. Manifold works have been written about the thirteen principles, analyzing them, explaining them, and showing how they apply to our daily lives.

In chasidic literature (or *Chasidus*) too, the thirteen principles have received a scholarly and methodical analysis. The present work has been based on the teachings and writings of several of the most prominent chasidic masters, notably those of the *Chabad-Lubavitch* dynasty. Each principle is treated as a meditation, a soul-illuminating insight into the very depths of our being, the nature of God, and His teachings, the Torah. In this sense the work before the reader is less of an exposition of the thirteen principles, and more of an expedition into them.

In a general sense, Chasidus views each of the thirteen principles as forming a whole. Each principle is treated as an integral part of all the others. Thus, if one of the principles is ignored, or misunderstood, all the others suffer as a result. Moreover, the principles follow a specific order since each idea is a basis for the one that follows, and each subsequent principle reveals and develops a further facet of the essence of Jewish belief; or, in chasidic terminology, each succeeding principle describes a further revelation of godliness.

However, this is not all. Chasidic philosophy views all of Torah as a manifestation of God Himself. Thus the thirteen principles are not merely a descriptive or philosophical statement of lofty Jewish ideals. Their intention is experiential—they are intended to be an encounter with ourselves, with the axioms upon which we base our lives (and not only our religious lives, but the very nitty gritty of our daily existence), with the wisdom of God, and ultimately, as a happy encounter with God Himself.

NOTES

1. See *Baruch She-amar* prayer book, p. 202, s.v. אני מאמין.
2. *Code, Yesodei HaTorah* 1:1.

Faith

A MATTER OF FAITH

Each of the thirteen principles of Jewish faith, as printed in most prayer books,[1] begins with the declaration, "I believe with complete faith...." What makes something a fundamental principle of Jewish faith? Why are only these thirteen principles considered the fundamental principles of our faith? In order to answer these questions, we must first understand what faith is, how faith is attained, and what effect it has on our daily life.

FAITH AND EXPERIENCE

Chasidic teachings[2] explain that the faith of the Jew stems from the fact that the soul experienced godliness prior to its descent into this physical world. God sends the soul down into a physical body where the soul no longer sees or experiences the same godly revelations.[3] But since the soul has already had direct experience of God, an indelible impression of this experience remains as the feeling of faith in God. Accordingly, it is innate in every Jewish soul, because every Jewish soul experienced God firsthand.[4]

There is nothing in the world that could change your mind or weaken your faith in what you yourself experienced directly. So not only is such faith not blind, as those who challenge or ridicule our faith would claim, but the experience of the soul having "seen" God cannot be denied or dismissed. Thus, Jewish belief is based on a personal, true, and heavenly vision.

However, an even more profound concept is contained within this idea. The soul's experience of godliness prior to its descent into this world was revealed to that soul by God and not accomplished through its own efforts.[5] This is a subtle but profound distinction. We are all finite creatures. The soul is also finite, even the highest and most sublime soul.[6] The understanding and realization of God that the soul can achieve as the result of her own efforts is finite and limited. But since this revelation comes from God Himself (i.e., He reveals Himself to the soul, rather than the soul achieving a revelation of God as a result of its own efforts) this revelation is without limitations or restrictions of any kind, since God has no limitations or restrictions.[7]

Accordingly, we see that Jewish faith is not based simply on a revelation of God but on an infinite revelation of God. This is of profound significance, because it means that every Jewish soul that comes into this world has been illuminated with divine revelation.

And once the soul begins to tap into this inherent divine revelation, there are no limitations as to the level it can achieve, because inherent in the soul is a revelation that is infinite!

It follows that anything that appears to be a limitation of the soul is only an illusion and that there is really no such thing as a limited soul.

Another idea we deduce from this is that belief or faith is not merely something that a Jewish person takes an active role in but that faith in God is a description of the essential nature of the soul itself. Active belief in God is actually only the second aspect of the Jew's faith. The first and primary aspect is that faith is the essence of the Jew (the Jewish soul).

We can now understand that it is impossible for a Jewish soul not to have this belief in God. The Jew's faith is not necessarily based on having heard or learned anything about God and has nothing to do with the person's observance of the *mitzvahs*. A Jew's essential faith has to do with its original experience of God—the experience that was granted to every soul by God Himself.

This, then, is the foremost characteristic of the Jewish soul: that God Himself revealed Himself to the soul. Hence, if a person lacks faith, he does not believe in God, or if he lacks any feeling or interest in matters of Jewish faith, it merely pertains to the second aspect of faith: active belief in God. However, as regards the first and primary aspect of faith, which is inherent in every Jewish soul, and is its most fundamental characteristic, every Jew shares the same experience of God and bears the same memories of its experience.[8]

Chasidic teachings reveal that there is another explanation of faith in God. The first Rebbe of the *Chabad-Lubavitch* chasidic dynasty, the Alter Rebbe, Rabbi Shneur Zalman of Liadi, author of *Tanya* and *Shulchan Aruch HaRav*, taught that the essence of a Jew is not only that he does not *want* to part from God but that he *cannot* be separated from God.[9] In these few concise words, the Alter Rebbe defines the essence of the Jewish soul, which is its attachment to God. This attachment is so intrinsic that it is impossible for the soul to ever detach itself from God, for it is one with God.

We can now return to the main theme of our discussion—the declaration, "I believe with complete faith. . . ." According to the above, this declaration is not merely paying lip service to religion. As regards a person's soul, this declaration is very real, for belief in God is part of the inherent nature of the Jewish soul, because the soul experienced a revelation of God prior to its descent into this world. Furthermore, and this is the primary reason, the essence of the Jewish soul is its attachment to God.[10]

THE ROLE OF *MITZVAHS*

What then is the role of the 613 divine precepts (the *mitzvahs*)? By doing the *mitzvahs*, we actively attach ourselves to God (the second aspect of our faith in God). The Hebrew word *mitzvah* comes from the root word meaning attachment, or bonding. Sin, on the other hand, implies separation and alienation from God, which, for the soul, is an impossibility. The soul wants nothing but to be close to God and does not want to be separated from God in any way, as we mentioned earlier, in the name of the Alter Rebbe.

A person's wish to do or not do something is not always an expression of his essential self; it does not necessarily reflect his very being. However, as regards the soul's desire to be attached to God, the Alter Rebbe declares that this is not merely a decision of the soul, or the will of the soul, but that this is the essence of the soul.[11]

Human beings want to live. There is nothing dearer to us than life. Yet, no one would say that we are making an active decision to be alive. The same is true of the soul and her attachment to God. It is not a decision that the soul makes. No other choice exists, for this is the soul's essence.

All this stems from the fact that the soul is really part of God Himself.[12] And because it is part of God, it is one with God. The soul knows God because it is part of Him. This knowledge is inherent in the soul. And this is the explanation of faith and belief as found in chasidic teachings.

According to our first explanation of the nature of faith—that faith in God is the result of a revelation of God to the soul—it follows that there are essentially two entities: the soul, and the revelation that is granted to her by God. It implies an I-and-Thou relationship. But according to our second explanation, faith is not merely the result of a divine revelation. Rather, it is an inherent aspect of the essence of the soul itself. Hence, every Jewish person has this attachment, for his very being is to be one with God. If someone says, "I do not feel it; I do not have this belief; I am lacking faith," he is simply mistaken, because every Jew is attached to God.

This definition of faith is very different from that presented by non-Jewish religions and philosophies. As far as Judaism is concerned, faith is essential to our being, the result of an infinite revelation and the soul's inner attachment to God, regardless of our level of awareness of it. However, faith in God as defined by others is the result of awareness of God, a product of understanding and active involvement. This is what brings a person to faith, according to the latter definition, and therefore, without understanding and active involvement, it cannot be said that one has faith.

FAITH AND SELF-SACRIFICE

With this as a preface, we can now understand the true meaning of self-sacrifice, which is also an essential aspect of the nature of the soul.[13] Simple observation tells us that there are many kinds of self-sacrifice. People give up their lives for their country, or for an ideal, or a principle, or another person. There are even people who care so little about their lives that they give up their lives for worthless pursuits. But when a Jew gives up his life for God, this is not self-sacrifice for gain, not for an ideal, not for any reward, but because he cannot possibly carry on living without being connected to God. Any other way would be contrary to the essence of his being. This is in contrast to giving up one's life for a country, however ideological and altruistic the person's motives, for the latter is merely an exchange. The person is exchanging his life for the gain of his country. And the same applies to an ideal or a political position. Here again, life is exchanged for gain, even if the gain is an ideal or a philosophy. There is the motive of gain, albeit of the noblest sort. And therefore, although one may be sacrificing oneself, it is nevertheless not what we refer to as self-sacrifice.

Rather, the true definition of self-sacrifice is to give up one's life with no motivation of gain but as the result of pure *emunah*—faith in God. The soul cannot depart from God. Since the soul is one with God, the act of self-sacrifice is not based on reason or circumstances (although, to be sure, we are commanded to surrender our lives under certain circumstances[14]).

We can now understand the view expressed in chasidic teachings concerning a person's doubts about his faith in God. There are, of course, many different approaches as to what to do to solve this spiritual problem. But chasidic teachings have a truly unique insight in this matter, teaching that a person should completely ignore the doubts that arise in his mind, realizing that the soul itself has no doubts. The soul is absolutely certain of the existence of God because it experienced God and is one with God. If there are doubts, they do not arise from the godly soul.

From where then do these doubts come? Chasidic teachings explain that the Jew possesses two souls: a godly soul and an animal, or natural soul.[15] The animal soul is by nature in a constant struggle with the godly soul, trying to overpower it and became the primary, or even exclusive, source of a person's motivations.[16] All doubts about God come from the animal soul. When a person has doubts, they are a clear sign that he must strengthen his godly soul in its struggle with the animal soul. As he strengthens the godly soul, he will begin to feel what the godly soul feels, faith in God. Therefore, doubts are no cause for concern, for they have nothing to do with the godly soul. They are merely an indication that the animal soul is presently prevailing over the godly soul and must be tamed. We would certainly have cause to be concerned if we had only one soul, for then the same soul that has faith in God at times may also lack faith in God and have doubts. This would indicate that the soul is weak or in trouble. But since there are two souls, and the godly soul is always aware of God and strong in its faith in God (as the result of its own experience and essential nature), a Jew never has to worry about lack of faith. It is always there, although it may be temporarily concealed.

This being the case, how is it that we find people who believe in God, claim to have faith, and yet do things that contradict this belief? This problem is something every individual faces. We live with contradictions of this sort. On one hand we are certain that God exists. Yet we do things contrary to the belief in God's existence. This inconsistency has been discussed in the Talmud. The Talmud[17] offers the example of a thief who stands at the threshold of the house he is about to break into and offers a prayer to God for success in his quest. He knows that God forbids him to steal. Yet he prays to God that he should not get caught stealing and that God should actually help him. What could be a greater contradiction than this?

We can understand the paradox here by realizing just how esoteric our faith in God really is. Since faith stems from our essence, it may remain esoteric, and it is possible that this esoteric faith is not translated into our daily life. One of the main tasks of a person in this world is to apply this faith to daily life.

Revealing this esoteric faith, which is the soul's attachment to God, in our daily lives, should be done in a most practical, albeit inward, way. This is one of the functions of a Rebbe, the revered leader of a chasidic dynasty. Our tradition teaches[18] that in each and every generation, there exists a Jewish spiritual leader who is an extension of the soul of Moses, who nourished the faith of the entire Jewish people. This is what a Rebbe does; he translates the faith that is innate in the soul of every Jew into practical terms for the members of his generation.

The intention, however, is not that the Rebbe does what is incumbent upon you to do. On the contrary, chasidic teachings demand that a person must make his own efforts to apply his innate faith to his daily life by contemplating the greatness of God in order to understand whatever may be understood by the human mind. The effort expended in trying to understand reveals his innate belief, making it permeate his daily life. This is because the intellect is a bridge between the esoteric world and this physical plane of existence. The Rebbe, however, delineates the methods by which this faith can be revealed.

Accordingly, the declaration "I believe with complete faith . . ." is not meant to be a mere statement of our innate belief in God. Rather, it is also meant as a declaration to actively cultivate this faith so that it permeates our daily lives. In order to do this, however, we must use our intellectual powers.

FAITH AND REASON

It is common knowledge that when a person has an experience that cannot be understood or explained, it remains cryptic, even to himself. But when the experience is defined and explained, it becomes more tangible to the person himself, as well as to others. This is one of the reasons why it is essential to contemplate the greatness of God. Through this, one is able to bridge the gap between faith and awareness and thus have an effect on one's daily life. This also answers the question, "If someone has strong faith with no doubts, is there any need for him to study and understand?" The answer is a resounding "yes," because even with wholehearted faith, study and meditation are essential to connect faith to reality and to resolve the discrepancy between this physical world and the spiritual esoteric nature of the soul.[19]

As we now can appreciate, the Jew's faith is expected to be tempered by reason. Besides the need to use the intellect to bring faith into practical understanding, if a person had so-called "blind" faith, having failed to use his intellect, then one of the greatest gifts given to man by God, intellect, would not be involved in the service of God. The person's belief and actions would be involved in serving God, but his intellect, and consequently his emotions, would be detached from God, since the latter are born of the intellect.[20]

If God created us with intellect and emotion, it is because He wants them to become vessels for godliness. It is His desire that they be utilized in serving Him. The only way this is possible is by trying to understand as much about God as is humanly possible. Not until a person's intellect is convinced about the greatness of God can he be said to be intellectually involved in serving Him. And when he becomes intellectually convinced of the greatness of God to such an extent that it affects his emotions and ultimately his actions, he will be serving God with every part of his soul and body.

FAITH AS A COMMANDMENT

According to our two explanations of faith in God—one, that it is the product of the soul's experience and two, that faith is the essential nature of the soul—the question arises as to why belief is counted as one of the *mitzvahs*. If faith in God is the essence of who we are, then why do we have to be commanded to be who we are? Furthermore, what exactly is the *mitzvah* to believe in God? Briefly, the answer is that if God's existence is something we can prove to ourselves, then we must prove it.

Maimonides begins his great code, the *Mishneh Torah*, by stating that we are able to prove God's existence. Moreover, the knowledge of God's existence is the most fundamental of all principles and the pillar of all wisdom.[21] Furthermore, we can prove it logically. This means that if a person believes in God but cannot prove to himself that God exists, then he is lacking a fundamental *mitzvah* of the Torah, or, at the very least, we are lacking a vital aspect of the *mitzvah*. We see from this that Judaism does not fear that a person will search and meditate and perhaps come to the wrong conclusions. Therefore, the Torah challenges us, and even commands us, to understand and prove God's existence logically.

Of course, the opposite question can also be raised: "If I can prove that God exists, then what need is there to believe in God? Of what value is belief when there is proof?" This question is really twofold. First, if we are born with essential belief, why do we need to be commanded to believe? Second, why do we need to believe when we can and must prove God's existence with logic? Similarly, one may ask, "How can we be commanded to believe at all? Is belief something that can come as a result of a directive?" To acknowledge such a directive presupposes acceptance of a Commander whose directives you follow. Otherwise, the commandment is also not believed or accepted.²²

To understand this, we must first clarify the nature of the innate faith of the soul (resulting either from impressions of what the soul saw and experienced prior to its descent into this world or because of the soul's inherent oneness with God). What exactly is the nature of this belief? God cannot be defined in any way. Even by calling Him the Creator or by referring to Him as infinite, or omnipotent, or whatever distinction or title we use, He is not limited by any of the qualities ascribed to Him. All qualities and titles, though they be true, are only a function of our limited perspective, because of the way we understand things.

To state that He transcends all titles is a limitation. To state that He cannot be compared to anything is still a limitation, categorizing Him in our terms of understanding of existence. The truth is that we have no words or descriptions at all for God. This ineffable existence of God, without form or title, is what is known to the soul prior to its descent into a body in this world. It is a belief based solely on the soul's direct experience of God, who has no form or title. In this sense, belief is far superior to intellect, for it is based on experience of the way God really is, experience of His essence, rather than on what is revealed to the mind.

But what comes next? What is a Jewish person supposed to do with the belief he or she is born with? Maimonides explains that the most fundamental principle of all, and the pillar of wisdom, is to meditate on the greatness of God as much as is humanly possible.[23] God's existence, that He is a Creator, and that everything is dependent on Him, can be proven and therefore must be proven. This is a commandment that every Jewish person is obligated to fulfill. It is a *mitzvah* for every Jewish person to exert himself to understand as much as he can.

And what about the realms that are higher than logic and do not operate according to the rules of logic? How does one deal with those levels? Yes, there is a *mitzvah* to believe certain matters that are higher than understanding. But the process that leads to the fulfillment of the *mitzvah* of belief begins with the attempt to intellectually understand as much as possible. Then afterward comes the belief that God is much more than can be understood by the human mind.

With this preface, we can now answer the questions that were asked above. The question, "If a Jew believes already, why does he need a commandment to believe?" can be answered in the following manner: there is no activity associated with our inborn belief. We do nothing to accomplish that belief. It is simply inborn. But only when we exert ourselves in study and meditation in order to understand the greatness of God as much as is humanly possible, and believe in that which our human intellect cannot grasp, only then have we fulfilled the *mitzvah* of belief. That is to say, an intrinsic part of the *mitzvah* of belief in God is to understand as much as we can, then transcend understanding through belief.

The question, "If one can prove God's existence, why is there a need to believe?" can be answered as follows: the belief we are talking about does not concern the knowledge of God's existence that a person can prove. It is belief that God's existence transcends that which can be proved intellectually. Belief in this sense is not really belief in His existence as such but in the nature of His existence. That He exists can be proved logically. But the nature of God's existence is grasped only by belief, which transcends understanding.

The question, "How can belief be commanded? Either a person believes or does not believe," can be answered in a similar way: the *mitzvah* is comprised of two stages—the effort to understand as much as possible, and then to believe that God transcends understanding. This is obviously not something that a person is born with. It is something that must be worked at, requiring intellectual effort as a preface to belief. Accordingly, the question, "Since fulfilling a commandment presupposes belief in a Commander, how can there be a commandment to believe? It is a contraction of terms," is also answered, since we are not talking about belief in God's existence here. A *mitzvah* is something we must *do*. Since the belief required comes about as a result of the prior exercise of intellect, it should be counted as a *mitzvah*.

From the foregoing, however, it is apparent that the belief that a Jew is born with is a far higher order than the belief that follows understanding. The former has no stages or levels and is equal in every soul. It is infinite, as it stems from God's revelation to the soul, whereas the belief that we acquire after understanding can never be infinite, for it is the result of human endeavor and logic, even though it transcends understanding and logic. Nevertheless, faith gained through understanding is superior to the infinite faith that is inborn, for this was a result of a man's own efforts.

In the faith that follows understanding and logic, there are various levels. Every day a person can grow in his belief. If he understands more today than he did yesterday, he has grown. What he believed yesterday, he can prove to himself today. Thus, faith becomes knowledge. And, by definition, his faith today is higher than it was yesterday.

With regard to this faith, no two people are alike. Even Moses, who experienced a direct vision of God and learned the entire Torah from God, had a limit to his understanding. Therefore his faith transcended his understanding.[24] So with regard to the *mitzvah* of faith, no two Jewish people are alike. From this, we can understand why even a person who pursues his belief and not his intellect needs to study and prove that there is a Creator. We can also understand why even a person with knowledge of the existence of God needs to believe. If a person's relationship with God is only one of belief, he does not serve God with his intellect. Conversely, if a person served God only through knowledge and understanding, he would be limited to what he is able to understand, which is very little indeed. This is the meaning of the adage[25] that the highest form of knowledge is to know that you cannot understand God.

One might ask another, perhaps simplistic, question: "Why do I need to understand to realize that I cannot ultimately understand? I will accept at the outset that I cannot understand. I will have blind faith." The answer is that when one understands that God cannot be understood, then one appreciates even intellectually that God transcends logic. Although one cannot define exactly what it is that one cannot understand, one senses with one's mind that there exists something that cannot be understood. This is the advantage of study. Since the nature of knowledge is that it is internalized and becomes part of us, the awareness that there is something beyond logic becomes part of our reality. We have made the belief that follows understanding part of our knowledge.

REASON AND GOD'S WILL

The *mitzvahs* of the Torah are divided into three categories: judgments (*mishpatim*), testimonies (*eidut*), and precepts (*chukim*).[26] The first category, judgments, are logical. Had we not been given the Torah, we still could have figured them out on our own. These are typified by commandments such as the prohibition of murder and theft or the commandment to honor one's father and mother. Testimonies demonstrate their value. We would not have derived them ourselves, but once performed, they prove their merit. Observing the Sabbath might never have deduced by human reason, but once experienced, its benefits are readily understood. Testimonies also serve as "witnesses" for God. The Sabbath is, again, a prime example, for it testifies that God created the world and rested from His acts of creation. Wearing *tefillin* (phylacteries) is another example, testifying that God placed His Name upon us. The third category, precepts, are laws that are beyond logic and often defy logic. Prime examples are the prohibition of wearing a garment that is a mixture of linen and wool. The laws of *kashrus* are also precepts. There is no understandable reason why a fish with fins and scales is permissible as food, but any species lacking either fins or scales is forbidden. The human mind cannot fathom the purpose of these *mitzvahs* at all.

One might ask, "Why should the *mitzvahs* be divided into three categories?" A *mitzvah* means God's will. All *mitzvahs* are commanded by God, meaning they are all His will. So why should any of them be logical? Inasmuch as God is not bound by logic, why should any of the *mitzvahs* be logical?

At first glance, it seems proper for all *mitzvahs* to be superrational. Since they originate in God's will, there is no reason at all that man should understand them. This is not to

Basis for mitzvah — it is God's will — period

say that the reason is so deep that we do not know what it is, but that it is not based on reason at all.[27]

If this is so, how does one understand the concept of a "rational" *mitzvah*? If it originates from God, who is beyond reason, how does the *mitzvah* then acquire a rational explanation? The Torah itself often gives reasons for certain *mitzvahs*. However, even where the Torah itself gives a reason for the *mitzvah*, this cannot be considered the origin of the *mitzvah*. Every *mitzvah*, even the most logical, is rooted in a source far beyond all reason or logic. All *mitzvahs*, the rational as well as the superrational, are rooted in God's Infinite Will, and transcend human reason to a degree unfathomable by our minds. The fact that certain *mitzvahs* can be understood merely means that they can also be understood. But this understanding has nothing at all to do with why we fulfill the *mitzvah*.[28] The basis for the *mitzvah* is that it is God's will. For example, the Torah commands us to observe the *Shabbat* because God created the world in six days and rested on the seventh.[29] Therefore, the Torah tells us, by resting on *Shabbat* we remember that God is the Creator. However, this is not the reason for resting on *Shabbat*. The essence of the law is far beyond that. When the law enters the realm of logic, it functions satisfactorily on that level as well.

Why then do some *mitzvahs* operate within the realm of reason at all? If every *mitzvah* really transcends reason, then why do we have to attempt to absorb its rational, intellectual dimension as well? It would be simpler to do the *mitzvahs* because they are God's will.

However, Judaism rejects the notion of faith completely devoid of reason because it wants our intellect and emotions involved in the fulfillment of God's will. If we were to perform the *mitzvahs* because of faith alone, the intellect would declare, "I cannot comprehend this. It is not relevant to me."

Our emotions would say, "I cannot feel this. It is not relevant to me." Even though the essence of the *mitzvah* is incomprehensible, the Torah wants some of the *mitzvahs* to be brought down to the level of logic so that a person can utilize his intellect and emotion in their fulfillment. Without the *mitzvah* of understanding God, belief in God would be devoid of intellect and emotion. And just as we said earlier, that belief had to be lowered to the level of logic in order to involve logic in a person's divine service, so too the commandments were brought down to the level of logic in order to involve logic.

There is yet another benefit to the commandments having a logical dimension. Logic is accessible, having an inner effect on the person. Belief, by contrast, is transcendent and esoteric, affecting the person more indirectly. By functioning in the realm of logic, the commandments allow a person to experience them even though they are beyond logic. Suddenly, the person can relate them to his own personality or situation in life, or to whatever frame of reference he wishes to apply them. In the same way that a person should strive to transform his esoteric beliefs into part of his daily experience, so too with the commandments; their rational aspect makes it easier to identify with them and relate them to everyday situations.

This personal identification with the commandments illuminates an understanding of the verse in the Book of Exodus (6:3), in which God spoke to Moses and said, "I revealed Myself to Abraham, Isaac, and Jacob by the name of Almighty. But I was not known to them by My Explicit Name" (the Ineffable Four-letter Name, or *Tetragrammaton*). A careful examination of earlier Torah verses in Genesis, in which God did appear to Abraham, Isaac, and Jacob will reveal that He did, indeed, disclose this Name to them.[30] However, there is no contradiction here. Chasidic teachings explain that there are two levels of God's Ineffable Four-letter Name. The lower level of God's Name transcends human intellect, but it is nevertheless the product of striving to understand, as explained earlier. This was revealed to the Patriarchs, who managed to achieve the maximum of human understanding and then transcended it through their belief in God, Who cannot ultimately be apprehended by the intellect.[31]

The higher form of the Four-letter Name of God, however, was not revealed to Abraham, Isaac, and Jacob. This is the Name as it relates to the pure belief innate in the soul, as we explained earlier. This is belief in God the way God is in His Essence. This was not revealed to the world, not even to the Patriarchs, before the Torah was given to the Jewish people on Mount Sinai. God's revelation at Mount Sinai (and subsequently as well) was this higher form of the Four-letter Name: God as He really is, infinitely removed from man's striving to understand. This level was first revealed by God to Moses and later at Mount Sinai.[32]

FAITH AND TRUST

All these ideas focus on belief as it is in the abstract, indicated by the Hebrew word *emunah*, faith. But there is a higher level than *emunah*, and this is *bitachon*, trust. It is possible to have faith in God but to lack trust. But it is not possible for a person to trust in God without having active faith.

What is the difference between faith and trust? As mentioned above, faith in God comes after understanding and after concluding that God is beyond understanding. In the realm of action, this means that a person believes that everything comes from God and accepts his lot, be it good or not so good, because it comes from God. If it is from God, it must be good, even if it does not necessarily appear that way.[33]

However, trust in God indicates confidence that God will grant only revealed goodness to him (i.e., that which appears good even in the eyes of the recipient).[34] Trust thus derives from the belief that God is the essence of kindness and mercy, and in this sense is even greater than faith, for a person who possesses faith, without trust, merely resigns himself to accepting whatever may come from God. Trust—*bitachon*—however, ensures a person that whatever will be, will be good in a revealed way. Thus it is the highest form of good, because it is good not only in the Creator's eyes but also in the eyes of the creation!

Let us make the distinction between belief or faith, and trust a little clearer. A person who believes in God (who has *emunah*) believes that whatever God does is for the good, even when, God forbid, something painful or negative happens. He believes that there is good hidden within it and that it is ultimately for his benefit, either to correct him, or to cleanse him, or for other reasons known only to the Creator. If, however, we believe that pain or discomfort comes for our own good, to correct or cleanse, for example, then we might ask, "What happens to the beneficial cleansing if God gives me good in a revealed sense? How can we be sure that it has the same cleansing and rectifying effect on us as suffering?"

This is precisely where trust fulfills its role. We trust that God, being the essence of kindness, will find a way to correct our mistakes pleasantly. We trust that whatever rectification that may come from pain and discomfort can be achieved through kindness instead.

As a whole, trust is based on God Himself, Who is not bound by any precedent or rule that a person must be corrected through discomfort. Inasmuch as our trust is in God the way He really is, beyond our understanding, then we can trust in perfect calm and confidence that whatever happens will be good even in terms of our level of appreciation and understanding. God is going to give what we want while satisfying His own purposes for our greater good.

TRUST AND POSITIVE THINKING

Interestingly, chasidic teachings explain that the very trust itself, when it is pure trust in God, has the merit of causing the hoped-for good to come about. The merit of such complete trust in God causes the hidden good, which can be accomplished through pain or discomfort, to be transformed from indirect good (that which is ultimately good for us, but that is not revealed as good) to good in a revealed way. This is one of the teachings of the Baal Shem Tov. Based on the verse,[35] "One who will trust in God, kindness will surround him," the Baal Shem Tov taught that when a person puts his full trust in God, the trust itself causes kindness to surround him.[36] This is the meaning of the chasidic adage: "Think good—and it will be good."[37] It is Judaism's ancient affirmation of the power of positive thinking.

Therefore, as soon as a person makes up his mind and remains determined to think positive thoughts, he has tapped into the power that will create positive results. Even when circumstances are such that hope seems futile, placing your complete trust in God will create a successful outcome.[38]

There are many stories of simple people who placed their trust in God and were able to accomplish things that far greater people were unable to do. The power of trust, since it is trust in God Himself, is literally unlimited. The Baal Shem Tov taught that where a person's will is, this is where the person really is.[39] Above, when they want to locate a person, they do not look up his address and telephone number. Rather, they find him by locating his inner will, for this reveals his true whereabouts.

Accordingly, when a person sincerely places his will and trust in the positive, then he is regarded as being there. He is on the level of the essence of God's kindness, a revelation that is not limited by adverse situations and circumstances.

It is far more difficult to attain *bitachon* than *emunah*. *Emunah* is abstract belief. *Bitachon* is the actualization of belief. A person with *bitachon* is calm; his equanimity and peace of mind are the result of his trust in God, which displaces all worries.

When addressing the subject of belief (*emunah*), we brought the example from the Talmud of a thief, as he is about to burglarize a house, praying to God for help. As mentioned, there can be no greater contradiction than asking God to help one commit the sin of stealing. Yet we commonly find this kind of contradiction. At times, one professes a belief in God and truly does believe, but in the very face of the belief transgresses God's will time and time again. This problem exists only with respect to belief, not trust. Trust, being the actualization of belief, has been internalized and has an impact on the total personality. Belief is Step One. Trust is Step Two.

FAITH AND LIFE

Belief in God, shining in the soul of every Jewish person, is the greatest gift imaginable. It can be compared to an enormous inheritance that one receives without having done anything to deserve it. We are born with it, receiving it as a gift from heaven. This is why the Prophet Habakkuk took the entire 613 commandments of the Torah and distilled them into one commandment—*emunah*, as he says in the verse, "A righteous person will live (*yichyeh*, in Hebrew) in his faith."[40] Now, we find the word *yichyeh* (will live) could also mean resurrect, to *bestow* life. If a person were to live with the joy of having this belief, it alone could give him the foundation and strength to overcome any obstacle in life. His immersion in this faith would allow him to transcend all obstacles. It is even more than an inheritance that a person acquires simply as the result of being the legitimate heir; it has been actively acquired and internalized by the person's own efforts. Therefore the person has integrated and merged his existence into that of God's.

There are great chasidic Rebbes who explain the verse from Habakkuk in the following way: They render the word *yichyeh* (will live) as a causative verb, so that the word now means not only that the person himself lives through faith but that through his faith he gives life to others.[41] This indicates that the saintly *Tzaddik* experiences his *emunah* in the fullest possible sense. Not only is he animated by his faith but those who are attached to him are also inspired and enlivened.

Some chasidim maintain that attachment to a *Tzaddik* is sufficient to fulfill the requirements of spiritual service. The *Tzaddik* does the spiritual work and everything is accomplished by relying on him. But others, notably *Chabad chasidim* (followers of Rabbi Shneur Zalman of Liadi, mentioned earlier), maintain that being attached to the *Tzaddik* is essential but that every person also has to utilize his own powers of mind and heart to meditate and understand as much as is humanly possible. Only then can one attain his own *emunah*. They reason that although the word *Tzaddik* means a uniquely righteous, saintly person, nevertheless, the word also refers

to every Jewish person, as the verse (Isaiah 60:21) states: "And your people are all *tzaddikim*" (plural of *Tzaddik*). This means that every Jewish person, through study and deep meditation, can come to live and rejoice in the faith that he inherited and that he strives to internalize in a revealed way. For if he does this, he feels the presence of God dwelling in his heart and soul.

THE INTELLECT ENHANCES FAITH

We learned above that reason and faith appear to be opposites, but the truth is that reason can assist belief in God. Intellectual reason seeks to rationalize everything. Faith is above intellect and far beyond any comprehension. And yet intellect can be used to enhance one's faith, causing it to be internalized instead of remaining esoteric and abstract. This point needs further clarification to be completely understood.

We must first explain the uniqueness of the intellect. In general terms, intellect as compared to emotion is more objective. Emotion is subjective, and can be defined as, "What something does for me." If it feels good to me, then I love it. If it disagrees with me, then I dislike it. Intellect tries to understand what the truth is regardless of its impact on me. This objectivity is a great gift God has given human beings. To possess this intellectual objectivity, a person has to reach beyond himself. The intellect can be likened to a window that allows daylight to shine into a house regardless of what is inside the house. If the window is clear, the light will penetrate to the interior of the house. In a deeper sense, intellectual objectivity presumes humility and self-effacement. By humility and self-effacement we do not mean that the person has an ego but tries to ignore it or reduce its activity. The pure definition of humility is lack of self-seeking. Humility is not self-expression but self-transcendence. The ability to totally abandon one's own interests is, itself, a godly gift.

Several forces are at work in the intellect. There is the force of wisdom (*chochmah*, in Hebrew), the force of understanding (*binah*), and the force of knowledge (*daat*). Knowledge follows understanding, a result of deep and prolonged contemplation. But nevertheless, it transcends understanding. Knowing in this sense is not merely understanding; it is understanding that has become sufficiently internalized to be experienced as an intuitive awareness.

When a person contemplates an idea deeply, he becomes absorbed in it and preoccupied with it until it becomes part of his very being. When a person contemplates the greatness of God, with total concentration and immersion, using his power of *daat*, he eventually attains an intuitive knowledge, which transcends normal understanding, touching the very essence of the soul, which is *emunah*, as explained above. Then belief is no longer a transcendent, encompassing force. It has become internalized to a very great degree. Hence, by meditating on concepts pertaining to faith, we deepen our understanding until it becomes internalized as knowledge, and so we have the advantages of both intellect and belief. Faith and knowledge merge and become one with us, reaching closer and ever closer to the inner aspects of our soul. Through *daat* we can reach the purity of *emunah*, the very essence of the soul.

NOTES

1. The thirteen principles, which Maimonides described as the roots and foundations of the Jewish religion, first appeared in his *Commentary*

on the Mishnah, as an introduction to the final chapter of the tractate Sanhedrin. They were subsequently abbreviated, possibly by the Rambam himself (see *Baruch She-amar* prayer book, p. 202, s.v. אני מאמין), and were later appended to many versions of the daily prayer book.

2. *Likkutei Sichot*, vol. 20, p. 58; vol. 10, p. 206; vol. 15, p. 247; see also *Tanya*, chap. 37.

3. *Tanya*, chap. 3.

4. See Ibid., chap. 18.

5. Ibid., chap. 19.

6. *Likkutei Sichot*, vol. 20, p. 56 ff; pp. 295–296.

7. See *Tanya*, chap. 18 ff.

8. Ibid., chap. 19. Explained in *Likkutei Sichot*, vol. 22, p. 249.

9. Explained in *Likkutei Sichot*, vol. 20, p. 6 ff, p. 50 ff.

10. *Tanya*, chap. 18 ff; *Likkutei Sichot*, vol. 20, p. 6 ff.

11. *Tanya*, chap. 19.

12. Job 31:2. Explained in *Tanya*, chap. 2.

13. *Tanya*, chap. 18.

14. Maimonides, *Code, Yesodei HaTorah* 5:1.

15. *Tanya*, chap. 1, citing Rabbi Chaim Vital's *Shaarei Kedushah* 1:1; *Eitz Chaim* 50:2.

16. This battle is described in *Tanya*, chap. 11.

17. *Berachot* 63a, according to the version found in *Ein Yaakov*.

18. *Tikkunei Zohar, Tikkun* 69. Cited and explained in *Tanya*, chaps. 42, 44.

19. See at length *Derech Mitzvotecha, Haamanat Elokut*, chap. 1 ff.

20. *Tanya*, chaps. 3, 12, 17.

21. *Code, Yesodei HaTorah* 1:1.

22. This argument is presented by Nachmanides in his commentary to Maimonides' *Sefer HaMitzvahs*, in the name of *Baal Hilchot Gedolot*; Don Yitzchak Abarbanel in *Rosh Amana*, chap. 4 (among others) against counting faith as one of the 613 *mitzvahs* of the Torah. See also *Derech Mitzvotecha, Ha'amanat Elokut*, chap. 1. The entire matter is discussed at length in the Lubavitcher Rebbe's *Chiddushim u'Biurim b'Shas*, vol. 3, sec. 44, chaps. 4, 5, 8.

23. *Code, Yesodei HaTorah* 1:1, as proven by his use of the word לידע, to know, rather than להאמין, to believe. See at length *Derech Mitzvotecha*, ibid., chap. 2 ff.

24. See Numbers 12:7; *Vayikra Rabbah* 9:9.

25. *Bechinat Olam* 13:45.

26. See commentaries on Deuteronomy 6:20; commentaries to the *Haggadah* for Passover, regarding the question of the wise son. Explained in *Likkutei Sichot*, vol. 1, pp. 282–283; vol. 3, p. 896 ff; vol. 4, *Chukat*.

27. See *Likkutei Sichot*, vol. 4, p. 1056 ff.

28. Ibid.

29. Exodus 20:8–11.

30. As in Genesis 12:1, 12:7, 26:2, 28:13, and so on.

31. Explained in *Likkutei Torah*, *Bamidbar* 16b; *Chukat* 57c.

32. See Exodus 6:2 ff.; 19:20 ff.

33. *Tanya*, chap. 26.

34. See at length the Lubavitcher Rebbe's *Shaarei Emunah*, chaps. 27–35.

35. Psalm 32:10.

36. See *Tanya*, *Iggeret HaKodesh*, end of chap. 11; *Tzemach Tzedek's Biurei HaZohar*, p. 194.

37. See *Igrot Kodesh* of Rabbi Yosef Yitzchak Shneerson, the sixth Lubavitcher Rebbe, vol. 2, p. 537, vol. 7, p. 197—in the name of the *Tzemach Tzedek*.

38. As in the story reported in the Talmud (*Taanit* 21a) regarding Nachum Ish Gamzu.

39. Explained in *Likkutei Sichot*, vol. 8, p. 348.

40. Habakkuk 2:4.

41. Reported in the name of Rabbi Shlomo of Karlin.

The First Principle

> I believe with complete faith that the Creator, blessed is His Name, creates and directs all created beings, and that He alone made, makes, and will make everything.

he first principle involves belief in the existence of God, that He is the Primary Cause and that all of creation derives only from His true being and exists only by virtue of the reality of His being.[1]

THE NATURE OF HIS EXISTENCE

It seems that Maimonides' intention is that there are two components comprising the commandment to believe in God: (1) that there is a Primary Existence, that is, belief in the actual existence of God; (2) that everything else in heaven and earth exist only by virtue of the reality of His existence.

However, other authorities, such as Nachmanides and Don Yitzchak Abarbanel,[2] argue that one cannot count belief in God as one of the commandments because only after we have accepted the existence of God can we accept His commandments. Thus, fulfilling the commandments actually presupposes belief in God's existence, and therefore belief cannot be counted as one of the 613 commandments.

Abarbanel therefore explains[3] that Maimonides' intention in including belief in God among the 613 *mitzvahs* is that we are not merely commanded to believe in the existence of God—for this, no commandment is required. Rather, we are commanded to believe that God's existence is perfect and complete. That is, once we already believe that God exists, we are commanded to believe that God's existence precedes all other existence, and His existence is the only absolutely perfect one. And what is this perfection and preexistence? That His existence is the only necessary (or primary, unconditional, and essential) existence. This is referred to in classical philosophy as *a priori* existence,[4] compared to which the existence of everything else is merely secondary or conditional.[5]

Anything dependent upon something else for its existence is not complete and not unconditional. God's existence is the only necessary and unconditional existence because it is of His essence, totally independent of anything else.

However, what does the fact that whatever else exists is necessarily dependent upon His existence add to God's completeness and perfection? What would be lacking in His completeness if there were something not dependent on His being for its existence? It might underscore the imperfection of created beings, since their existence is only possible, not necessary, and is therefore conditional. But in what way is the perfection and unconditional being of the Creator thereby expressed?

The explanation is as follows: when we say that His existence is "necessary," we mean that His existence is an absolute, unconditional necessity that must be everywhere, on every plane of being. It is not dependent on any circumstance whatsoever.

Thus, were we to say that there was some object whose existence was independent of God, this would imply that God is not found within that particular entity. And this would mean that God's existence is not necessary and unconditional in essence, and therefore equal everywhere, but only possible and conditional. Accordingly, the idea that "everything else in heaven and earth exist only by virtue of the reality of His existence" is an inseparable aspect of the concept of His necessary, unconditional existence.

CONTINUOUS CREATION

We explained above that everything in heaven and on earth exists only by virtue of the reality of God's existence and is thus totally dependent on Him for its own existence. This requires some clarification. Not only is every aspect of creation dependent on God for its initial existence, its "coming into being" *ex nihilo*, as Maimonides explains in his *Guide for the Perplexed* (2:13), but once it has been created, it requires constant input from Above to keep it in existence. God did not simply create the world at some point in history and then leave it to its own devices while He occupies Himself with other business.[6] Rather, the creation is a continuous activity, so that if it were suspended even momentarily, all of creation would return to its former state of nonbeing, just as before the creation.[7]

Initially, God alone existed,[8] and there was nothing else. He then created everything that exists from absolute nothingness. The world did not exist before it was created, and it continues to exist only as the result of God's constantly recreating it. This is what Maimonides means when he says[9] that "if one could conceive that He was not there [i.e., within the creation], then neither could anything else be there."[10]

Therefore, the world is not something separate from God; it is completely dependent on God for its continued existence, for if He were to remove His creative power from a rock or a fly or any created entity, it would instantaneously cease to exist. This means that the rock or the fly or the whole world has no existence other than the creative power of God that brings them into existence constantly.

In the second part of *Tanya*, called *Shaar HaYichud v'HaEmunah* (The Gate of Unity and Faith), Rabbi Shneur Zalman of Liadi[11] elaborates on this teaching in the name of the Baal Shem Tov.[12] He explains that according to the Baal Shem Tov, the creation of the world through the Ten Utterances of Creation,[13] "There shall be light," "There shall be a firmament," and so forth,[14] was not a historical event that took place only once upon a time. Rather, it is a constant process that continues to take place at every moment, as expressed in the verse, "Your word, O God, constantly stands in the Heavens."[15] We gain an extraordinary realization from this—that the entire universe is nothing less than a divine declaration.

But Rabbi Shneur Zalman goes further and explains that the word of God is very different from the words of man. When a human being speaks, his words leave him and travel outward, and eventually disappear. But the words spoken by God never leave Him. God is everywhere and no place is void of Him:[16] "Do I not fill heaven and earth, says the Lord?" (Jeremiah 23:24). Therefore, the words of God, even after He utters them, are still within Him, because there is no such place as "outside of God."

Thus, the relationship between God and His world is that they are not two existences at all, with God on the one hand and the world, enlivened by God, on the other. It is not that God looks down from His holy abode and cares for everything from a distance. Rather, the entire existence of every creation at every moment is entirely dependent on God for its life and its existence. This is unlike the relationship of the soul to the body.[17] A lifeless body is still a body, but without God, there would be no body at all. He is its existence.

Let us contrast this with our own experience. When a person makes a vase, for example, the finished object no longer needs the input of the craftsman who made it. If he goes out for lunch, or even if he passes away, the vase will continue to exist independent of him. Thus, it is very difficult for us to understand why the creation needs constant input. Why can we not assume that once the universe was created it no longer requires a Creator to constantly re-create it? What is the difference between *our* creating and God's?

Chasidic texts[18] explain this by way of an analogy. When a person throws a stone up into the air, the stone continues to rise up to a certain point, and then falls again to the earth. Why did it not continue rising and flying through the air? Because the power of the person who originally threw the stone into the air eventually diminishes, until it ceases to have enough power to keep the stone moving, and at that point it begins falling back to earth. But why is a stone thrown through the air any different from a vessel made by a craftsman? Why does the latter continue to exist long after the craftsman himself has left the scene, and perhaps even the world, but not the former? *Chasidus*[19] explains that when a craftsman takes a lump of silver and fashions it into a beautiful goblet, he has merely changed its shape. Previously it was a bar of silver, or a ball of silver, or a formless lump, and now it is the shape of a goblet. The malleability of silver allows it to have potentially any shape. Thus the craftsman merely actualized one of the myriad shapes that the lump of silver could have had.

By way of contrast, when a person throws a stone up into the air, no one would argue that he has merely actualized one of the potential states of being that the stone possessed. A stone does not naturally possess the ability to fly through the air, which is merely revealed by an expert craftsman. On the contrary, its natural tendency is to fall to earth—in more scientific terms, to remain in a state of rest unless acted upon by an outside force. As long as the power of the thrower is invested in the stone, it will continue to fly through the air. But as soon as the energy that lifted it aloft dissipates, it will fall to its natural former state. *Chasidus* explains that this is an analogy for creation *ex nihilo*, something from nothing.

We can now understand the concept of continuous creation. If it is true that a stone is kept aloft only as long as the power of the thrower continues to make it fly through the air, then how much more so is this true of the act of creation *ex nihilo*. The divine energy that created the world from nothing must constantly maintain the world in existence, and if it were to cease for even a moment, the world would not continue to exist as a dead world but would simply cease to exist as if it had never existed in the first place.[20]

The author of *Tanya* explains this concept with a further analogy.[21] The light of the sun that shines down to us on earth appears to be an independent entity, whereas in reality, as everyone knows, it is totally dependent upon the sun for its existence. If the sun were suddenly extinguished, its rays would simply disappear, for they have no independent existence. They are merely an extension of the sun itself.

The same is true of creation. If God were to stop saying the ten utterances through which the world was created, the entire creation would instantaneously cease to exist. This is expressed in the daily liturgy as follows: ". . . Who, in His goodness, constantly renews the work of creation." (And this is the true meaning of the verse,[22] "Hear, Israel, the Lord our God, the Lord is One." By the word "One" we do not merely mean that there is only one God, but "One" means that there is only one existence, God, as we will discuss at greater length in the second principle.)

The idea of God's constant creation can serve as a preface to understanding the Torah's teachings regarding Divine Providence. God brings about everything that happens to every creation, including human beings, at all times. It is obvious that if no creation can exist even for a moment without God, certainly no creation can accomplish anything without God giving it life and bringing it into being. If a body is dependent on God for its existence, it is obvious that the same body cannot perform an action without God, for action certainly demands higher power than simple existence. Therefore, the Jewish belief in Divine Providence is a logical conclusion of the concept of God's unity, as will be explained in our discussion of the tenth principle.

CREATION AND THE SABBATH

A verse in the Torah (Genesis 2:2) states that "God finished by the seventh day His work which He had done, and He rested on the seventh day from all His work which He had done." Similarly, "For six days God created the world . . . and on the seventh, He rested" (Exodus 31:17). According to what we have said above, this presents a problem: how does the world continue to exist on the Sabbath? We explained at length that God constantly renews the creation, from moment to moment, so that if the life force that brings all of creation into existence disappeared for even a moment, all of creation would cease to exist and would return to a state of absolute nothingness. What, then, does the Torah mean when it states that God "rested" and "finished" creating?[23]

In order to understand this, it is necessary to explain the difference between the three categories of activities termed in *Chasidus* the "garments of the soul." These are thought, speech, and action. Action, the most elementary of these three categories, is not unique to man alone. Animals, and creatures on an even lower plane of being, also act—they move, search for food, eat, protect themselves, and so on.

Although most animals and other creatures also have some means of communication, they do not possess the power of speech, and certainly not to the extent that man possesses this faculty. In fact, the verse describing the creation of man and how God breathed the soul into his lifeless body, so that he became "a living soul," is rendered in the Aramaic translation as "the man became a speaking soul."[24] Speech is a form of communication, of revelation.

Thought is of an even higher order. The story is told[25] that one *Shabbat* afternoon, the famous kabbalist from Safed, Israel, Rabbi Yitzchak Luria (better known as the Arizal), lay down to take a nap. His chief disciple saw that he was dreaming, and when the master awoke, the disciple questioned him as to the contents of his dream. The Arizal told him that to communicate in speech what he had experienced in his short dream would take him more than eighty years. Speech is far more limited than thought, and action is far more limited than speech.

Moreover, thought is much more intimate than speech; unless someone can read your mind, your thoughts will remain private. While thought remains within, speech relates to another person or to persons. Action extends even further, to the level of inanimate objects upon which we act.

Similarly, the levels of thought, speech, and deed correspond to different levels of godly revelation, which are referred to in chasidic and kabbalistic terminology as "worlds." Each of these represents a different "layer" of creation. The outermost layer derives from action, as the verse states, "My *hand* established the *earth*" (Isaiah 48:13, emphasis added). A more internal and spiritual layer is created by speech, as the verse states, "By the word of God the heavens were made, and with the breath of His mouth, all of the heavenly host" (Psalm 33:6). The innermost level is indicated by thought, "Whatever God *desired*, He made" (Psalm 135:6, emphasis added); and "the Patriarchs, the Israelites, the Temple, and the name of the Messiah rose in *thought*" (*Midrash Rabbah*,[26] emphasis added).

Chasidic works[27] explain that on *Shabbat*, the Holy One, blessed is He, "retires" from the plane of action and of speech, withdrawing to a far more spiritual level, corresponding, in human terms, to the level of thought.

It is for this reason that we are forbidden to speak about profane (and even mundane) matters on *Shabbat*.[28] Since man was created in the image of God,[29] man too must rest on *Shabbat*, refraining from forbidden action and modes of speech.

Nevertheless, the world continues to exist on the Sabbath, albeit on the level of thought. (Incidentally, this is also the reason that a Jew acquires an extra soul on the Sabbath, as our Sages taught[30]—for the soul derives from this level, as mentioned above: "Israel arose in thought."). Furthermore, the energy that was invested in speech and action during the six days of the week becomes elevated on the Sabbath, ascending to the level of thought. Thus, the Hebrew word for Sabbath, שבת, has the identical letters to the word "return," תשב, for the life force of the world returns to its source on the Sabbath.

However, one should not make the error of thinking that there are two separate realms, the spiritual and the physical. The physical too, has its inner, spiritual dimension (as we will explain at length in our commentary to the thirteenth principle), which becomes its primary, revealed life force on *Shabbat*, whereas it is hidden in the background during the week.[31] Furthermore, not only is the previous week elevated with the advent of the Sabbath, the following week is also blessed by the Sabbath that precedes it, as stated explicitly in the Talmud[32] and the *Zohar*.[33]

TIME

We explained above that the world is in a state of continuous creation. However, this does not mean that the creation is uninterrupted. While *Chasidus* refutes the idea that the universe was created once upon a time and simply continued to exist, chasidic texts[34] explain that the renewal of the world from moment to moment is not actually a continuous process but a continual renewal. That is, although the world appears to be like a stream of water that flows constantly, without any gap, this is not quite correct. A more appropriate analogy for this would be the flow of electricity that is produced by turbines, or the movement of pistons by internal combustion. Each spin of the turbines, or each explosion of a quantity of gasoline, produces a specific "packet" or quantum of energy, which lasts until it is used up. The same thing is true of creation. Each "pulse" of divine energy creates and enlivens the world until it is "used up" (or, to be more accurate, until it is recalled), and then the next packet of energy flashes the creation into existence again. This is the meaning of the verse, "And the *chayyot* were going and returning" (Ezekiel 1:14). *Chasidus* explains that the word *chayyot* (חיות in Hebrew, literally "animals") can also be read as *chiyyut*, life force, which is in a constant state of flux, of flashing in and out of creation, in and out of existence.[35]

This is also true on an individual level. Each individual creature is re-created from moment to moment, as the previous packet of energy and life force returns to its source and a new one descends, re-creating and enlivening each creature individually.

This flashing in and out of being is the origin of time. Time, as we know from modern science as well, is a measurement of change. The change brought about when one flash of divine energy succeeds another is what creates time. Thus, according to *Chasidus*,[36] time is created and did not exist prior to creation.[37]

PLANES OF REALITY

We can now understand further ramifications of the concept of creation. The Talmud[38] states that wherever you find the greatness of the Holy One, blessed is He, there you find His humbleness. Elsewhere,[39] the Talmud explains that "greatness" refers to the work of creation out of nothing. Accordingly, when juxtaposed, these sources in the Talmud inform us that the work of creation is an expression both of God's greatness and of His humility: greatness in regard to us, for His greatness is revealed through the tremendous vastness and complexity of His creation, but as regards Himself, it is an act of great modesty and humility, for "it is not the practice of a king to engage in casual conversation."[40] This refers to the ten utterances through which the world was created.[41] These utterances are referred to as "casual conversation," for in order to create a finite world, God limited and contracted the infinite and undivided revelation of Himself (referred to in Kabbalah as the *Or Ein Sof*, the Infinite Light[42]) into a mere "ten utterances." The question that is eternally asked—Why did God create the world?—is even more of a question. God obviously had no need for the world to exist—He was complete without its existence. He created it only out of His desire to do so.[43]

Kabbalistic texts[44] explain that to create a finite, limited world, God contracted and concealed His Infinite Revelation. This act of contraction and concealment to create the world is referred to as the *tzimtzum*[45] (explained more fully in the following chapter). *Chasidus* explains that the word for "world" in Hebrew, *olam*, stems from the same root as the word *he'elem*, concealment or hiddenness. The process of creation is a process of progressive concealment of God from His creation, so that various planes and levels of reality come into being. However, it should be kept in mind that God did not remove Himself from creation. He merely concealed Himself in progressive stages.

Chasidic and kabbalistic texts mention four planes of reality in general, one lower than the next, which are referred to as the four "worlds," although there are actually an infinite number of worlds and spiritual gradations.[46] The difference between a higher world and a lower world is only in terms of the revelation of God's Infinite Light within that world. The more godliness is revealed, the higher the world. The more it is concealed, the lower the world, and the greater the feeling of self, ego, within that world. Thus, the feeling of self, or ego, is in inverse proportion to the revelation and comprehension of godliness. The greater one's self-consciousness, the lesser one's pure awareness of God. Our physical world is the lowest aspect of the lowest world and therefore exhibits the greatest degree of ego, in inverse proportion to the degree of godliness revealed in the world.

Holiness is defined in a similar manner: that which reveals the presence of God. A holy person does not necessarily mean one who possesses holy powers, the power to see the future, or to perform miracles. The definition of a holy person is one who is without any ego in the presence of God and is totally humble because of his awareness of God's unity. He lives his life with an awareness that God is all that there is. When a person is holy, it means that his ego is totally crushed. He has no sense of "me." His entire being is directed at carrying out God's will. So when one speaks about a person as holy, one means that he has no existence of his own. Understandably, such a person can also perform miracles or see into the future and do all that is associated with holy beings. But of himself, he has nothing. It is all God. He is a servant of God, carrying out His will to the fullest.

God is thus really within every one of us, or, to be more accurate, everything is within Him, but He remains hidden because we place ourselves in the way. A holy person takes himself out of the way. He removes his ego and allows the reality of the omnipresence of God to shine through.

WHY *THIS* WORLD?

Why did God create this physical world? It was pointed out above that God obviously had no need for the world to exist for He was and is perfect and complete without its existence. But He obviously had some purpose in creating the world, or He would not have done so.

Jewish Sages have discussed this question at length and have provided several answers. The *Zohar*[47] explains that the reason for creation is that through it the creatures that God creates will come to know Him. Rabbi Yitzchak Luria (the Arizal) explains that the reason for creation is that since God is absolutely complete and perfect in every way, had He not actualized all of His deeds, and His power through creation, He would not be called perfect and complete in all His deeds, Names, and appellations.[48] Elsewhere,[49] the Arizal explains that God created the universe in order to do good to His creatures and give them the opportunity of recognizing His greatness. The *Midrash*[50] explains that God created the world because He desired a dwelling place in the lower worlds.

Let us examine these views a little more closely. The view of the *Zohar*, that God's reason for creating the world is that through the process of creation God becomes known, surely applies to a much greater extent in the higher planes of reality, where godliness is revealed to a far greater extent. Therefore, this does not explain why He created this physical world. If His intention was that He should be known to his creatures, this condition was already fulfilled with the creation of the higher planes of reality, the higher worlds, and there was no need to create this physical world, where godliness is, by definition, concealed to the greatest extent (since it is the lowest of all worlds in terms of divine revelation). How, then, can this be His main intention in creating this world?[51] Moreover, the level of godliness that is revealed in the process of creation is severely contracted, to the extent that the entire creation is an act of humility for God, as explained above. And therefore the level of godliness that is revealed in the act of creation is a relatively low one. Accordingly, the knowledge we can have of Him through the creation is also extremely limited.[52] Thus, it does not seem justified to assume that this is the reason for, and purpose of, the entire creation.

Similarly, the argument that creation actualizes God's powers and divine Names, which were only in a state of potential prior to creation, also applies specifically in the higher worlds, where these powers and Names are revealed, and not to this lower world, where they are concealed. Moreover, one cannot argue that God was incomplete prior to the actualization of these Names and powers, for He was complete and perfect prior to creation, and the entire creation adds nothing to His perfection.[53] Furthermore, it is only on this plane of existence that there is a distinction between the potential and the actual, but not on higher planes of existence.[54]

Chasidus therefore opts for the explanation offered by the *Midrash*, that God wanted a dwelling place in the lower worlds. However, this idea requires some explanation.

As explained above, as far as God Himself is concerned, the distinction between "higher" and "lower" has no validity, for God pervades all worlds equally.[55] Before the world was created, He was One Alone, One and Unique, filling all of existence in which the universe would later be created. It is still the same now, insofar as He is concerned. For the change relates only to those who receive His life force and light, which they now receive after various levels of contraction and concealment of the light and life that emanate from Him. Eventually, this material and gross world was created—a world capable of manifest evil, where God's Infinite Light is almost totally concealed.

The purpose of this descent is not for the sake of the

higher worlds, because for them this is a descent from the light of His Presence. Rather, the ultimate purpose of creation *is* this lowest world, for such was His will—that the darkness and evil be subdued and the Infinite Revelation of God (the *Or Ein Sof*) be revealed in the lowest of worlds to an even greater extent than in the higher worlds. This is the revelation of His Essence rather than the revelation of the Infinite Light.

Now, why God wanted this we cannot answer; the *Midrash* informs us that this was God's desire, האוה in Hebrew. Regarding desires, there are no reasons or explanations.[56] Thus, although we do not know why He wanted this, we do know what it is that He wanted:[57] for godliness to be revealed on this lowest plane of existence.

THE ROLE OF MAN

We must now clarify what man's role is in God's plan. If the reason for creation had to do with understanding or recognizing God's greatness (as proposed by the *Zohar* and the Arizal) then man would obviously have an important place in the act of creation: through him the purpose of creation (knowing and recognizing God) would be fulfilled. However, since the reason for creation is simply that this is what God wanted, and why He wanted it cannot be understood by man, what importance does man have in God's universe? None whatsoever! Accordingly, God's "dwelling place in the lower worlds" is formed by man's self-nullification, by his absence of ego. Only in this way is the transcendent, inexplicable will of God revealed, not through reason and comprehension.[58] And this is brought about only by submission to His will as expressed in the Torah and its commandments, as will be explained in our commentary to the eighth and ninth principles.

NOTES

1. Maimonides, *Commentary to the Mishnah, Sanhedrin*, chap. 11, first principle; *Code, Foundations of the Torah*, 1:1.

2. In his commentary to Maimonides' *Sefer HaMitzvahs*. He cites this opposing view as the opinion of *Baal Hilchot Gedolot*; Don Yitzchak Abarbanel in *Rosh Amana*, chap. 4. See also the Tzemach Tzedek's *Derech Mitzvotecha, Ha'amanat Elokut*, chap. 1. The entire matter is discussed at length in the Lubavitcher Rebbe's *Chiddushim u'Biurim b'Shas*, vol. 3, sec. 44, chaps. 4, 5, 8.

3. In *Rosh Amana*, chap. 8.

4. See also the *Pirush* on Maimonides' *Code, Yesodei HaTorah* 1:1.

5. Chasidic writings agree with the Abarbanel in a general sense, with one major difference: Although they agree that the commandment to believe in God's existence cannot be taken literally, and must be understood as commanding us to believe in God's existence as perfect and complete, they nevertheless disagree with Abarbanel's explanation of what this perfection and completeness entails. That God's existence is "necessary" is a matter readily understood by the human intellect and is therefore in the realm of understanding, not of faith. Accordingly, there are no grounds for defining the commandment to believe in God's completeness and perfection as belief in His being the First Cause and necessary existence. Rather, belief in God's completeness and perfection is on a far more elevated plane, completely transcending human intellect. See *Derech Mitzvotecha, Ha'amanat Elokut*, chap. 1ff.; *Chiddushim u'Biurim b'Shas*, ad loc.

6. *Tanya*, pt. 2 (*Shaar HaYichud v'HaEmunah*), chap. 2, pt. 4 (*Iggeret HaKodesh*), chap. 20. This is also alluded to in Maimonides' words in his *Code, Yesodei HaTorah* 1:1: ". . . Who *brings* (ממציא) everything into existence," not ". . . Who *brought* (המציא) everything into existence."

7. See also Nachmanides (Ramban) to Genesis 1:1.

8. Compare the morning liturgy: "You are He before the world was created. . . ."

9. *Yesodei HaTorah* 1:2.

10. *Tanya* ad loc.; see also the *Pirush* to *Yesodei HaTorah* 1:3.

11. Author of *Tanya*, and *Shulchan Aruch HaRav*, among many other major chasidic works, he was one of the chief disciples of Rabbi Dovber, the Maggid of Mezritch, successor to the Baal Shem Tov. Rabbi Shneur Zalman founded the *Chabad*-Lubavitch chasidic dynasty.

12. Note that although this teaching was emphasized by the Baal Shem Tov and is regarded as one of the foundational principles of chasidic philosophy, it was nevertheless a view maintained by other authorities prior to the Baal Shem Tov, as is evident from the *Pirush* cited above.

13. *Pirkei Avot* (Ethics of the Fathers) 5:1.
14. Genesis 1:3 ff.
15. Psalm 119: 89.
16. *Tikkunei Zohar, Tikkun 57*. Explained in *Tanya*, chap. 21, *Shaar HaYichud V'haEmunah*, chap. 7.
17. Cf. *Vayikra Rabbah* 4:8.
18. See Rabbi Dovber's *Shaar HaYichud*, chap. 13.
19. See *Tanya, Shaar HaYichud v'HaEmunah*, chap. 2.
20. Ibid., chaps. 3, 7.
21. See ibid., chap. 3.
22. Deuteronomy 6:4.
23. These questions, and the answers that follows, are presented in *Likkutei Torah, Drushim l'Shabbat Shuva*, p. 66c; *Maamarim* 5703, p. 38 ff.; *Likkutei Sichot*, vol. 9, p. 220 ff.
24. *Targum Onkelos* to Genesis 2:7.
25. In *Emek HaMelech*, Introduction.
26. *Bereishit Rabbah* 1:7.
27. Ibid.
28. See Isaiah 58:13; *Shabbat* 113b, as ruled in *Shulchan Aruch, Orach Chaim*, chap. 307.
29. Genesis 1:26; 9:6.
30. *Beitzah* 16a.
31. *Likkutei Sichot*, vol. 9, p. 221.
32. *Beitzah* 17a.
33. Vol. 3, 63b.
34. *Maamarim* 5666, p. 41 ff.
35. See also *Tanya, Iggeret HaKodesh*, chap. 14, where this is explained in terms of the energy and life force that is assigned to creation as a whole on an annual, monthly, and daily basis.

36. And according to many Jewish Sages: Maimonides, *Guide*, pt. 2, chap. 30; Rabbi Saadia Gaon, *Emunot v'De'ot*, third discourse, 4th proof; Rashba, *Responsa* 418; Menachem Azaryah deFano in *Asarah Maamarot, Maamer Em kol Chai*, chap. 16.

37. *Siddur im Dach (Tefillot l'kol HaShanah*, by Rabbi Shneur Zalman of Liadi, author of *Tanya*), p. 75b in the name of the Rabbi Dovber, the Maggid of Mezritch; *Igrot Kodesh* of the Lubavitcher Rebbe, vol. 2, p. 224; *Likkutei Sichot*, vol. 18, p. 109; *Derech Mitzevotecha, Ha'amanat Elokut*, chap. 11. Note that this does not contradict the *Midrash* (*Bereishit Rabbah*, chap. 3) that prior to creation there was a progression or sequence of time. See *Shomer Emunim* 2:17.

38. *Megillah* 31a.

39. *Berachot* 58a.

40. *Zohar*, vol. III, p. 149b.

41. *Likkutei Torah, Acharei*, p. 25d.

42. See "Mystical Concepts in Chassidism" by Rabbi J. I. Schochet, chap. 2, also printed at the end of the English edition of *Tanya*.

43. *Midrash Tanchuma, Nasso*, chap. 16, cited in *Tanya*, chap. 36. Explained at length in *Discourses* 5666, p. 3 ff.

44. *Eitz Chaim, Otzrot Chaim*, beginning.

45. Discussed extensively in *Tanya*, chaps. 21–22, 48–49; *Shaar HaYichud v'HaEmunah*, chaps. 3–4; 6–7; 9–10; and especially in *Torah Or, Vayera*, 13c ff.; *Likkutei Torah*, addenda to *Vayikra*, p. 51b ff. For a brief but thorough treatment of this subject, see "Mystical Concepts in Chassidism" ad loc., chap. 2.

46. See "Mystical Concepts in Chassidism," ad loc., chap. 4. Note that five worlds are mentioned there and in numerous sources in Kabbalah and *Chasidus*. Nevertheless, chasidic texts generally discuss only the four lower worlds, excluding the world of *Adam Kadmon*.

47. Vol. 2, p. 42a, b.

48. *Eitz Chaim*, at the beginning; *Shaar HaHakdamot*, Third Introduction.

49. *Eitz Chaim*, beginning of *Shaar Haklallim*. See also *Emek HaMelech, Shaar Sha'ashuei HaMelech*, chap. 1.

50. *Tanchuma*, op cit. See also *Midrash Rabbah, Nasso* 10:1.

51. *Discourses* 5666, pp. 5–7; *Discourses* 5702 ד"ה שוקיו, chap. 17.

52. *Discourses* 5666, pp. 4–5.

53. Ibid., pp. 5–7; *Discourses* 5702 ד"ה שוקיו, chaps. 17–18.

54. Ibid. See also Rabbi Moshe Cordovero's *Pardess, Shaar HaTzach Tzachot*, chap. 3; *Derech Mitzevotecha, Haamanat Elokut*, chap. 11.

55. *Tanya*, chap. 36. The explanation that follows is also based on this chapter.

56. See the Tzemach Tzedek's *Or HaTorah, Balak*, p. 997.

57. See *Likkutei Sichot*, vol. 14, p. 123.

58. Ibid., vol. 6, p. 21 n. 70, p. 23 n. 75.

The Second Principle

I believe with complete faith that God is One. There is no unity that is in any way like His. He alone is our God—He was, He is, and He will be.

aimonides' second principle concerns the unity or oneness of God, His relationship to the world, and everything else that is seemingly outside the essence of God. The principle of belief in the oneness of God is even further reaching, and has a more profound effect on our lives, than belief in God as such. This is because the true unity of God encompasses all of creation, including our very selves,[1] at the same time that He and His creation appear to be separate "entities." When we understand this clearly and fully, our commitment to God is deepened.

THE FINITE FROM THE INFINITE

In our discussion of the previous principle, we explained that the creation comes about *ex nihilo*, from absolute nothingness. Although we examined this idea at some length, we did not analyze some of the important ramifications of this concept: how was the finite produced by the Infinite, the material from the Immaterial, and above all, how we can reconcile the creation with the oneness of God? Does the creation exist outside of Him and therefore constitute a duality? The latter question is of particular importance as regards the second principle, but in order to attempt an answer, we must first explain how the finite can be produced from the Infinite and the material from the immaterial.

Jewish philosophers[2] and kabbalists[3] alike have tackled this problem. Among the solutions that they have offered are what are called in philosophical terminology "intermediate agency" and "emanationism," that is, that creation came into being by way of a series of intermediate steps, emanated by the Creator, which place a sufficiently great distance between Him and that which He created, that the corporeality and the multiplicity of the latter are disassociated and set apart from God Himself. In other words, the creation came about by way of a long chain of evolutionary processes, a chain of cause and effect, emanated by the Creator as the First (and very distant) Cause, until eventually the elements of this material world came into being.

However, *Chasidus*[4] points out that as long as there is some causal relationship between the Creator and the created, between the first link in the evolutionary chain and the last, no matter how long the chain might be, there always remains some association between one level and another and thus between the first link and the last. The aspect of infinity remains. Because each successive level is emanated or produced by the previous level, it "inherits" the infinity of its predecessor. And finite material being could not have been created from infinite spiritual being, no matter how many causes and effects interpose between the Creator and the created.

Rabbi Yitzchak Luria therefore proposed the doctrine of *tzimtzum*.[5] In the Arizal's view the process of creation was not an uninterrupted sequence of causes and effects or a gradual descent of emanations. Rather, the primary act of creation was to establish a "gap" between the Creator and the created, a "leap" (*dilug*) that breaks the gradualism and establishes a radical distinction between the First Cause and all subsequent effects.[6] This is called the *tzimtzum* (as mentioned briefly in the commentary to the previous principle). The doctrine of *tzimtzum* was expounded by the Arizal in the following way: Before the universe was created, there was only the Infinite One, whose infinite revelation of Himself (termed the *Or Ein Sof*, the Infinite Light) filled all of existence. In the Infinite Light there was no place for finite existence. But when it arose in God's will to create finite worlds, He withdrew His Infinite Light, so to speak, in order to create a void (*chalal*) wherein finite existence could be created by means of a reintroduction of finite light into the void.[7]

Rabbi Shneur Zalman of Liadi adopts this idea, adding some important qualifications. First, the *tzimtzum* is not to be understood literally, that God actually withdrew Himself from the void. He explains that God merely concealed His Infinite Light within Himself, raising it up to a level beyond revelation.[8] Moreover, since the *tzimtzum* took place only in the Infinite Light and not in God Himself, no change whatsoever is effected in Him by the *tzimtzum*, and the verse, "I, God, have not changed" (Malachi 3:6) is upheld.[9] He remains exactly as He was prior to the creation.

Thus a finite, material world was produced *ex nihilo* and not from some preceding spiritual substance by a process of gradual descent. Since the creation came about *ex nihilo*, by way of the *tzimtzum*, we understand how the finite could have come about from the Infinite and the material from the Immaterial.

THE ONENESS OF GOD

In one of the classical formulations of the doctrine of God's unity and oneness, Maimonides (*Sefer HaMitzvot, Mitzvah* 2) explains that we have been commanded to believe in the oneness of God—that He who brought existence into being, the First Cause of everything, is One, as the verse states, "Hear, Israel, the Lord is our God, the Lord is One. . . ." From his words, we understand that this *mitzvah* (commandment) forbids us to believe in partnership (*shittuf* in Hebrew), that is, we are forbidden to believe that God has any "partners" in creation, unlike the nations of the world, who are permitted to believe in other powers as well.[10] As far as we are concerned, however, God has no partners. There is nothing that assists God, making it easier for Him to create or sustain the world.

Nature is therefore not a power at all. For example, the sun shines and radiates heat and light, but not because it intrinsically possesses light and obeys God's command to shine. Rather, the source of the light of the sun is God's will. Only His will that the sun radiate light and heat permits the sun to shine. God could remove the sun or destroy it, but He wants the sun to exist and to radiate light, and so it does. The earth, similarly, has no intrinsic power to produce crops but produces fruits and vegetables according to God's will.

From these examples, we can understand that there is nothing in the world that assists God or is His partner. This definition of *echad*—one, God's unity—indicates that no power or force is a self-existing entity. Rather, every power and every force is merely the manifestation of godliness as that power or force. Thus, the sun and the moon and the earth have no choice concerning the roles they play in creation or in any aspect of their existence. They radiate light or reflect light, or produce fruits and vegetables without choice, being bound by the nature with which they have been created.

(However, God Himself is not bound by the laws of nature that He created. Regarding the Ark of the Covenant that stood in the Holy of Holies of the First Temple, the Ark occupied no space although it had definite dimensions, as we find in Exodus (25:10). When one measured from each end of the Ark to the nearest wall, one discovered that the sum of the two measurements was exactly equal to the measurement across the width of the room, without taking the size of the Ark into account. Accordingly, we must conclude that although the Ark had physical dimensions, and existed in time and space, it nevertheless did not occupy any space. This is an indication that God is not limited by the limitation He placed on the laws of nature.[11])

We do find one hint in the Torah of the possibility of a partnership with God, and this is the *mitzvah* to honor one's parents. There are three "partners" in the creation of every child: the father and mother create the body and God gives the body a soul; therefore we are commanded to honor them. Yet even here it is not really a partnership because just as the sun and moon give light only because of their God-given power, a man and woman are able to procreate only because this power is invested in them by God. The difference is that they have a choice to use this power or prevent its actualization, and for their choice, parents are worthy of being honored. But any power that we see is merely God Himself as He clothes Himself within these powers. There is no partnership. He is the sole proprietor, running the entire show alone.[13]

DUALITY AND ONENESS

Thus far we have discussed the classical view of the oneness of God. However, there is another perspective of the unity of God. The *Zohar*[14] explains that once we have understood the *mitzvah* of belief in God in a general sense (i.e., that He is the Creator of the world, etc.) as clarified in our commentary to the first principle, we can now examine the ramifications of these ideas in a more specific sense, based on the verses "Hear O Israel, the Lord our God, the Lord, is One" (Deuteronomy 6:4), and "Know this day and take unto your heart that the Lord is God. In the heavens above and on the earth below, there is nothing else" (Deuteronomy 4:39).

The *Zohar*,[15] one of the earliest and most important kabbalistic texts, explains that the two appellations, Lord (י-ה-ו-ה in Hebrew) and God, are essentially one. However, in numerous places the *Zohar* and *Midrash* comment that the former Name indicates infinite revelation and expansion without any limitation whatsoever, whereas the latter Name is indicative of the attribute of severity and restriction, concealing and contracting the infinity of the former. The latter Name (אלוקים) is also the source of multiplicity and immanence (God within nature or creation), whereas the former is indicative of unity and transcendence (God as He transcends creation). Nevertheless, the *Zohar* states categorically that they are absolutely one!

Chasidus[16] clarifies the meaning of the *Zohar*'s statement by way of an analogy. A human being also has the power of revelation and the power of limitation and concealment. The power of thought, for example, is capable of producing an endless stream of thoughts. However, it also has the capacity to limit and define concepts, for every concept must have some limitations and must be categorized in some way if it is to be understood at all. Similarly, a teacher must possess the ability to conceal and limit his own understanding of a concept in order to instruct his students, who are not yet at the level of understanding to grasp all the details and ramifications of the idea the way the teacher understands it.

In both of these examples, the source of the idea of the concept is the very same source that limits it. This may be compared to a teacher who understands on a much higher and much deeper level than his student and uses an analogy to explain it to his student. Although the teacher presents the student with a coarse physical analogy to illustrate his point, the teacher is in no way affected by the analogy. He still thinks the same way as he did before. The analogy does not limit his thought and understanding at all. But what the analogy does is reach down to help the student who must operate on such a level to begin to understand something in a limited way. And if it is a good analogy, the student will begin to understand the teaching that is hidden within the analogy. Thus, in order to educate his student, the teacher contracted his thoughts and presented them in a manner accessible to the student.

In exactly the same way, these two divine Names also derive from the identical Source, God Himself. Just as the power of Infinite Revelation is drawn from His Essence, so too, the power of concealment and contraction is also drawn from His Essence.[17] Thus, both divine Names are in reality two different manifestations of divine energy that stem from the identical source.[18] This is the *Zohar*'s explanation of the unity of

God: that the two apparently opposing forces are in reality two sides of the same coin, so to speak.

One of the ramifications of this idea is readily seen in the *mitzvahs* of the Torah, which operate in a world of time and space. With rare exceptions, the *mitzvahs* are time bound and are subject to the limitations of place, of degrees and measurements, including when and how to perform it, so that if the *mitzvah* is done outside of these boundaries, it is not regarded as a *mitzvah* at all. Now the *mitzvahs* are the Supernal Will[19] of God, Who is beyond time and beyond space. How then do we reconcile the two?

The answer is that God is beyond time and space, but He is nevertheless the cause of time and space. It is not a paradox at all, for everything has its source in God. For though He is beyond time and space, He chose to create time and space. They are real to us only because He hides His infinite and eternal light from us so that we can exist within the limitations of time and space. But since He so chooses God can even dwell in the dimensions of time and space, even though they have no reality for Him.[20] They are His creations and He completely transcends them, yet He chooses them for a dwelling place.[21] Although He always remains beyond time and space, He desires that in the reality of time and space, it should be known that He is one.[22] And this is not a contradiction for Him.

This is how the *Zohar* defines the oneness of God, that the infinite and the finite are in reality one.

BEING AND NOTHINGNESS

The Baal Shem Tov, the founder of *Chasidus*, explains the oneness and unity of God in an even deeper sense,[23] on the basis of what was explained above regarding the first principle: that because the world is created *ex nihilo*, the continued existence of the world must be the product of a constant input of divine energy. This divine energy, which we referred to as the ten utterances through which the world was created, is in reality the true existence of the world.

We must make a distinction between "speech" as applied to God and speech as it applies to man.[24] When a person utters a word, the breath emitted in speaking is something that can be sensed and perceived as a thing apart, separated from its source in the ten faculties of the soul. But, as regards the Holy One, blessed is He, His speech is not separated from His Self, for there is nothing outside of Him, and there is no place devoid of Him.[25] Therefore, His speech is not like our speech and is only called speech by way of analogy: the light and life force He emits in a revealed way to create worlds and sustain them is called "speech," the ten utterances with which the world was created. His speech, unlike ours, is united with Him in absolute union, comparable to the way a person's speech and thought are united with him while they are still *in potentia* in his wisdom and intellect, where they are totally united with their source, the wisdom and intellect in the brain.

The speech and thought of the Holy One, blessed is He, is absolutely united with His essence and being, even after His speech has already become materialized in the creation of the worlds, just as it was united with Him before the worlds were created.

Created beings are brought into existence by way of the *tzimtzum* mentioned above, which obscures and conceals the light and life force that are derived from His "words." It appears that this life force is something that has become separated from Him after it issued forth from Him, just as the speech of a human being issues from him and becomes separated from him. This, of course, is not true, for "even darkness is not dark for You" (Psalm 139:12); all forms of concealment are only relevant to us and not to Him. Accordingly, before Him, everything else is of no account whatever. Creation has no existence at all other than the divine energy that brings it into being from moment to moment.

Rabbi Shneur Zalman of Liadi takes this teaching even further. He explains at length that the entire physical creation is not the independent existence it appears to be. Although this is the way it appears to us, this is only because we do not see the divine energy that brings the physical creation into being and keeps it in existence. In comparison with this divine energy, our existence is as if absolutely nothing.

This can be understood[26] by way of an analogy. The rays of the sun shine down upon earth and all its inhabitants. The sun's rays are the radiance and light that spreads out from the body of the sun and is visible to all as it gives light to the earth and the entire universe. Since light diminishes and dissipates the further it travels, logically then, if the sun's rays shine here, some 93 million miles away from their source, they must be much brighter in their source, the sun's surface. However, if we were standing on the surface of the sun, we would, in fact, see no rays, because where the sun itself exists, its mere rays are completely and absolutely swallowed up in the brightness and radiance of the sun itself and are regarded as naught and complete nothingness. They are absolutely nonexistent in relation to the body of the sun globe, since this light and radiance is merely the illumination that shines out from the body of the sun itself. It is only in the space of the universe, and down here on earth, where the sun itself is *not* present, that this light and radiance appears to us to have actual existence. Only here can the terms *yesh* (being or existence) be applied to them at all. When they are in their source, in the body of the sun, however, the term *yesh* cannot be applied to them at all, and they can only be called naught and nonexistent. There the rays of the sun are indeed naught and absolutely nonexistent, for there, within their source (the body of the sun), only the sun itself gives light, and there is nothing besides it.

Only the *tzimtzum* conceals from us the fact that we are constantly within our Source and there is nothing besides God.

Thus, according to Rabbi Shneur Zalman, not only does God have no partners, and not only do all opposing forces have but one source, and not only is existence completely and totally dependent on the divine energy that brings it into being, but the world itself is also one with God, since the existence of the entire creation is absolutely nullified in His existence.

In terms of the analogy used by the Baal Shem Tov: the words of God that bring the existence of the universe into being are always within God and never leave Him. Not only does the world have no independent significance or have a life of its own, being completely dependent on God's life-giving force, the world has no independent existence at all because it never leaves God. The whole world then is included in the presence of God Himself.

This is analogous to the light of the sun within the sun, as explained above. Of course, as Rabbi Shneur Zalman of Liadi explains,[27] the analogy is imperfect because the sunlight that shines on earth is a great distance from the sun. But the world is never at a distance from God and is always within its source, always completely nullified within its source. When meditating on this idea, one will realize that the world, from God's perspective, has no essential reality and does not really exist at all. Only He exists.

This concept is the exact opposite of the natural feeling and understanding of each and every creation. Every created entity feels that it is a true, independent existence of some significance and importance. Each created being is very dear to itself. This, incidentally, is why we are charged with the *mitzvah* to meditate on the greatness of God—in order to nullify the ego and realize that there is only one imperative, essential existence, God. There is only God, as the verse states: "And you shall know this day, and take it to your heart, that the Lord is God in the heavens above and on the earth below, there is nothing else" (Deuteronomy 4:39). Regarding the last two words in the verse, *ain od*, meaning "nothing else," or "there is no other," Rabbi Shneur Zalman of Liadi explains[28] that *od* in Hebrew signifies a secondary existence. Thus the words *ain od* tell us that the world does not even have the status of *od*—a secondary existence—in the presence of God. In comparison to the soul, the body is also referred to as *od*, for without the soul there would merely be a lifeless body, and therefore we call it a secondary existence. But the world has nothing of its own to allow us to consider it even a *secondary* existence. There is only God.

BEING AND TRUE BEING

However, if a person were to constantly meditate on the world being nothing and without intrinsic value, he might have difficulty in understanding the importance of Torah and *mitzvahs*. And he would certainly have difficulty in understanding that the purpose of Torah and *mitzvahs* is to make the world a holy place. Why bother when the world has no true reality and is completely dependent on the godly life force that brings it constantly into being? How can Torah and *mitzvahs* be considered absolute if they are based upon a merely illusory reality? It is for this reason that Maimonides translates *ain od* differently in his *Mishneh Torah*,[29] which is a book of *halachah*, instruction on how to lead one's life. Maimonides does not interpret *ain od* as meaning that there is nothing besides God or that there is not even something that is secondary to God, as we explained above. Rather Maimonides renders *ain od* as meaning that there is nothing as true as God.

Everything in the world is a creation of God's and is dependent on God for its existence. Since the existence of everything else besides God is directly dependent on Him, its existence is not part of its essence; its existence is, so to speak, incidental in that it exists only by virtue of the will of its Creator. Therefore, its existence is not regarded as "true." The word "true" does not only mean that it is not a lie. True also means that it must be.[30] Something that is dependent on another existence does not have to be, and thus, in this sense it is not true. On its own, it does not exist. Truth means that it is true on every level. An existence that is there because something else makes it exist is not a true existence. Since God is the only imperative or necessary existence, and everything else exists because of His existence, only He is a true existence.

This definition of the oneness of God—that there is nothing as true as God—is nevertheless incomplete in that it does not describe God's relationship to the world, and therefore it is really not a definition of His oneness.

Why then did Maimonides present us with this interpretation of *ain od*? The answer is that this view is necessary if we are to perform the *mitzvahs* with proper feeling and dedication. For if a person were to maintain only the awareness of the ultimate reality—that all existence, including his own, has no intrinsic value or true being—he will not be able to perform *mitzvahs* properly. Proper performance of the *mitzvahs* demands a respect and concern for the world. Therefore, a person must also understand the other side of the coin, that God intentionally created a world in which creatures feel that their existence is real. Therefore, we are not living in a dream. Existence is not an illusion. This is not merely an imagined world. It is God's will that this world exists in reality, and therefore, it exists in reality. If we thought otherwise, we could never fulfill the *mitzvahs* properly.[31]

This entire idea hearkens back to a point we made earlier: that it is no paradox for God to do two complete opposites. He is quite capable of creating a world where creatures have an awareness of their own existence as a reality, while at the same time they can be aware that the world is entirely dependent on His existence. Thus, our world feels itself to be a creation, and yet this is not a lie. It is a reality that God created. God based His entire Torah and all the *mitzvahs* on this idea. We are supposed to feel our existence. It is part of our inborn nature. There is nothing wrong with this consciousness. To think we exist is not a sin. It is a God-given reality. But it is nevertheless our privilege and obligation to come to the higher realization that the ultimate truth is that only God exists.[32]

When we in this reality come to a realization of the truth, that the only existence is God, then we have made this world into a dwelling place for God. This reality has invited God into the world.

Although chasidic teachings explain at great length the implications and ramifications of God's oneness (*Hashem Echad*)—that God is the only true existence—they nevertheless simultaneously affirm the value of this world, as a reality created by God, even though it is not the ultimate reality. From this perspective we can live in this world and make this world into a dwelling place for God.[33]

THE HUMAN EGO AND THE UNITY OF GOD

We have described above the significance of our declaration of faith in the unity of God. But the matter does not end with merely understanding the significance of these words. Obviously, there are many ramifications of this central theme in Jewish thought, and the most important of these ramifications has to do with the way a Jew lives his life in this world.

The idea of God's unity is what every Jew should live with and strive to imbue in his daily life. It is certainly the approach that is stressed in chasidic teachings. If one were to stop a *chasid* in the midst of his meditation or interrupt his study of *Chasidus*, the unity of God would always be the topic with which he is engaged, directly or indirectly.

Although our aim is to instill this awareness of the omnipresent unity of God within our minds and hearts, the human ego presents a barrier to this realization. Ego allows a person to follow the dictates of his heart. Ego is not merely a person's self-adulation, so that one regards oneself as greater than the next fellow. Ego is also the individual's wanton obedience to his own heart. And nothing is a greater barrier to God's unity than the individual's doing whatever he feels like doing. This is diametrically opposed to the truth, for one of the ramifications of God's omnipresence and absolute unity is that we are obligated to behave in a way that is consistent with this truth. And when a person follows the whims of his heart, he denies that reality.

Rabbi Shneur Zalman of Liadi once made the following statement in public: "*Shema Yisrael, Hashem Elokaynu, Hashem Echad*. The letter *dalet* of the word *echad* resembles a hatchet. And why does the *dalet* resemble a hatchet? Because you have to knock the *echad* into your mind." As soon as he finished those words, he went back to his room. The idea of knocking the *echad* into one's mind is the central theme of *Chasidus*. The unity of God is the basic theme of all existence and it should be the basic theme of our lives.

HE ALONE IS OUR GOD

The above discussion focused on the nature of God's unity, and its ramifications on the life of a Jew in this world. Situations may arise, however, as they certainly did in the past, where a Jew is faced with the necessity to proclaim the principle of God's unity as binding upon him to the extent that he is willing to forego his own life in order to uphold this principle. This is called *mesirat nefesh* in Hebrew, self-sacrifice. In certain circumstances one is expected to give up one's life for God.[34]

This is directly connected to the first principle, faith in God. If a person is told to worship an idol, God forbid, he is expected to give up his life rather than worship the idol because of the principle of faith. What is the connection, however, between self-sacrifice and the unity of God?

One of the meditations on the words "*Shema Yisrael, Hashem Elokaynu, Hashem Echad*" (Hear, Israel, the Lord our God, the Lord is One),[35] is that as we say the word *echad* we declare our willingness and readiness to give up our life for God. This is based on the awareness that *echad* means that there is nothing else whatsoever besides God Himself. Everything else is created by God and has no independent, intrinsic being. We therefore commit ourselves wholly to God and nothing else.

On a deeper level, the idea of *mesirat nefesh*, self-sacrifice, as explained by *Chasidus*, means sacrificing your own will.[36] *Mesirat nefesh* does not necessarily have to entail literally giving up one's life. Sacrificing one's own will, while remaining alive, is also regarded as *mesirat nefesh*. *Mesirat nefesh* literally means giving up, or surrendering, one's *nefesh*. The word *nefesh* is used in several places in Scripture to signify will. Thus, *mesirat nefesh* in this sense means that the individual has no will other than his will to fulfill God's will.

This does not mean that he merely surrenders his will to God's will. This would imply that in reality he would rather fulfill his own will, but because of his devotion to God, he is willing to forego his own wishes and comply with God's. Rather true *mesirat nefesh* means that he has no will other than God's will; his will is to do what God wishes him to do. This is the way that the Baal Shem Tov explains the *Mishnah*,[37] "Fulfill His will as you would your own will," that is, the ultimate fulfillment of His will is when you have adopted it as your own. In this way, a person's entire existence is the fulfillment of the divine will. This indicates that the Oneness of God has permeated the person to such an extent that he actually becomes an extension and expression thereof, and he ceases to exist as an independent entity.

By meditating on surrendering one's will in this way when reciting the *Shema* prayer, one actually affirms the unity of God. This means not only the unity of God as He is in Himself, but also the unity of God as He relates to this world and to our daily lives, to the extent that a person's entire life is directed toward fulfilling the divine will rather than seeking self-fulfillment, or worse, self-gratification. Teaching ourselves to live with this *mesirat nefesh*,[38] so that everything we do throughout our lives is an expression of our faith in the oneness of God, is the real affirmation of this principle. This is true self-transcendence.

This is no more in evidence than when a person runs up against an obstacle and realizes that the obstacle itself is also from God. When he manages to overcome the obstacle, his inner strength, to the very depths of his soul, becomes revealed. This is why God placed the obstacle in his path—so that the depths of his soul could be revealed. The verse states, "For God tests you to know. . . ." *Chasidus* explains that the intention of the verse is not that by means of the test God will know whether you believe in Him or not, whether you are faithful to Him or not. God already knows what lies concealed in a person's heart and mind. Rather the intention is that *we* should know what our real relationship to Him is. In order to overcome a test, a person must use the innermost parts of his soul. Therefore, by means of the test, he comes to know more about himself and who he is.

We explained earlier that the function of *mitzvahs* is to reveal godliness in the world, which means making the world itself reveal godliness,[39] because the natural process of creation entails a concealment of godliness. Conversely, sin and transgression create another layer to cover up the reality of God's omnipresence. This is why evil is sometimes referred to as *kelipah*. *Kelipah* is the Hebrew word for shell or husk. A shell or husk is something that covers and conceals the fruit, so that the fruit remains invisible and inedible. The same is true of *kelipah* in a spiritual sense. It hides and conceals godliness, preventing us from relating directly to Him.

The word that best describes evil is *kelipah*, for this is the worst aspect of evil. It is a cover-up that denies the truth and refuses to let it be revealed. It prevents the unity of God from being revealed.[40] When the word hidden is used in a spiritual context, it does not mean that something moved to a different place. It means that the hidden thing is in the same place but hidden from recognition. When a treasure chest is hidden in the sand, it is there, but we do not see it. We describe this world the same way. Because of the process of creation it does not reveal God. God is here just as the treasure chest is in the sand, but just like the sand hides the chest, the world hides God. Evil not only hides God in the sense that it does not reveal Him, it actively conceals God. Holiness, by contrast, reveals God, and this is why a holy person is humble in the presence of God, for his humility is the natural result of an awareness of the greatness of God and His unity. When a person is aware that God is everything he naturally feels humble and insignificant. This is why Moshe Rabbeinu, our teacher Moses, who was the greatest prophet who ever lived, was also considered the most humble person who ever lived.[41]

NOTES

1. See *Torah Or*, p. 55b; *Imrei Binah, Shaar Kriat Shema*, chap. 8ff.
2. Cf. Maimonides' *Guide*, pt. 2, chaps. 4–12.
3. Cf. Moshe Cordovero's *Pardess Rimonim* 4:9.
4. *Tanya*, chap. 48; *Tanya, Iggeret HaKodesh*, chap. 20; *Likkutei Torah, Devarim* p. 46c, 20d.
5. See the beginning of *Etz Chaim, Otzrot Chaim, Mevoh Shearim*, and so on.
6. See *Torah Or, Esther* 90a, 116c; *Likkutei Torah, Shir HaShirim* 40b ff., 41d, 42b, ff.
7. See the beginning of *Etz Chaim, Otzrot Chaim, Mevoh Shearim*,

and so on; *Tanya*, chaps. 21, 48, 49; *Likkutei Torah, Vayikra*, p. 51bff., and especially 52c.

8. *Shaar HaYichud v'HaEmunah*, chap. 7; *Likkutei Torah, Vayikra*, ad loc.

9. *Tanya*, chap. 20; *Shaar HaYichud v'HaEmunah*, chap. 7.

10. See Maimonides' *Code, Hilchot Akum*, chap. 1; Rama in *Shulchan Aruch, Orach Chaim* 156.

11. Ibid.

12. Exodus 20:12.

13. See *Likkutei Amarim, Tanya*, chaps. 20–23.

14. Vol. 1, p. 25a, in *Raya Mehemna*; Introduction to *Zohar*, vol. 1, p. 12a. See also vol. 2, 25a (*Raya Mehemna*).

15. The following is based on the explanation found in *Derech Mitzevotecha, Achdut Hashem*, p. 59bff.; *Veyadata*, Moscow, 5657.

16. *Veyadata*, Moscow, 5657, p. 7.

17. Ibid. See also Rabbi Meir Ibn Gabbai's *Avodat HaKodesh* 1:8.

18. See also *Tanya, Shaar HaYichud v'HaEmunah*, chaps. 6–7.

19. See *Likkutei Amarim, Tanya*, chap. 23.

20. See *Tanya, Shaar HaYichud v'HaEmunah*, chap. 4ff.

21. See *Midrash Tanchuma, Nasso*, chap. 16. Cited and explained in *Tanya*, chap. 36.

22. See *Midrash Tanchuma, Nasso*, chap. 16.

23. *Tanya*, chap. 20. See also *Tanya, Shaar HaYichud v'HaEmunah*, chap. 1ff.

24. See *Berachot* 40a.

25. *Tikkunei Zohar, Tikkun* 57.

26. *Tanya, Shaar HaYichud v'HaEmunah*, chap. 3.

27. See ibid., chap. 3; *Tanya*, chap. 21.

28. *Tanya, Shaar HaYichud v'HaEmunah*, chap. 1.

29. *Yesodei HaTorah* 1:4.

30. See the *Pirush* to *Yesodei HaTorah* 1:1, 4.

31. See the Lubavitcher Rebbe's *Chiddushim u'Biurim b'Shas*, vol. 2, p. 135ff.; *Likkutei Sichot*, vol. 26, p. 114.

32. See *Derech Mitzevotecha, Achdut Hashem*, last chapter.

33. See *Likkutei Sichot*, vol. 29 p. 33ff.

34. See Maimonides' *Code, Yesodei HaTorah* 5:1.

35. Deuteronomy 6:4.

36. See *Likkutei Sichot*, vol. 2, p. 456.

37. *Avot* 2:4.
38. See *Likkutei Sichot*, vol. 3, p. 990ff.; vol. 4, p. 1281; vol. 8, p. 5ff.
39. See *Tanya*, chaps. 36, 37.
40. See ibid., chap. 6.
41. Numbers 12:3.

The Third Principle

> I believe with complete faith that God does not have a body. Physical concepts do not apply to Him. There is nothing whatsoever that resembles Him at all.

Maimonides' third principle addresses the issue of anthropomorphism. Many verses in the Torah apparently describe God as having distinctly human characteristics. Thus, He watches with His eyes, listens with His ears, stretches out His arms, speaks with His mouth, and so forth.[1] This principle therefore informs us that none of these expressions should be understood in their literal sense because God has no physical form whatsoever.[2]

HUMAN TERMS FOR GOD

Nevertheless, we must understand why the Torah uses these terms. One of the classical answers[3] is that the Torah speaks in human terms so that we can have some knowledge of God. Since our human frame of reference is based on the experience of our physical senses, the Torah speaks to us in physical terms, even with reference to God.

There in an inner meaning to the terms used in the Torah, however. When we say that the Torah speaks in the language of humans, it is not to be misconstrued that this is merely for the sake of allowing us to understand godliness and is merely a device that serves a certain purpose but has no intrinsic truth. This is certainly not so, for since the Torah is God's Will and Wisdom, it is a Torah of truth, and everything in the Torah is absolute truth.[4]

The explanation offered in chasidic writings[5] is that everything in the physical world has its source in the spiritual world. There is no created being in this world that lacks a specific source Above from which it derives. As the Talmud states, "There is no blade of grass below that does not have a *mazal*, a spiritual source Above, which makes it grow."[6] If there is an eye or an ear in this physical world, it is because there is an "eye" or an "ear" in the spiritual world.[7] Naturally, the "eye" in the spiritual world is not a physical eye. Rather, what an eye does or what an ear does down here on earth has its source Above from which it derives. But "seeing" Above, or "hearing" Above is on a far higher, more spiritual plane. For "seeing" and "hearing" as they are Above to be manifested as seeing and hearing down below in this world, they must undergo a long process of descent, coarsening and contracting, until they become seeing and hearing in the physical world. But the true life force of a physical eye or a physical ear is its spiritual counterpart Above, in the spiritual spheres. Thus, when we say that the Torah speaks in the language of man, we do not mean that it uses expressions alien to the true intent of the words of the Torah. On the contrary, the true "eye" or "ear" is Above, in the spiritual worlds, whereas the eye and ear down here are merely a dim reflection of their source Above.[8]

When we say that God does not have a body, or the likeness of a body,[9] we do not mean to repudiate only the body in a physical sense. This much is obvious and needs no proof. *Chasidus* explains that we repudiate the idea of a "body" in a spiritual sense as well, referring to the higher spiritual worlds and the supernal emanations known as the *sefirot*, which are manifestations of divine energy but are not God Himself,[10] as the *Zohar* states explicitly: He is not any of these qualities at all.[11]

A DEEPER EXPLANATION

An even deeper explanation is found in chasidic literature. This can be understood by way of analogy to the faculties of a human being. In a human being, the act of seeing is the manifestation of the power of sight inherent in the soul. The eye itself is merely the vessel for this particular soul power. The same is true of the ear—it is a vessel for the power of hearing that utilizes it. Therefore, even when we speak about the eye seeing, or the ear hearing in a purely physical sense, we do not mean that it is only the physical eye that sees, or the physical ear that hears, for someone may have the necessary organs of sight and hearing and still not be able to see or hear. Rather, when the power of sight is invested in the organs of sight, a person sees, and when the power of hearing is invested in the organs of hearing, a person can hear. Accordingly, even when we refer to the physical organs of sight and hearing, we are also referring to the powers of sight and hearing that are invested in those organs.

Thus, when the Torah uses human terms, these are merely a metaphor for the spiritual power that is eventually manifested as human sight by a process of descent and coarsening, and so on.

Moreover, the faculties of sight and hearing possessed by the human soul are *also* metaphors for "seeing" and "hearing"

Above, which are not "powers" in the same sense as seeing and hearing are faculties of the soul. Maimonides states clearly[12] that not only does God not have a body but that no physical concepts apply to Him.[13] This includes any spiritual structure or form, for these are merely physical attributes described in an abstract form. God does not *possess* the attributes of wisdom, understanding, kindness, strength, mercy, and so forth, in the same way that the soul possesses the faculties of sight, hearing, thinking, and so on. For "there is nothing whatsoever that resembles Him at all." The attributes that we mention are merely acts of God that have been manifested on the spiritual plane.

The *Midrash*[14] tells us that when God revealed Himself to Moshe (Moses), Moshe asked Him by what Name he should call God. And the answer he received was, "According to My deeds I am called!" When He radiates the attribute of strict justice, He is called *Elokim*, when He illuminates the world with the attribute of kindness, he is called *E-l*, and so on. However, God's true nature is beyond the grasp of human intellect, as the verse states; "Can you fathom God by searching? Can you fathom the Almighty to perfection?" (Job 11:7).

TIME AND CHANGE

A further ramification of our belief that God has no body is that He does not exist in time. Such concepts as beginning and end and change therefore do not apply to Him, as it is stated in the verse, "I am God, I do not change" (Malachi 3:6). This means that since He is infinitely removed from the world, nothing in the world affects Him.[15]

Quite naturally, the question will arise about what the Torah means when it states that God's anger burned, or that God regretted something He did. Concerning the generation of the Flood, it states that God regretted having created the world.[16] It also says in context of the sacrifices, that God derives pleasure from the offerings we bring Him.[17] All these indicate that human behavior affects Him, and that, therefore, He is changeable. Certainly, if He is angry then it follows that at another time He is not angry. If regretful, then, at times, He is satisfied, and so forth. The same principle applies to God's will. When we pray to God and ask Him to change His will and bring us a cure or sustenance, we say clearly in our prayers, "May it be Your will . . ." that is, that His will should change. And yet, we maintain that God has no body or any of the limited and changeable forces that are associated with a body.

To explain this, *Chasidus* gives us the metaphor of light, which has no intrinsic color, shining through colored glass. When it shines through red glass, the light will appear to be red. When it shines through blue glass, it will appear to be blue, and so on. In fact, the light itself remains colorless, merely taking on the hue of the colored glass.[18] In a similar manner, God set up a system of attributes that function like colored glass. By themselves, the attributes cannot create or give life. But what they can do is limit and "tint" the attribute with certain qualities and characteristics. This does not change the nature of the energy that is invested in that attribute. It still remains the same unchanged energy in its source. But it takes on the appearance of that particular attribute when invested in it. For example, the attribute of kindness: if God bestowed kindness upon us directly, that is, by bypassing the system of attributes, the light would be too strong and too all encompassing for us to appreciate the kindness. It is a little like finding a person who likes chocolate cream cake and shoving three hundred pounds of chocolate cream cake down his throat. This might not really be considered kindness. So, for our own benefit, God arranged a system wherein His light shines through attributes that constrict the light in order for it to be utilized and appreciated by His creations.[19] When the Torah states that God was "angry" or "had regret," it means that His Infinite Light (i.e., His revelation of Himself), which has no form whatsoever, shone through the attribute of strict justice, or that He withdrew His revelation of light. This is described as "anger" in the Torah.

This means that our deeds, so to speak, automatically cause the light to come to us through vessels or attributes that correspond to our actions. Therefore, when the Torah says that God saw or God heard, or God was happy, it means that the manner in which the flow of light and revelation was received came through those particular attributes.

This system of our deeds affecting the attributes is a result of God's kindness. Intrinsically, we lack the power to influence Him in any way. On our own, we are too insignificant to affect those attributes at all. But as an act of gratuitous kindness, God wants us to feel that what we do really makes a difference in heaven. To accomplish this, He set up a system wherein our actions really do make a difference. As a result, our service to God is far more meaningful, since we know that we are really affecting the spiritual worlds. So when we act in a certain way, we affect the manner in which God's light will flow forth to us. (This will be explained at length and annotated in our discussion of the eleventh principle.)

The foregoing also explains the meaning of our prayer, "May it be Your will that. . . ." We are not asking God to change His mind, so to speak. We are asking Him to reveal Himself to us through different vessels and attributes.

TWO SYSTEMS

All of this is, then, the description of a system of relationships set up by God. In this system, whatever happens is based on our actions, how we affect the attributes, and how we are answered. This is how God constricts Himself and relates to us in a limited way, in a way that we can relate to and even, at times, comprehend. The revelation is "shaped" and defined by the vessel or attribute in which it is invested. In technical terminology, this is referred to as the immanent, or indwelling revelation of God.

But there is another system, an infinite system, the transcendent revelation of God as He is in Himself. In the infinite system, God is revealed in every detail and aspect. Here, He does not have to constrict or limit His revelation of Himself according to the ability of the recipients to receive that revelation. And at the same time He is revealed in His full glory, He is not contained or grasped by anything.[20]

These two systems are the two different ways with which God relates to the world. One system is characterized by a boundless, infinite revelation, wherein God is in everything while at the same time He remains unchanged and ungraspable. The other system is the one in which God relates to us according to our behavior, the revelation being limited by the capacity of the recipients to receive. In this system, the actions of humans below make a difference. It is only with respect to the second system that we speak about God seeing or hearing or getting angry. It refers only to God's relationship to us, as a product of our actions. But, concurrently, we acknowledge that there is another reality as well, as God is in Himself, in a completely unknowable and indescribable way.[21]

Even in the lower system, however, where godliness appears to be limited and constricted, we do not mean that the light itself (God's revelation of Himself through various attributes) is constricted. It merely appears to be constricted because it is perceived by the world as shining through a vessel or attribute. Metaphorically, it is seen from the other side of the glass. Therefore, it appears to the world that is receiving the flow of God's light through these attributes that God is angry, or happy, or has regrets, or that He is spoken of as having human or even physical attributes (the hand of God, God spoke). Even here, the light is not really constricted or changed in any way. The vessel has no effect on the light itself, only on the way in which we perceive the light, so that it should change and be affected by our deeds.[22]

NOTES

1. As in Exodus 24:10, 31:18, 9:3; Deuteronomy 2:15, 11:12, etc.
2. See at length Maimonides' *Code, Yesodei HaTorah* 1:8ff.
3. *Berachot* 31b; Maimonides, *Commentary to the Mishnah Sanhedrin* 11:1.
4. See Rabbi Menachem de Fano's *Asarah Maamarot, Maamar Chikur HaDin*, pt. 3, chap. 22; *Shnei Luchot HaBrit*, p. 13bff.; 161aff.
5. *Likkutei Torah, Tazriah* 22bff.
6. *Bereishit Rabbah* 10; *Shir HaShirim Rabbah* 1.
7. References in footnote 4.
8. See the Lubavitcher Rebbe's *Shaarei Emunah*, chap. 42:3.
9. From the poem *Yigdal*.
10. *Torah Or Bereishit*, vol. 6, p. 1023b; *Derech Mitzevotecha Haamanat Elokut*, chap. 7.
11. In *Patach Eliyahu*, Introduction to the *Tikkunei Zohar*.
12. *Code, Yesodei HaTorah* 1:9, 11; *Teshuvah* 3:7.
13. It may be pointed out that in terms of God's omnipotence, He could have chosen to have a body of some sort too (not necessarily in the purely physical sense). However, the Torah testifies to the fact that He did *not* choose to do this (cf. Exodus 20:4; Deuteronomy 4:16–19).
14. *Shemot Rabbah* 3:6.
15. *Code, Yesodei HaTorah* 1:11.
16. Genesis 6:6.
17. Genesis 8:21.
18. See Rabbi Moshe Cordovero's *Pardess Rimonim, Shaar Orot v'Keilim*.

19. See also *Patach Eliyahu* (Introduction to the *Tikkunei Zohar*): "... You brought forth ten *tikkunim* (garments), which You called the ten *sefirot* (attributes), by which You conduct the world...."

20. See *Likkutei Amarim, Tanya,*, chap. 48.

21. Ibid.

22. See *Derech Mitzevotecha, Haamanat Elokut.*

The Fourth Principle

> I believe with complete faith that God is first and last.

he fourth principle is a declaration of faith in the absolute eternity of God. There is nothing else that shares this eternal quality. God always was, and always will be.[1] A verse states, "I am first and I am last" (Isaiah 44:6). The concept of God as "first" does not mean first in time or first in number. It is obvious that God transcends time, for even human thought transcends time and space, as is proved by the fact that we can easily imagine ourselves in the past or in the future, and as occupying a different place from the one that we in fact occupy now. Accordingly, this cannot be what Maimonides had in mind when he declared that God is first and last, for this is not a matter in which we must believe since it can be proved logically. Rather, he must have meant something else entirely, in which we are obligated to believe.

TIME AND SPACE

Before we can understand what is meant by the words "God is first and last," we must first clarify what we mean by time, in order to know why time is *not* what we are talking about. Both time and space are merely creations that came into being when God created the world, as the Rambam points out in his *Guide for the Perplexed* (2:13).[2] What is time? Essentially, time is a measure of change. The world is in a state of constant change and flux. The passage of time is simply the measurement of the way the world changes. Before and after, the basic ingredients of time, are merely descriptions of what the world was like before a certain change took place, and afterward.[3]

Time and space define each other, as is recognized by modern science. Time is defined in terms of space: a single object cannot occupy two different places at the same time, and space is defined in terms of time: two objects cannot occupy the same space at the same time. Thus, practically speaking, there can be no time without space or space without time.

This answers the classic question about the creation of the world. According to the Torah, the world was created 5,756 years ago (this being year 5756 of creation). The question asked is, "Why didn't God create the world any earlier? Why not 6,000 years ago or 7,000 years ago or even a minute earlier?" The answer is that before God created the world, there was no such thing as time, and therefore it does not make sense to ask why He did not do it before, for there was no "before." Time is only as old as Creation.[4]

Time itself is finite. It did not always exist. Time consists of finite increments, sixty minutes in an hour, twenty-four hours in a day, and so forth. No matter how one divides time, whether by minutes, seconds, or milliseconds, it is always definable in increments. Add one more finite minute and there

> The gap between the new pulse of light & the next is what defines next moment — the space between the letters

The Fourth Principle

is more time. Subtract one finite second and there is less time. Time is thus a finite creation, as dependent on the Creator as any other creation. Accordingly, time and infinity are mutually exclusive concepts.

Each and every moment of time in this world represents a new pulse of light and energy from Above. Each pulse of energy, of creative force, has a defined order and sequence as to when it is manifested in creation. The "gap" between one pulse of energy and another is what defines a new moment, or a new hour, and so on. When the creative energy of the previous moment returns to its original source, and a new pulse of energy flows down into creation, a change has taken place. The measurement of this change is what we call the passage of time.[5]

From God's perspective, all of these energies are all there at the same time. It is metaphorically like the difference between thinking and speaking. Speech must come forth in the proper order and sequence to be intelligible. But in thought there need not be the same sequence of words, or any sequence at all, for that matter, for the idea can be thought of all at once.

The concept of time as a measure of change means that we are measuring changes of new energies. The way things were before is different from the way they are now. New energies are in play. But the energies are new only to us. We see the change as being something new that was not here before. But from God's perspective, transcending time, all these energies exist simultaneously. Time does not exist from an eternal perspective. When past, present, and future are all one, there is no time. Incidentally, this is one of the explanations as to how the Prophets of Israel were able to foresee things that would happen in the future. They were raised to a visionary level above time wherein all events occur at once. Therefore, events that would happen in the future in

> When past present & future exist simultaneously there is no time

a time-based world were evident to them in their above-time, prophetic experience.

TIME IN THE SPIRITUAL WORLDS

There is, however, another level or concept of time, based on order and priority, rather than on change.[6] This is the concept of time in the spiritual worlds—a function of the relationship between the supernal attributes, which are called the *sefirot* (emanations) in kabbalistic terminology. Kabbalistic works explain that one *sefirah* develops from another, in a specific order, so that the second attribute cannot be manifested without the prior manifestation of the first one. Or, in other words, a lower attribute descends and develops from a higher attribute. This ordering of priorities is time in the spiritual worlds.

This can be compared to the progression from intellect to emotion. In the order of development, emotions are a product of the intellect, which necessarily precedes emotion. In this sense, time is a cause-and-effect relationship. The cause is called "before" (earlier), and the effect is called "after" (later).

Based on this explanation of time, when we say that God is beyond time, we are saying that although to us one thing seems to be the cause of another—its effect—nevertheless, this is only the way that *we* perceive it. But as far as God is concerned, the cause and effect exist simultaneously.[7] In the commentary to the second principle, we explained that the nature of the divine order is not like that of a creature of flesh and blood.[8] By way of analogy: when a person utters a word, the breath emitted in speaking is something that can be sensed and perceived as a thing apart, separated from its source, the faculty of speech possessed by the human soul. But as regards the Holy One, blessed is He, His "speech" (i.e., the ten utterances through which the creation came into being[9]) is not separated from Himself, since there is nothing outside of Him, and there is no place devoid of Him, and all the utterances are nullified in His Essence and are united with Him in absolute union, just as a person's speech and thought are united with him while they are still *in potentia* in his wisdom and intellect. Accordingly, there is no distinction between earlier and later. This is also the explanation of the divine Name י-ה-ו-ה, which is explained as being a compound of the words for past present and future (היה, הווה, יהיה) all at once. This Name therefore indicates that at this level, past, present, and future are all merged into one without any beginning, middle, or end.[10]

ABOVE AND BELOW

Based on a statement of the *Zohar*,[11] that the Infinite Light (the *Or Ein Sof*, God's Infinite Revelation of Himself) is above without beginning, and below without end, we can offer a deeper explanation of the concepts of "first" and "last." When we state that God is first we mean that He is "above without beginning," and when we state that He is last, we mean that He is "below without end."[12] *Chasidus* explains that "above without beginning" means that whatever elevated spiritual level one would be able to attain, level after level above, the original source is always above and beyond that level. This therefore refers to God as He is in His Essence, totally transcending time and space. On the other hand, "below without end" means that the revelation of godliness spreads out and continues, even within time and space, so that even the most minor detail of creation is nothing less than a manifestation of godliness. This is the meaning of the verse, "If I ascend to heaven, You are there. Even if I make my bed in *She'ol* (hell), You are there!" (Psalm 139:8). This is also what the *Zohar*[13] states: "There is no place devoid of Him," for if there were some aspect of existence in which God were not found, this would be a limitation of His omnipotence.[14] Although this is not something we can see with our eyes at present, it will be revealed in the era of the resurrection of the dead, as explained in our commentary to the thirteenth principle.

Let us examine this in greater depth. In discussing the first and second principles, we cited kabbalistic texts[15] that explain that a finite world could not have existed side by side with the revelation of God's infinity. Thus, to create a finite, limited world, God contracted and concealed His Infinite Revelation. This act of contraction and concealment to create the world is referred to as the *tzimtzum*.[16] The doctrine of *tzimtzum* was expounded in the following way: Before the universe was created, there was only the Infinite One, whose infinite revelation of Himself (termed the *Or Ein Sof*, the Infinite Light) filled all of existence. In the Infinite Light there was no place for finite existence. But when it arose in God's will to create finite worlds, He withdrew His Infinite Light, so to speak, in order to create a void (*chalal*) wherein finite existence could be created, by means of a reintroduction of finite light into the void.[17]

Chasidus points out that the *tzimtzum* is not to be understood literally, that God actually withdrew Himself from the void. He merely concealed His Infinite Light within Himself, raising it up to a level beyond revelation.[18] Moreover, since the *tzimtzum* took place only in the Infinite Light, and not in God Himself, no change whatsoever is effected in Him by the *tzimtzum*. Accordingly, although "God is first" in the sense of being prior to the *tzimtzum* and the creation of the spiritual and physical worlds, nevertheless, "He is last" is also true, for there is no aspect of creation that is devoid of Him. The entire *tzimtzum* does not hide anything from God Himself,[19] for it exists only as far as we are concerned, as the verse states, "Even darkness is not dark for You (Psalm 139:12), as we explained at length in our commentary to the second principle.

THE FIRST CAUSE

Chasidus explains further that in a deeper sense "God is first" means that He is the cause of everything, as the *Zohar* states, "You are the Cause of all causes, and the Producer of all effects."[20] Because God is the cause of everything, He is first. The translation of the word "first" thus means that He is the cause of everything.

By stating that God is the cause of everything, the first of everything, we imply that any concept we could possibly imagine is preceded by God, who is eternal. God can do the impossible because the "impossible" is also a creation, and is only impossible in terms of the "laws" of nature, which are also created by God, and to which He is not subject. All descriptions, including the statement that He can do the impossible, are also created and are defined by our concept of what is impossible.

Just as He created the concept of greatness and the concept of finite, so He created the concept of eternal and infinite. Therefore, even eternity is not what God is. He is the "first" of everything, meaning that nothing caused the existence of God. He exists because He is.[21] If God were an effect of a prior cause, He would have a limitation. Anything created is limited in the sense that its existence is dependent on something creating it. But God's existence is but Himself and was not caused by some other factor. Therefore, He is first.

Implied also is the idea that He was here before the world, before the physical world, before any spiritual world. He was first before any kind of title or definition.

Thus, the true definition of the word "first" as applied to God is precisely the opposite of the common usage of the word "first"—that there is a second that follows the first. As regards God, He is first and there is no second. This is because all levels, titles, and terminology were caused by Him. He is the Cause of all causes.[22]

Thus, when Maimonides refers to God as being first, he does not mean that He is first in time but that He is the First Cause. Since the First Cause is not itself the effect of a previous cause, it does not make sense to speak of time even in the spiritual sense explained above, in the sense of precedence of cause and effect. God cannot be defined even in terms of the effects that He brings about, since He is not part of the system of cause and effect.[23]

This resolves the seeming contradiction concerning God's immutability. The Torah states that God does not change: "I am God, I do not change" (Malachi 3:6). In the *Siddur* (prayer book), it states that He is exactly the same before He created the world as after He created the world.[24] This is certainly a paradoxical idea. How can it be that there is no difference or any change? Before the world was created, there was only God, alone. Suddenly, God creates the world and He brings into being every single creation in the world and every detail of every creation. How is it possible that this effects no change in Him? How can He be exactly the same before and after He created the world? The paradox can be understood according to the above explanation of God as "first." As the Cause of all causes, He is so removed that everything is but a reflection, and whatever happens within the reflection has no effect on the source of the reflection. This can be compared to a ray of

a creation that has a beginning but no end

sun shining into a room through the window. If one closes the shutters, so that the sun no longer shines into the room, the sun itself is unaffected by this change. In a similar way, God's creating the world and everything in it effects no change in Him whatsoever, so that He is the same before He created the world and after He created the world.[25]

FIRST AND LAST

We can understand this principle in an even deeper sense. Maimonides states that God is "first" and is also "last." *Chasidus* explains that "first" means that God always existed and is therefore utterly removed from any comparison with His creation. His being "last" means that He will always exist. It indicates that God is eternal. We need to state the idea of "last" in the context of "first" because it is possible to conceive of a creation that had a beginning but has no end. It is possible for there to be a creation that is eternal even though it had a beginning in time. If God were to will something to be eternal, then it would be eternal. The sun and the stars, for example, are creations, and therefore, of themselves would eventually burn out, disintegrate, and disappear, just like any other created thing. However, by the will of the Creator they exist eternally, and do not grow dimmer or disappear with the passage of time.[26] Empirically, they are eternal. As a theory, the theory of entropy, meaning that the universe is slowing down, growing more and more disordered, and is naturally dying out, is acceptable and even correct. But as a fact, it is utterly rejected by Judaism, for God is constantly re-creating His universe.[27]

Maimonides himself points out in his *Guide for the Perplexed* (2:13) that everything was created by God out of absolute nothingness, a subject that we examined in our commentary to the first principle. According to this doctrine, initially, God alone existed, and there was nothing else. He then created everything that exists from absolute nothingness. This is an outright rejection of the idea that there was some kind of raw, undeveloped matter that was formed and developed and "evolved" into our world as it exists today.[28] (It is difficult to understand how some scientists, people with intelligence and learning, are prepared to believe in some preexistent gas, the origin of which they cannot explain, which formed the universe, but not in a preexistent, transcendent divine Being. Jewish belief, says Maimonides, is that the world was created complete and out of absolute nothingness—it did not *evolve* into its present state.) However, it is also a rejection of the idea that the universe will naturally die out and disappear with the passage of time, for its entire existence is completely dependent on a constant creative force that brings it into being at every moment by the will of the Creator. If He chose, the world would vanish in an instant (and not die out over billions of years), and since He chooses to maintain its existence, its existence remains as potent as it was at the beginning of creation, without losing any energy in the process.

Thus, if it is God's will, it is possible for there to be a creation that is eternal even though it had a beginning in time. Nevertheless, even though there is a concept of forward eternity (i.e., where something has a beginning, but no end), this is not what Jewish thought calls eternal or infinite. If something had a beginning, a moment in time when it was created, then it already has a limitation. If something will exist forever but was created, then it is not infinite. The complete idea of infinity implies something that always was and always will be.

In fact, any created entity is not truly infinite because it has two limitations. The first limitation is that it did not create itself but was dependent on a Creator (and therefore is still dependent on the Creator, as we explained in our commentary to the first principle). The second limitation is that its "infinity" is limited, for it had a beginning. In this sense, therefore, it is finite.

This is what we mean to exclude when we say that God is first and last. He was not created, nor did He have a beginning, even in the spiritual sense of beginning as "preceding." Since His being is of His essence, He always existed and will therefore always continue to exist.[29] Accordingly, the idea of His being "first" in the sense that He always was automatically includes the idea of His being "last"—He always will be.

Moreover, the concept of "always will be" in relation to "always was" is far more elevated than the "always will be" of a created being that continues to exist forever merely by virtue of God's will. In the latter case, the very matter of the created entity naturally dies out eventually, as Maimonides explains at length in his *Guide*.[30] Accordingly, even though some entity might exist eternally by the will of the Creator, this is in opposition to the laws that the Creator set for material existence. Its continued existence is miraculous in the sense that it does not follow the natural course of events that the Holy One, blessed is He, implanted in the creation. In contrast, the "eternality" of He who has no beginning is of His Essence.

Furthermore, since He has no beginning, the fact that He has no end is not a separate issue, as if to say, "God has no beginning, and guess what? He has no end either!" Something that has no beginning cannot have an end, by definition. Thus, "I am last" is an *a priori* corollary of the fact that "I am first," in the sense just explained.

Although we cannot understand all of this clearly, we nevertheless take it on perfect faith that God is eternal, without a beginning and without an end. He is first and last.

NOTES

1. See Maimonides' *Commentary to the Mishnah, Sanhedrin,* chap. 10.
2. See also R. Saadia Gaon in *Emunot v'Deot,* 43—the fourth proof; Rashba *Responsa* 418; R. Menachem Azaryah de Fano in *Asarah Maamarot, Maamar Em kol Chai,* chap. 16. See also Shomer Emunim, *Vikuach* 2:17, for a kabbalistic discussion of this matter.
3. Discussed at length by the Lubavitcher Rebbe in *Igrot Kodesh,* vol. 2, p. 224; *Likkutei Sichot,* vol. 18, p. 178; *Derech Mitzevotecha, Haamanat Elokut,* chap. 11.
4. *Siddur im Dach, Shaar Kriat Shema* ד"ה להבין פ"ר דק"ש. *Igrot Kodesh,* vol. 2, p. 224.
5. *Derech Mitzevotecha, Haamanat Elokut,* chap. 11; *Igrot Kodesh,* vol. 2, p. 224.
6. Referred to as "seder zmanim" the order of time in *Bereishit Rabbah* beginning of chap. 3. Explained in Rabbi Moshe Cordovero's *Pardess Rimonim, Archei HaKinuim,* s.v. Seder Zmanim; *Avodat Hakodesh* (Rabbi Meir ibn Gabbai) pt. 4, chap. 5. Explained in *Chasidus* in *Derech Mitzevotecha, Haamanat Elokut,* chap. 11.
7. The following explanation is based on *Tanya,* chap. 21.
8. *Berachot* 40a.
9. *Avot* 5:1.
10. *Or HaTorah VaEra,* p. 200.
11. *Zohar Chadash Yitro,* 45c; *Tikkunei Zohar, Tikkun* 19.
12. See *Shaar HaEmunah* (Rabbi Dovber of Lubavitch), chap. 16; *Torat Chaim, Shemot,* p. 235a; Discourses 5666, pp. 188–189; *Sefer HaArachim,* vol. 4, p. 371 ff.
13. *Tikkunei Zohar, Tikkun* 57.
14. Cf. *Avodat HaKodesh* (Rabbi Meir Ibn Gabbai) pt. 1, chap. 8.
15. *Eitz Chaim, Otzrot Chaim,* beginning.
16. Discussed extensively in *Tanya,* chaps. 21–22, 48–49; *Shaar HaYichud v'HaEmunah,* chaps. 3–4; 6–7; 9–10; and especially in *Torah Or, Vayera* 13c ff.; *Likkutei Torah,* addenda to *Vayikra,* p. 51b ff. For a brief but thorough treatment of this subject see "Mystical Concepts in Chassidism," ad loc., chap. 2.
17. See the beginning of *Etz Chaim, Otzrot Chaim, Mevoh Shearim,* and so on; *Tanya,* chaps. 21, 48, 49; *Likkutei Torah, Vayikra,* p. 51b ff., and especially 52c.

18. *Shaar HaYichud v'HaEmunah*, chap. 7; *Likkutei Torah*, *Vayikra*, ad loc.
19. See at length the discourse *Veyadata*, Moscow, 5657.
20. *Patach Eliyahu*, Introduction to *Tikkunei Zohar*.
21. See Maimonides, *Code*, *Yesodei HaTorah* 1:3.
22. Compare Rashba, *Responsa* 418.
23. This is clearly the intention of *Guide for the Perplexed* 2:13.
24. Morning liturgy.
25. Explained at length in *Likkutei Amarim*, *Tanya*, chap. 20; *Shaar HaYichud*, chap. 7; *Iggeret HaKodesh*, chap. 26
26. As is clear from the verses in Genesis 8:22; Isaiah 40:26.
27. As stated explicitly in the morning liturgy (end of the first blessing before *Shema*): ". . . Who in His goodness renews the creation constantly, each day."
28. The complications and fallacies of the theory of evolution are examined at length by the Lubavitcher Rebbe in *Shaarei Emunah*, chap. 63.
29. Rabbi Menachem Azaryah deFano in *Yonat Elem*, Introduction; *Pelech HaRimon* 4:3, cited in *Likkutei Torah*, *Pekudei* 7b, et al.
30. Pt. 3, chap. 8.

The Fifth Principle

> I believe with complete faith that it is proper to pray only to God. One may not pray to anyone or anything else.

The fifth principle teaches that God is the only one who we may serve and worship. We may not have recourse to any intermediaries but must pray to Him directly.[1]

PRAYER AND HUMAN NEEDS

We pray to God to help us with our needs, and we may not pray to anything else, even a servant of God, such as an angel, a star, or a holy person. This principle of faith presupposes our acknowledgment that everything that happens in the world happens only through God. Therefore, when we pray to Him because we have a need or a problem, we confirm the fact that all things are in His hands.[2]

It is a fundamental principle of Jewish faith that every person knows that he or she is directly connected to God and that God Himself cares for all of a person's needs. Accordingly,

He is the one to whom we must turn in prayer. For this reason, chasidic texts[3] compare our relationship with God during the hour of prayer to a father–son relationship (whereas when we are learning Torah, our relationship to God is comparable to a student–teacher relationship). Nevertheless, it is reasonable to ask, "Why would God bother dealing with us and our needs?" It also seems reasonable to be altruistic in the matter of prayer and refrain from asking for our own needs, preferring to ask on behalf of the Jewish people in general, or for other people, but not bothering God with our own needs, particularly our material needs.

Both attitudes are dismissed when we realize that God, who is truly infinite, can care for any being without any effort at all. It is no more strain for Him to care for a mosquito than an angel in heaven. Both are equally removed from God. On the contrary, when we turn to God for help with our physical necessities, we emphasize our belief that material matters are also in His charge, and not under the jurisdiction of some other power. It is for this reason that we are commanded to turn only to God when in need, and He will provide us with our needs.

Chasidus teaches[4] that a person should not have doubts whether God will answer our prayers or not. Every time we pray, it must be with the certain knowledge that God definitely answers us. This is why in the *Amidah* prayer, the central prayer in the Jewish liturgy, we request various things, then conclude the request with the declarative blessing, "Blessed are You, God, Who heals the sick," or "Blessed are you, God, gracious and generous in pardon." Although it seems contrary to our experience that our prayers are *always* answered, this explanation is soundly based on a principle of *halachah* (Jewish Law): When a person is in doubt as to whether or not he should make a blessing, he must refrain from making the blessing.⁵ Otherwise it might be a blessing said in vain, which is taking God's Name in vain, and a serious transgression. If there were the slightest doubt about our prayers being answered, then we would be forbidden to make this kind of blessing of thanks to God, for it might be a blessing in vain! Therefore, since the Sages of the Talmud taught⁶ that this is the correct formula for prayer—to ask, and then thank God, using His Name—it is certain, without doubt, that He answers us each time. Sometimes we openly comprehend the answer, and other times we do not. But this difference is only with regard to us and our perception. As far as God is concerned, whenever we pray to Him, He answers us. In addition, our Sages declare that the verse, "Behold God is mighty, and does not despise any" (Job 36:5) refers to communal prayer, which is never turned away empty-handed.⁷

PRAYER AS SERVICE OF THE HEART

There are many aspects to prayer. There is prayer in which we request the fulfillment of our needs. But there is also prayer that is a means of serving God. Although the fulfillment of every commandment (*mitzvah*) of the Torah is an act of service to God, prayer specifically is referred to as service—"service of the heart," in the words of our Sages.⁸ It is unique in that its whole theme is the service of God. When a person prays to God, even if he does not ask for anything, the activity of prayer alone is regarded as serving God.

Why is prayer, more than any other *mitzvah*, singled out as service to God? How is it any more of a service to God than putting on *tefillin* or waving a *lulav* and *etrog* or eating *matzah* on Passover? All of these are regarded as actions of service to God, but none are specifically called such except prayer.

The answer is that as "service of the heart," prayer attaches one emotionally to God, and one is affected and revived throughout one's being. Reciting the words is a necessary component of prayer, but the love or awe one experiences are what characterize the *mitzvah* of prayer as service of the heart. Prayer is not merely moving the lips and reciting a set formula, although these are also necessary.[9] Rather, prayer is characterized as service of the heart.[10] When a person prays, he is emotionally attached to God. He is attached often through love or through awe (or fear) of God. This means that the person is not merely performing a mechanical action but that he is also experiencing something. He is moved.[11]

MEDITATION

It is impossible to have a true feeling of something and be thoroughly moved by it unless one first understands it and contemplates it or meditates upon it in order to develop this true feeling. When one recites those parts of the liturgy relating to loving God with all one's heart and all one's soul, it can hardly be felt in truth without proper contemplation of those subjects that arouse one's love and awe of God, as Maimonides states explicitly.[12] Why prayer alone is called service of the heart is that love and awe are the main objective of prayer, but only supplementary components of the vast majority of other *mitzvahs*.[13] When prayer is enriched by contemplation, the feelings described in words of prayer, feelings of love, and awe of God, become revealed in the heart, and this entire process is called serving God.

However, it could then be asked, why is there so much importance attached to pronouncing the words of prayer, if the main objective of prayer is feeling? The expression "lip service," meaning empty rhetoric, can apply nowhere so aptly as here. If it is the emotion that really matters, then why not simply pray with our minds, utilizing mental concentration alone? Why express the thoughts through speech at all? And yet, we learn that mental concentration alone does not fulfill the *mitzvah* of prayer. Prayers must be expressed verbally.[14]

Chasidus explains that vocalizing the words, although the act may appear to us as superficial compared with thought or emotion, affects the innermost recesses of the soul.[15] Although thought and emotions are more inward powers than speech, for words themselves are essentially physical entities, produced by the passage of breath over the vocal cords, formed and defined by the tongue, teeth, and lips. Nevertheless, the power of speech is one of the deepest powers of the soul, to the extent that the human soul is referred to as "a speaking soul."[16] Moreover, in relationship to the rest of creation, man is singled out as "the speaker" (*medaber*). One of the explanations of this is that his essence is revealed in speech even more than it is revealed in thought, for the latter is merely a "garment" or power of the soul but does not express its essence.

We often find that a person's feelings of love for another will become even deeper as a result of expressing it in words. The same is true with the emotion of anger. If one expresses the anger in words, the anger becomes felt with greater depth. In a similar way, explaining a matter to another person clarifies it to the person presenting the idea as well, to the extent that he even gains new insights into the subject that he was not aware of previously. The reason that speech is able to affect both the intellect and the emotions is that the source of speech is from a higher spiritual level than either the intellect or the emotions.[17] Thus, when a person speaks, he connects to a deeper part of his soul than he connects to through either intellect or emotion. When man speaks, it is not speech alone that comes forth but energy from the inner essence of the soul. This inner essence of the soul is revealed in his speech, giving added life and strength to his intellect and emotions. It is for this reason that the Torah instructs us to actually speak the words of prayer. Since the objective of prayer is feeling, when the prayers are vocalized, deeper feelings are expressed. Speech, therefore, is not a substitute for feelings but a means of expressing deeper feelings than are aroused by meditation alone.

TO GOD ALONE

This brings us back to the original principle as stated by the Rambam: "It is proper to pray only to God." *Chasidus* explains the inner meaning of this idea: When a Jew prays to God, he should pray only to His Essence and not to any of His revealed or hidden characteristics, in the words of our Sages, "to Him, and not to His Attributes."[18] The story is told that the Alter Rebbe, Rabbi Shneur Zalman of Liadi, would say, "God, I don't want Your lower *Gan Eden* [Paradise]. I don't want your higher *Gan Eden* [according to Kabbalah, Paradise has two major levels, an upper and a lower]. I only want only You."

Chasidic teachings use the following analogy to describe this approach: When a person has been granted the privilege of entering the palace of a king, he must pass through many rooms and halls until he reaches the inner chamber of the king himself. It is possible to be so overwhelmed by the beautiful furniture and paintings, the marble floors and the gold tapestries in the outer halls and corridors, that he stands enraptured and forgets completely about the king. But if he keeps his mind on the purpose of his entering the palace, he will not stop and linger, admiring the decorations in the outer halls and corridors, but will go straight to the king himself. This is the meaning of the Baal Shem Tov's adage that a person's prayer is his desire to stand before God and pour out his heart. The person rich in knowledge of the various levels of spirituality can, indeed, be entertained by the spiritual worlds that he experiences. But the simple Jew who knows nothing about spiritual attributes prays directly to God, like a child who knows nothing about levels and meditative perspectives or godly attributes.[19] He knows only that he is praying to God Himself!

The more knowledgeable a person is, the greater the danger that he will make conclusions about God, defining Him and limiting Him according to his personal perception of who God is. Although He is the Creator, the Infinite One, the Eternal, the Omnipotent, these terms do not define or limit Him in any way. These are what God *has* but not what God *is*. This is what a Jew strives to realize when he prays to God. When a person prays to the Essence of God, he connects his own essence to God's Essence. Conversely, when one has established parameters for God in one's mind and one prays to Him within the confines of these parameters, he not only fails to reach God's Essence but he also fails to reach his own essence. The essence of a person relates only to the Essence of God. This is the inner meaning of the Rambam's words, that we pray only to God—not to any preconceived or learned idea of God but just to His Essence. And this is what is meant by prayer as attachment, as explained below. The ultimate attachment is when the pure essence of the soul connects with the Essence of God.

But if such simplicity and innocence in prayer is what is desired, then why does Jewish mysticism, so closely associated with prayer, explain all the godly attributes and worlds, and moreover, instruct us to contemplate about them during prayer and when saying God's Name? In each of the stages of prayer we are expected to think of a different attribute and spiritual world. How does all of this mesh with the idea of praying only to the Essence of God? And by Essence, we mean to the exclusion of all Names and attributes.

The answer is that it is never to those worlds or attributes that one prays. The Names and the worlds and the attributes are only there to channel the flow of God's bounty, to direct His answers to our prayers through the right channels. By contemplating the various Names and attributes, the mystic creates vessels for the bestowal of God's flow of goodness and bounty. The prayer is directed only to God, but the answers come by way of the channels and vessels that are God's Names and attributes,[20] through the system that He set up by which He distributes whatever it is that we need, spiritually and materially, as explained above. These are, metaphorically, the vessels that will contain the blessings. But the prayer itself is always directed to the Essence of God alone.

However, most people do not have this mystical knowledge, and so when we pray, it suffices to direct the thoughts to God in a general way:[21] "God, may my prayer to You be regarded as if I had all the correct mystical thoughts." If a Jew says this to God, he or she can be assured that it is enough to guarantee that God will accept their prayers.

PRAYER AS BONDING

There is a third aspect of prayer. The Hebrew word for prayer, *tefillah*, is derived from the word meaning bonding or attachment.[22] When one meditates, and prays to God, experiencing feelings of closeness to God, the soul experiences a feeling of deep bond and attachment to Him. For the soul, having descended from its original lofty level to become clothed in a human body, where its former closeness to God is now hidden, this bonding is like a breath of fresh air. It is as if the soul has shed itself of its imprisoning body and experiences once again what it had formerly, prior to its descent into the human body.[23]

This aspect of prayer is best illustrated by Jacob's dream, in which he saw a ladder standing on earth, its top reaching to the heights of heaven, and on the ladder were angels ascending and descending.[24] The *Zohar*[25] explains that the angels ascending is a reference to prayer, and the angels descending refers to Torah study.

What is the difference between prayer and the study of Torah? In prayer the "direction" of our service is ascent. When we pray, we strive to raise ourselves to a higher level of awareness of, and attachment to, God. In prayer, man seeks God. In the morning, for example, as soon as we wake up, we first recite the short prayer *Modeh ani*, acknowledging that God has restored our soul to us, and expressing our gratitude for this. Then we recite a series of blessings that thank God for giving us all of our faculties such as intelligence, sight, the power to stand erect, and so forth. Afterward, we continue through the order of the morning prayers until we reach the point of realization of the all-encompassing presence of God in the recital of *Shema*,[26] as explained in our discussion of the second principle. From the outset, the entire process has been one of raising our base, animal soul from the point of little or no consciousness of God and elevating it to a greater awareness of, and closeness to, God.

Torah study is entirely different. First, the Torah is of divine origin, containing the will and wisdom of God, as is discussed at length in the Scripture, Talmud, *Midrash*, and Kabbalah; learning Torah means eliciting godliness, drawing it down, so to speak, into this physical world from above. This is in direct contrast to prayer, which raises the soul to its former level of attachment, as mentioned above.[27]

REVEALING DIVINE ATTRIBUTES

A fourth aspect of prayer is our praise of God. During prayer, we call Him kind, wise, great, mighty, awesome, and many other terms of praise. The idea of praising God seems to be a peculiar one. Why do we do this? Are we trying to flatter God? Does it really make a difference to Him when we call Him kind and wise and mighty?

Chasidic teachings explain that this practice can be understood through the analogy of a wise or kind person who is always so preoccupied with other affairs that he does not visibly demonstrate his wisdom or kindness. One way of making him reveal his hidden qualities is by praising him for these qualities. The praise itself elicits and reveals these qualities because a person naturally tries to live up to the expectations and image we have of him. Thus, by praising the person, one does not merely flatter him but helps him develop and reveal these worthy traits.[28]

With respect to God, however, there is a notable difference in the analogy. God is infinite, the ultimate simplicity of Oneness without form. Not only is He beyond physical form but he does not have any spiritual form to define him—neither wisdom, nor kindness, nor any other attribute or quality (as we explained in our commentary to the third principle). Any description of traits we might give him would indicate something other than Oneness. So the praises we utter are not a description. The praise has a purpose. When we ask God for something, we desire it on a level and within limits that we can appreciate. We want Him to bestow revealed good upon us, not good that is recognized as such only Above. But, since God is infinite, what He bestows upon us would, logically, also be limitless. Since we are limited creatures, however, bound by time and space, we cannot benefit from gifts of infinite magnitude. They would be more than we could handle.

By praising God for His kindness or His wisdom, we are inducing God to work within the system He established wherein we can receive His blessings in a limited fashion. The system is the one mentioned earlier, whereby a system of finite vessels gives character and quality to God's infinite light the way a colored pane of glass lends a hue to light shining through it. Therefore, by praising God for His kindness or mercy or wisdom, we are in effect requesting Him to radiate His light to us through those vessels. Praising God elicits His relating to us through the system. (However, as we explained in the third principle, this does not imply any change in Him, God forbid.)

The very idea of asking God for our needs requires some explanation. Does He not already know what we need? If so, just let Him give it to us. Of course, this would not be a problem for God. The problem would be that we would not know how to receive what He is willing to bestow! By praising God for His kindness, we are actually praying for kindness from God and, in a way, we are creating the attribute by providing a "receptacle" through which His kindness can be revealed.

The prayer itself is thus an extremely creative act. It is not merely a means of getting something off one's chest or to effect a cleansing. When we pray, we make things happen. When we ask God to fulfill a specific need, we are soliciting Him to constrict His infinite power to address our particular need. Although He already knows our needs, through the merit of our prayers, we create the vessels through which God will relate to us.

However, this too needs explanation. Surely God could have set up a system that functions without needing our praise to create and accomplish things, without our needing to articulate each request in order to bring about its fulfillment. But we see that the system itself is established this way because of God's kindness. He wants us to know and feel that we can contribute to our own welfare, that our participation makes a difference. This is what the verse in Psalm (128:2) states: "When you eat the fruits of your own labor, you are happy, and it is good for you." When a person receives a valuable gift without doing anything to deserve it, it does not sit well with him. But when a person feels that he did something, even if he is getting more than he deserves, more than his actions merit, nevertheless it sits much better with him. It is a much greater act of kindness to help the person receiving charity feel worthy of it. The system of prayer allowing us to be the ones who cause the bestowal to happen is the highest form of kindness. Through it, we know that we are in some sense worthy of the shower of good that descends from Above.

IS PRAYER A COMMANDMENT?

Authorities have a difference of opinion as to whether daily prayer is a scriptural commandment or a rabbinical ordinance. Most scholars are of the opinion that it is only rabbinical.[29] *Chasidus* explains[30] that prayer, if it is only rabbinical, is not lesser because of it, but greater. It has even more importance than if it were from the Torah itself. There are 613 *mitzvahs* commanded by the Torah. This is in direct correspondence to the 613 basic parts of the body: 248 limbs and 365 sinews and organs.[31] Similarly, there are 613 spiritual "limbs" and "organs" of the soul. The 613 commandments correspond to the 613 "limbs" and "organs" of the soul. Just as the limbs of the body correspond to the "limbs" of the soul, the "limbs" of the soul correspond to the *mitzvahs* of the Torah. But there is one part of the human body that is not counted as one of the 613—the spine.[32] Yet the spine is much more than just another limb. It is the fulcrum of the entire body, holding it up and connecting everything. This is why it is not counted as an individual limb. It is like the hub of all the limbs. Prayer may similarly be regarded as the spine of the Jewish religion. It is the hub of everything, holding everything in place, connecting everything and sustaining everything. According to some explanations it is for this reason it is not counted as one of the 613 commandments from the Torah.[33]

Therefore, although prayer may only be a rabbinical injunction, it is, in a sense, much more than a scriptural commandment. Just as the spine is the conduit from the brain to all the limbs of the body, and from the limbs to the brain, prayer is the Jew's conduit to and from God. When a person prays properly, with intention, and with love and awe, his prayer becomes the hinge pin and the driving force for all the *mitzvahs* he does throughout the day. It is his prayer experience that gives the person his inspiration, directing the day's activities toward one purpose.[34]

But if prayer is of such central importance, then why was it only instituted by the Rabbis rather than by the Torah? *Chasidus* stresses the idea found in Talmud that rabbinical law should not be understood as any less important than scriptural law.[35] On the contrary, rabbinical injunctions come from an even higher source than scriptural precepts, as the Talmud declares in the name of God.[36] Rabbinical injunctions are so sublime that their light could not be brought into the world through a formal scriptural commandment, so they came in a hidden way, through rabbinical enactments. The third Rebbe of Chabad-Lubavitch, the holy Tzemach Tzedek, once said, "Anyone who is of the opinion that prayer is merely rabbinical law never saw the essence of light in his life." The Lubavitcher Rebbe of our generation, Rabbi M. M. Schneerson, added that *mitzvahs* in general are referred to as a candle—"The *mitzvah* is a candle (*ner*), and the Torah a great light" (Proverbs 6:23), whereas the Tzemach Tzedek referred to prayer as a luminary (*ma'or*)—the *source* of light.

PRAYER AND BLESSING

There is a fifth aspect of prayer, wherein we bless God.[37] Again, this appears to be a peculiar action. Usually, the recipient of a blessing is thought of as one who is lower than the one giving the blessing. The blessing he is given serves to fulfill a need or lack that the recipient of the blessing has. This obviously cannot be the meaning here. According to *Chasidus*, the Hebrew word for blessing, *brocha*, also has the meaning of elicitation, drawing down from above to below.[38] And this is the idea of blessing God. It does not mean that we are giving something to God, but that we are drawing down into the world what is already stored up for us on a higher spiritual level. Blessing God elicits and channels what has already been granted us on a spiritual plane.[39]

Prayer in a general sense can accomplish more than this, for when we pray, we accomplish things for which no allocation in the spiritual world was made. Even if, heaven forbid, it was decided Above that a person should not get what he needs, nevertheless, through sincere prayer, a person can in effect create a new will in God in order to receive what he needs. This is one of the explanations of the phrase commonly used in our prayers:[40] "May it be Your will. . . ." That is, even though this was not Your will until now, may our prayers have been effective in causing our requests to become Your will.

But there is a further complication concerning the efficacy of prayers relating to our needs. Judaism teaches that everything that is going to happen to us throughout the year is decided on Rosh Hashanah and the decision is sealed on Yom Kippur.[41] If this is so, then what good can it do for us to pray for what we have already been given? There are two possible answers. The first is that whatever a person is granted on Rosh Hashanah is on a *spiritual* level, and remains in potential until we elicit it from Above by making the appropriate channels and vessels through prayer. If we fail to bring it down, then it remains on a spiritual plane. But three times a day, we are judged whether we are worthy of receiving the allocation that was given on Rosh Hashanah,[42] that is, if we are worthy enough for that which has been granted on a spiritual plane to become actualized on the physical plane. Interestingly, some authorities maintain that the Hebrew word for prayer, *tefilah*, stems from the word "judge," *pilel*. Our daily prayers therefore express our hopes and requests that we be judged worthy of the materialization in this world of the spiritual outflow from Above. Therefore, praying for our needs daily is no contradiction to the idea that the allocation for our needs was determined on Rosh Hashanah.

A second explanation is that through sincere daily prayer it is possible to create a new will that grants a new allocation. It is as if the power of prayer allows the person to create a "new line," so to speak, and a new allocation through the line. Thus, even if a person was not granted the fulfillment of his needs on Rosh Hashanah, God forbid, he should still pray daily, for his sincere prayer may result in a new allocation.

The idea of a new allocation is, in fact, mentioned on several occasions in the Torah, particularly with regard to our Patriarch Isaac, whose prayers were effective in changing the status of his barren wife.[43] This, incidentally, is also why *chasidim* go to a Rebbe for a blessing in the face of a problem. Perhaps it was clearly decided that a particular couple should not have children. They could have been married for many years but remained childless. So they would go to the Rebbe and ask for a blessing to have children. He would pray for them, even though it seemed to be their portion to be childless. The prayers of the righteous *tzaddik* effected a new allocation, and they had children. There are literally thousands of personal accounts of this nature in our generation as well as in past generations.

A SUBSTITUTE FOR SACRIFICES

The central idea of prayer, however, as service to God, is related to the idea of prayer as a substitute for sacrifices, as we find in the words of the Prophet Hosea (Hosea 3:14), "We will render the prayer of our lips in place of the sacrifice of bullocks." Prior to the destruction of the Temple in Jerusalem, there were daily sacrifices offered in the name of all the Jewish people. Since we no longer have a Temple, prayer was instituted daily as a substitute for the daily sacrifices in the Temple.[44] The sacrifices were an integral part of the daily service. In fact, Maimonides[45] explains that the essential purpose of the entire Temple was that it provided a set place for offering sacrifices.

The word that is always used in the sacrificial service of the Temple is "*avodah*," service. It is the identical word used to describe prayer, *avodah shehi b'lev*,[46] service of the heart. *Chasidus* explains that there is a deeper association between the two than merely sharing the same descriptive term. Every Jewish person has two souls, the godly soul and the animal soul.[47] The godly soul is totally selfless, devoted to God with no motives other than to cleave to its Source. This soul is often compared to fire, which, by nature, always reaches upward, seemingly yearning to leap off the wick and return to its source on high. It is the wick that holds the fire down in this world. And if the fire does return to its source, it loses its own identity, merging with its source—it ceases to burn. The nature of fire to return to its source is clearly for no selfish reason. The proof of this is that it becomes nullified when it accomplishes the goal. It is the same with the godly soul, unselfishly wanting to return to God.[48]

The animal soul has exactly the opposite nature. Its interests are always selfish. This does not mean that it always wants to do evil or to sin, but at the very least, the animal soul is always seeking its own benefit, its own comfort.[49] God gave us the two souls in order to give us a choice as to which inner voice motivates us. To which one will we listen?

But there is another reason for having two souls. Our goal is to transform the animal soul into one that also loves God. The godly soul is able to convince the animal soul that it should also love God, even for selfish reasons. When this is accomplished, instead of a battle between two inner opposing forces, there are two spiritual powers within pulling in the same direction. This is the ultimate purpose of prayer.[50]

In the days of the *Beis HaMikdash* we took an animal and gave it as an offering to God, and fire descended from heaven to consume the offering. In exactly the same way, when a person prays with concentration, sincerity, and fervor—the fire of the godly soul—his service parallels the sacrificial offerings, in which fire descended from heaven (in our analogy, the fire of the godly soul) and consumed the offering (in our analogy, the self-seeking, animallike aspect of a person, which is offered to God). In the sacrifices, we offered an animal to God. In prayer, we offer our animal soul to God. In this way a person elevates his animal soul to the level of holiness and achieves a level of love for Him comparable to that experienced by the godly soul.[51]

In addition, *Chasidus* explains[52] that not all of the soul is manifested in the body. In fact, only the lowest levels of the soul are generally enclothed in the body or attached to it, whereas the most sublime levels of the soul are generally not, except at the time of prayer. In the words of Rabbi Shneur Zalman of Liadi: "The essence and being of the godly soul do not constantly hold undisputed sovereignty over the 'small city' [the body], except at appropriate times, such as during the recital of the *Shema* or the *Amidah*. . . ."[53] This is also the meaning of the statement of our Sages[54] that one should beware of a person "whose soul is in his nose," that is, who has not yet recited the morning prayers, for until he has done so, the higher levels of soul are unattached to the lower levels.

Now, although our Sages refer[55] to prayer as the "life of the moment," whereas Torah study is referred to as "eternal life," nevertheless, prayer must precede study, as our Sages state,[56] "From the hall of prayer to the hall of study. . . ." One of the talmudic Sages even expressed the hope that "his prayer be close to his bed," that is, that he would have the opportunity to pray immediately on rising, prior to any other activity. This is because prayer is compared[57] to the spine; although it is not regarded as one of the limbs of the body, it is nevertheless the connecting link between all parts of the body and is vital in actualizing the decisions made in the brain and transmitting them to the rest of the body.

The efficacy of prayer is not only as regards spiritual matters. On the contrary, since one is commanded to "know God in all your ways" (Proverbs 3:6), that is, even in matters that are not directly connected to our service of God, such as making a living (hence, "all *your* ways") before we begin our daily jobs and chores, we are told, "Know God," that is, attach[58] yourself to Him, unite with Him, through prayer, for this will give you direction in your ways and enable you to serve God even while involved in mundane matters.

NOTES

1. See Deuteronomy 4:19; *Code, Avodat Kochavim* 2:1.
2. *Code, Avodat Kochavim* 1:1.
3. Cf. *Tanya*, chap. 44.
4. *Iggeret HaTeshuvah*, chap. 11. This is the unprecedented but indisputable interpretation of the talmudic statement cited in the following footnote.
5. *Berachot* 33a. See also Radbaz, *Responsa*, vol. 2, chap. 642.
6. *Berachot* 49a.
7. *Berachot* 8a. See also *Sefer Hakkarim*, pt. 4, chap. 10.
8. *Talmud Yerushalmi, Berachot* 4:1; cited in *Tur, Orach Chaim* 98.
9. *Berachot* 20b; *Shulchan Aruch, Orach Chaim* 62:3, 185:1, 2. Cited in *Tanya*, chap. 38.
10. *Taanit* 2a.
11. See *Avot* 2:13.
12. Maimonides *Code, Yesodei HaTorah* 2:2.
13. *Tanya*, chap. 38.
14. *Berachot* 20b; *Shulchan Aruch, Orach Chaim* 62:3, 185:1, 2. Cited in *Tanya*, chap. 38.
15. See *Discourses* 5672, chap. 59; 5678 ד"ה ועתה ינדל.
16. *Targum Onkelos*, Genesis 2:7.
17. *Likkutei Amarim, Iggeret HaKodesh*, chap. 5.
18. *Sifri* to Deuteronomy 4:7, cited and explained at length in *Chasidus* in *Derech Mitzevotecha, Shoresh Mitzvat HaTefilah*, chap. 1, ff.
19. See *Pirkei Heichalot*, chap. 32.
20. See *Derech Mitzevotecha, Shoresh Mitzvat HaTefilah*, chap. 1, ff. at length.
21. *Likkutei Amarim, Tanya*, chap. 41.
22. See Rabbi Sholom Dovber's *Kuntreis HaAvodah*, chap. 1.
23. *Tanya*, chap. 39.
24. Genesis 28:10 ff.
25. *Zohar*, vol. I, *Hoshmatot* to *Vayetze*; *Midrash HaNe'elam, Vayetze*.
26. The standard order of the morning liturgy.
27. *Likkutei Amarim, Tanya*, chap. 37.
28. *Derech Mitzevotecha, Hallel*; see also *Lehavin Inyan Lag b'Omer*.
29. The various opinions are listed in *Minchat Chinuch Mitzvah* 434.
30. *Likkutei Torah, Balak*, p. 67c ff.

31. *Tikkunei Zohar, Tikkun* 30 (p. 74a). Cited and explained in *Tanya*, chaps. 23–24.

32. See at length the essay titled *Iyyun Tefillah*, by Rabbi Dovber of Lubavitch.

33. Ibid.

34. *Tanya*, chap. 40.

35. *Eruvin* 21b, 77a, 85b; *Yevamot* 36b, etc.

36. *Eruvin* 21b: "Take more care regarding the words of the Sages than regarding the words of the Torah itself!" and as stated in *Bava Metzia* 59b: "You have overruled Me, My sons."

37. See *Avodah Zarah* 7b.

38. See *Likkutei Torah, Eikev* 16a.

39. Ibid.

40. Cf. the request for the restoration of the Temple recited at the end of the *Amidah* prayer.

41. *Beitzah* 16a.

42. See *Likkutei Torah, Eikev* 16a.

43. Genesis 25:21.

44. *Berachot* 26b.

45. *Beit HaBechirah* 1:1.

46. *Taanit* 2a.

47. *Tanya*, chaps. 1, 2.

48. Ibid., chap. 35.

49. Ibid., chaps. 1, 6, 7.

50. Ibid., chaps. 9, 10.

51. See *Berachot* 54a: ". . . with *both* of your inclinations."

52. *Likkutei Torah, Shir HaShirim* ד"ה יונתי.

53. *Tanya*, chap. 12.

54. *Berachot*.

55. *Shabbat* 10a.

56. *Berachot* 64a.

57. *Iyyun Tefilah*, by Rabbi Dovber of Lubavitch, at length.

58. The word דע (know) is first used in the Torah (Genesis 4:1) to denote attachment and union. Accordingly, this could be regarded as its primary meaning. See *Tanya*, chap. 3 (p. 7b).

The Sixth Principle

I believe with complete faith that all the words of the Prophets are true.

The sixth of the thirteen principles of faith concerns prophecy and divine inspiration. Believing that the words of the Prophets are true means that we believe that God grants prophecy to man.[1] Why should this concept be one of the fundamental principles upon which the faith of the Jewish people is built? And why should this principle take precedence over the belief that the Torah was given by God, which appears only in the eighth principle?[2]

BELIEF IN THE PROPHETS IS BELIEF IN GOD

Chasidus explains[3] that the precept (*mitzvah*) of believing in the prophecy of the Prophets has more to do with belief in God than with the greatness of the prophet. There are two explanations of this. First, we believe that prophecy is a testimony to His infinity. Second, because we believe in God we believe that He provides guidance for mankind in general and the Jewish people in particular, and this is done through His Prophets. This second explanation will be discussed in chapter 10.

Let us examine the first idea in greater detail. The first explanation is that prophecy is a testimony to His infinity. *Chasidus* teaches that God is infinitely exalted and removed from anything in creation, and yet, at the same time, He is able to lower Himself endlessly in investing His life force and energy in an infinite number of levels.[4] This means that even if one were able to ascend an infinite number of levels, one would not get any closer to God. On the contrary, the more elevated the spiritual level one reaches, the more one would realize how removed God is. As we learned in the third principle, "God does not have a physical body, and physical concepts do not apply to Him."

Conversely, God lowers Himself to every level so that there is nothing that is incapable of revealing godliness. He lowers himself into this world, considered the lowest of worlds, and He lowers himself into the lowest part of this world.[5] He truly has no limit in either direction. This is why our Sages state, "Where you find His greatness, you also find His humility."[6] It is a corollary of our belief in God that we believe that He transcends everything and is nevertheless intimately involved with everything, for nothing could exist without Him, as we learned in the second principle. This is the meaning of the chasidic aphorism, "God is everything, and everything is God!"[7]

One of the ramifications of this is that God is capable of illuminating the mind of a prophet with His wisdom, to the extent that the prophet's mind unites and becomes one with His wisdom, and yet the prophet is able to be perceive and even communicate this wisdom.[8] This means that God, Who is limitless and transcends the grasp of human logic, can **also** be revealed within the realm of human logic. It is a testimony to God's greatness that He is able to elevate a finite mind and cause it to unite with infinity.[9]

Hence, belief in the words of the Prophets is a principle of Jewish faith, because it is an extension of our belief in God's omnipotence. This also explains why Maimonides placed this principle before the principle of faith in the Torah (the eighth principle)—for this principle does not relate to the prophet as prophet but as an extension of the greatness of God.[10]

THE PROPHETIC EXPERIENCE

The principle that we have to believe that God reveals himself to the Prophets still needs clarification. There seems to be a contradiction. Maimonides explains[11] that when a prophet experiences prophecy, his normal intellect and emotions cease to function. But we see that when he transmitted the identical words to the Jewish people, their intellect and emotions did not cease to function. Why then did the prophet's intellect and emotions cease to function?

We also have to understand why a prophet is called *meshugga*,[12] "insane." This is not meant in an offensive, negative sense, that the prophet experiencing prophecy is literally insane. Rather, it means that his actions are not based on reason but transcend reason. This also appears to indicate that normal human activities are suspended in the prophetic experience. In chasidic terminology, that which transcends intellect is revealed in the intellect of the prophet, so that his intellect experiences something that is beyond intellect.

God, being infinite, also manifests within the finite, in this case within the finite intellect of the prophet. It is possible for something to be restricted and limited and yet reveal the essence! As the famous teaching of the Baal Shem Tov states: "When you grasp even a little bit of the Essence, you have all of the Essence."[13] Accordingly, when we speak about the "word" of God, this does not mean that there is any less of God's Essence in them than in God's "thoughts," for example. As far as God is concerned, He is as much in His words as He is in His intellect or any other attribute. This is precisely what our Sages point out in the Talmud: regarding the first of the Ten Commandments uttered on Mount Sinai, our Sages explain[14] that the first word of the First Commandment, the word *Anochy* (אנכי, "I am . . :") is an acronym, that is, the letters of the word spell out an entire sentence, *Ana nafshi chetavit yehavit*, which *Chasidus* interprets as meaning, "I gave Myself in writing." That is, when I uttered the Ten Commandments, says God, I gave you Myself![15] The same applies to prophecy: "I give you Myself," resounds in the words that the prophet hears. He experiences the essence of God's words. It is not that he just understands that these are God's words, but he receives the Essence of God through His words.[16]

Furthermore, the same essence is transferred to the words that the prophet then communicates to the people to whom he repeats his prophecy. The words he uses do not limit or condense the message he was sent to convey. They still contain the Essence of God.

Chasidus explains[17] that prophecy is what is called knowing the *mahut*, the essence of something, rather than simply knowing the *metziut*, the existence of something. The former term refers to *what* it is and the latter term merely to the fact *that* it is. There are many things whose existence can be proved. However, of what is it that exists, we may not have a real appreciation.

A prophet experiences the *mahut*, what it really is, and nevertheless, Maimonides explains that the prophecy is manifested in the prophet's intellect. But how can this take place? How does the intellect grasp the Essence of God, which completely transcends the intellect? The answer to this question is that we do not mean that the prophet used his intellect to attain the prophecy, that he arrived at his prophecy through a process of reasoning. Rather it means that the intellect of the prophet experienced something that transcended intellect. Thus, prophecy is not a mere revelation of words. It is a revelation of God Himself.

PROPHETS AND SAGES

We can now understand the difference between a prophet and a sage who understands the most sublime spiritual secrets, such as the famous Arizal, Rabbi Yitzchak Luria Ashkenazi, the great kabbalist of the 1500s who lived in Safed, Israel.

Chasidus explains[18] that the difference between a prophet and a sage is exactly the difference between *metziut* and *mahut*. A sage has knowledge of the *metziut*—about the thing, but he does not experience the thing itself. The prophet's understanding, however, is in a manner of knowing the *mahut*, the thing itself. Although he understands with his mind, he nevertheless *experiences* his prophecy, rather than merely understanding it. This is the superiority of the prophet over the sage.

PRECONDITIONS FOR PROPHECY

In his *Code* (*Yesodei HaTorah* 7:1) Maimonides writes that prophecy can only be attained by someone who sanctifies himself and works upon himself until his mind is directed constantly toward God. Why is this so? If prophecy is a revelation of God, by God through the prophetic experience, what difference does the preparation of the prophet make? Isn't the prophecy dependent on God, not on man? However, the very idea of prophecy—God revealing Himself to a prophet—indeed demands extensive preparations and refinement by the prophet.

This idea can be grasped by what *Chasidus* has to say about a *tzaddik*, a holy person. When a person is described as holy in Jewish terms, it means that he is so self-effacing and humble, and so dedicated to God, that he is worthy of God revealing Himself to him.[19] In Jewish thought, a person is regarded as holy not because of his abilities to do miracles or because he can foresee the future. Rather, a holy person is so because he has nullified his ego.[20] What makes him holy is that he is not in the way, he does not, so to speak, block the light. The godliness within him illuminates his actions, his words, and even his countenance.[21] In fact, the same godliness resides within every person, but the ego within the person covers up what is inside.[22] A holy person works upon himself and makes sure that he does not conceal the godliness that is within him. Therefore, when we praise a holy person, we are taking note of his lack of ego, his nothingness, which is the only true vessel for the presence of God.[23]

What we have said above also applies to a prophet. In order to become a vessel for divine revelation, for prophecy, he must work on himself and refine himself to such an extent that he becomes "transparent," so to speak. The slightest trace of ego prevents the prophetic experience from manifesting itself so that if he is there, then God is not. The Talmud states that God exclaims, "I and an arrogant person cannot dwell together!"[24] His prophecy is simply the revelation of God within and through him.

NOTES

1. See Maimonides *Code, Yesodei HaTorah* 7:1ff.
2. As asked by the Lubavitcher Rebbe in *Likkutei Sichot*, vol. 23, *BeHaalotecha* 3 (p. 82ff).
3. See *Likkutei Sichot*, ibid.
4. See Tzemach Tzedek's *Sefer HaLikkutim*, s.v. אין סוף.
5. This is the doctrine of the *Tzimtzum* mentioned in the beginning of the Arizal's *Etz Chaim* and explained at length in Rabbi Shneur Zalman's *Shaar HaYichud v'HaEmunah* (*Likkutei Amarim*, pt. 2). See also *Likkutei Amarim, Iggeret HaKodesh*, chap. 25.
6. *Megillah* 31a.
7. *HaYom Yom*.
8. Maimonides, *Commentary to Mishnah Sanhedrin*, chap. 11, sixth principle.
9. See *Guide for the Perplexed*, pt. 2, chap. 36ff.
10. *Likkutei Sichot*, ad loc., chap. 11. Explained at length in the Tzemach Tzedek's *Sefer HaLikkutim*, s.v. נבואה.
11. *Yesodei HaTorah* 7:2.
12. 2 Kings 9:11; Jeremiah 29:26; Hosea 9:7.
13. *Keter Shem Tov*, Kehot, addenda.
14. *Shabbat* 105a.
15. *Likkutei Torah, Shelach* 48d, ff.
16. See *Shemot Rabbah* 33:6; *Tanchuma Terumah* 3; *Tanya*, chap. 47.
17. *Likkutei Amarim, Iggeret HaKodesh*, chap. 19.
18. Ibid.
19. See *Tanya*, chap. 10.
20. *Likkutei Amarim, Tanya*, chap. 30.
21. Maimonides *Code, Deot* 5:1, 5:8.
22. See *Tanya*, chap. 42.
23. See *Code, Deot* 2:3.
24. See *Sotah* 5a; *Arachin* 15b.

The Seventh Principle

I believe with complete faith that the prophecy of Moses is absolutely true. He was the chief of all the Prophets, both before and after him.

his principle states the Jewish belief that Moses (or Moshe, as we will refer to him) was superior to all other Prophets, both those preceding and those following him. He attained the highest level possible for a human being to aspire to and he spoke to God face-to-face[1] (the meaning of this will be explained later) whenever he so wished. Thus, should a conflict arise between the words of Moshe and the words of any of the other prophets, we heed only the words of Moshe.[2] In fact, we believe in the words of the prophets *because* the Torah that Moshe taught instructs us to believe in them.[3] Therefore, if a person should come and perform miracles or do supernatural things, yet instruct us to deviate from the laws of the Torah, this in itself would be conclusive proof that he is a false prophet.[4]

MOSHE (MOSES) AND THE OTHER PROPHETS

The prophecy of Moshe differs from that of the other prophets in several important ways. First, God spoke to Moshe face-to-face (see Exodus 33:11; Numbers 12:6–8), that is, while Moshe was in a fully conscious, waking state rather than in the prophetic trance or dreamlike state that characterized the prophecy of all other Prophets.[5] Thus, most of the prophecies that Moshe was instructed to convey to the Jewish people begin with the words, "God spoke to Moshe saying. . . ." That is, his prophecy was direct—God, and not an intermediary, spoke to Moshe, and exactly what God said is what Moshe heard. Other Prophets, however, did not receive their prophecies directly but by way of angels and in trances and visions. And therefore they received their prophecy in words, which implies distance between the prophet and the object of his prophecy—"Thus says the Lord." Only Moshe experienced the direct revelation of the essence of godliness.

In addition, the other Prophets could not receive their prophecy while standing. They fell to the ground and could not rise. The prophetic experience overwhelmed them and affected their physical health. Only Moshe had the spiritual strength to stand while he experienced his prophecy. Moreover, Moshe did not need special preparation in order to receive prophecy, whereas all the other Prophets did.

THE STATURE OF MOSHE'S PROPHECY

A qualitative difference between the prophecy of Moshe and that of the other Prophets concerns the degree of God's greatness that the prophecy expressed. With the other Prophets, the experience of prophecy was a uniting of the mind and intellect with God, Who transcends the intellect (as explained in our commentary to the previous principle). All the Prophets' senses and instincts, and their normal waking intellect, were paralyzed by the prophetic vision.[6] But Moshe received his prophecy while functioning within the normal parameters of human life, with all his faculties intact and functioning. He experienced God on the highest level and not through an intermediary. God was fully revealed to Moshe while Moshe remained Moshe, a finite human.[7]

This fact reveals an aspect of God's Essence. The Hebrew word for truth is *emet* and consists of three Hebrew letters: *alef*, *mem*, *tav* (אמת). *Alef* is the first letter in the Hebrew alphabet, *mem* is the middle letter, and *tav* is the last letter. Truth is defined not as the opposite of a lie but as something that does not change. From the beginning to the middle to the end, it is the same. Only God is everywhere at the same time and remains totally unchanging.[8] And this is what we see in His relationship with Moshe. If godliness can be revealed only within the infinite, where there are no limitations, then it is in a sense limited—limited to being revealed on an infinite plane but not on a finite plane. Then it would not be absolute truth, for absolute truth must remain unchanged everywhere, even in a physical world, within the bounds of time and space.

This is the level of Moshe. That the unlimited essence of God was revealed to a human being while he was awake, standing, with all his human faculties intact, indicates that God is God everywhere and is not confined to the infinite or excluded from the finite.[9] The infinite was revealed to the finite without nullifying the existence of the finite. Of all the Prophets of Israel, only Moshe was on this level. Moshe accomplished this because he comprehended the fact that God is the only existence, and that he, Moshe, is merely a vessel.[10] Moreover, his comprehension of the fact that God is the only existence was not knowledge in the usual sense of human knowledge—something additional to the person's essence. Rather, his essence was the comprehension that God is the only existence. In other words, this awareness was his entire being.[11]

LEVELS OF PROPHECY

Moshe's power of prophecy derived directly from the Essence of God, whereas the prophetic power of the other Prophets derived from an indirect "reflection" of God. By definition, the essence is the same everywhere. A reflection, however, changes in intensity as one moves closer to, or further away from the source. A reflection is brighter when close to its source and grows dimmer as it is seen farther from its source. Therefore there are different levels of prophecy. The Prophet Isaiah, for example, prophesied on a more elevated plane than the Prophet Ezekiel. Each prophet's prophetic experience corresponded to the level of his soul and the level of divine revelation that he comprehended. However, all of their prophecies, besides Moshe's, were a uniting of the mind and intellect with God, whereas the prophecy of Moshe was a total nullification of his intellect to God.

Chasidus explains that Moshe was of the level of *chochmah*,[12] Wisdom, the highest of the Ten Divine Attributes and soul powers. *Chochmah* is the highest attribute and soul power because it manifests the greatest awareness of God. The greater the awareness we have of God, the less we are aware of ourselves and the less significant we are in our own eyes. This can be understood in somewhat more technical terms: the sudden flash of insight that indicates the brief illumination of *chochmah* by that which transcends it is so overpowering that at the moment that it takes place, all other thought processes are suspended, and the person is aware only of the flash of insight that illuminates his mind. (Now we can understand why the legendary Greek philosopher jumped out of the bath as the *eureka* of sudden insight regarding the displacement of water by solid bodies suddenly occurred to him!) It is for this reason that *chochmah* is regarded as the most sublime power of the soul, for it is capable of receiving that which is beyond it, and therefore (relatively) infinite.

Chochmah can be broken down into two Hebrew words: *koach*, meaning potential, and *mah*,[13] meaning what, that is, that which remains undefined and unlimited. Because *chochmah* feels nothing of itself, it remains undefined and therefore has infinite potential. Therefore the true unity of God is revealed in *chochmah* with the greatest of purity; it is the most worthy vessel for godly revelation.[14] Moshe is referred to in the Torah as the humblest man on earth,[15] for he embodied this aspect of *chochmah* more than anyone else and was therefore aware that there is nothing besides God, as we explained in our commentary to the second principle. Because Moshe was totally nullified in the omnipresence of God, his prophecy derived from God's essence.

Now we can comprehend the reasoning behind Rambam's orderly progression in the principles of faith. First, he deals with prophecy and the Prophets in a general sense to indicate that God is able to unite with a prophet's intellect. Then the Rambam deals with prophecy on a far higher level, the level of Moshe, with whom God was revealed in totality in the physical world. And this physical world is simultaneously finite and limited while feeling that God is the only true existence.[16]

Chasidus points out that after the advent of the Messiah, we will experience the greatest revelations of godliness possible, and all of them will be in the physical world.[17] Moreover, this is in fact the ultimate purpose of creation—that godliness will be revealed in the physical world.[18] The reality of God, beyond time and space, will be felt. But the revelation will not negate or destroy time and space. Time and space will be permeated with the awareness of God: that God, Who is beyond time and space, is constantly creating time and space. In that era, the relationship that existed between God and Moshe will be the relationship God has with all of His creations.[19]

MOSHE AS THE MEDIATOR

This brings us to an understanding of how Moshe could act as a mediator between God and the Jewish people.[20] At first glance, the entire idea is difficult to understand. Judaism teaches as a fundamental principle that we should communicate directly with God and serve God without recourse to intermediaries and middlemen, no matter how great or charismatic they might happen to be. But we nevertheless find that Moshe informs us, "I stand between you and God. . . ." This seems to imply that we reach God only by way of intermediaries!

Chasidus explains, however, that there is really no contradiction here, since there are two types of "mediators."[21] The function of one type is to bring together two different parties, whereas the other type serves to keep them apart. The latter is indeed anathema to Jewish thought. The idea of a being (human or angelic) who stands between the Jewish people and God is unacceptable. Emphasis is placed here on the word "being." This refers to a being that feels itself. When a person prays to an angel or a power, that angel or power is felt as an entity, a separate being. This, then, is a mediator. But Moshe, although he was a soul in a body, did not feel himself as a separate being. His whole existence was nullifed in God's. It was not an I-and-Thou relationship. When Moshe spoke, it was God speaking from Moshe's throat. When Moshe lifted his hand, it was because God wanted his hand to be lifted.[22] For this reason he was able to say, "*I will give you rain for your land at the proper time . . .*" (Deuteronomy 11:13, emphasis added), for it was not Moshe himself speaking but God speaking through him. This is not like a personality who merely adheres to God's will. Here, the personality is nothing but God's will. Therefore, regarding other Prophets we do not speak of a mediator between God and the Jewish people, as we do with Moshe. And so it is in every generation, for in every generation there is always an extension of the soul of Moshe.[23]

Rabbi Shneur Zalman of Liadi explains[24] that he heard from his teacher (Rabbi Dovber, the Maggid of Mezritch) that the Infinite Light of God (the *Or Ein Sof*) does not become unified with even the highest of all worlds until it clothes itself first in the attribute of *chochmah*. The reason for this is that God's true unity—that He is alone and unique, and apart from Him there is nothing—is revealed in the attribute of *chochmah*. Because *chochmah* is the attribute least involved with consciousness of self in the thought process and is a simple flash of an idea, objective and without extension in the intellect, it is termed *bittul*, or nullified. Because it is *bittul*, it reveals the unadulterated truth concerning the unity of God. Since this was the level Moshe was on, he was illuminated by the eternal truth of God.

The foregoing explains why everything Moshe did was permanent—a quality of truth. The Tabernacle he built in the desert was never destroyed. And when the *Mashiach* comes, the Tabernacle will be recovered and erected. This is a reason why Moshe had so great a yearning to enter the land of Israel, to bring the Israelites into Israel. He knew that if he brought the Jewish people into Israel they would never be expelled, and there would not be another exile. Had Moshe led the people into Israel, the redemption from Egypt would have been a permanent redemption, without any exile following it. For the very same reason, Moshe himself had to translate the Torah into seventy languages.[25] He could have appointed others to translate it, but he wanted the Torah to have the Essence of God in each of the seventy languages. It was not enough that the translation be merely an interpretation. It had to be of the essence. The only way to ensure this was for Moshe himself to be the translator. From then and forever, whoever would learn Torah, even in languages other than Hebrew, would be united with the Essence of godliness. And so the Torah is called *Torat Moshe*, the Torah of Moshe.[26] Similarly, this is why God taught the entire Torah to Moshe. God could have given us the entire Torah directly, instead of only the Ten Commandments. But had God given us the Torah directly, it would not have gone through the intermediary of Moshe—who was a physical vessel for the highest levels of holiness. Without this all-important level of the physical as a vessel for ultimate holiness, the Torah could not be said to be absolute truth.

At Mount Sinai, the Jewish people heard God say the Ten Commandments: "I am the Lord your God Who took you out of the land of Egypt," and so forth. But the people were so overwhelmed by the experience, they all died and their souls had to be restored to their bodies.[27] From the perspective of the Giver, God, everything was given, but the receiver was not a fitting vessel, and therefore the first two commandments, which were given to the entire people, did not yet demonstrate the truth of the Torah. That is, it was not yet shown that the Torah applies also to the physical, material world. This was accomplished by giving the Torah to Moshe, a vessel that was completely permeated by the Torah yet remained physical, a living, functioning human being.

When the Torah tells of the birth of Moshe, it says that he was born as *tov*—good.[28] One opinion teaches that this means the house in which he was born was filled with light.[29] Another opinion says that it means he was born circumcised.[30] Both opinions teach that Moshe was holy from birth. This, too, is an indication that Moshe was the embodiment of absolute truth, for truth is unchanging from beginning to end.

When a Jew learns Torah, he attains the level of Moshe. Moshe was not merely like a servant, loyal to the king. To Moshe, there was only one reality, God. When one's mind is completely absorbed in Torah learning, he is unified with God in the same way.[31] This is different from a Jew performing a *mitzvah*. During the performance of a *mitzvah*, there are two elements. There is the Commander, God, and there is the person who is obeying God by performing the *mitzvah*. Even though God and the Jew become united through the performance of the *mitzvah*, they nevertheless remain two entities. But Torah study is different. As the Jew studies Torah, the only thing that exists in this person's mind is the comprehension of God's knowledge. When one is deeply absorbed in a concept, the only thing that exists is the concept. The person does not feel himself. The concept is the only reality. This level of unity or oneness was the whole existence of Moshe, not only when he studied Torah but throughout his life. For this reason, it is a principle of our faith to believe that the prophecy of Moshe was absolutely true. And through this principle, we bring an added dimension to our belief in the greatness of God.

It is important to note that chasidic teachings[32] explain that each and every Jew has a spark of the soul of Moshe with him, by virtue of the fact that every soul is nurtured by Moshe, the "faithful shepherd,"[33] who brings knowledge of God and attachment to Him to each of His flock.

NOTES

1. Exodus 33:11.
2. Maimonides *Code, Yesodei HaTorah* 8:1, 3.
3. See *Guide for the Perplexed*, pt. 2, chap. 39; the Lubavitcher Rebbe's *Shaarei Emunah*, 37:3.
4. Ibid.
5. *Code, Yesodei HaTorah* 7:6.
6. Maimonides *Code, Yesodei HaTorah* 7:6.
7. Ibid.
8. *Malachi* 3:6.
9. See *Avodat HaKodesh*, pt. 2, chap. 8.
10. See *Devarim Rabbah* 2.
11. As we explained in our commentary to the second principle.
12. *Likkutei Amarim, Iggeret HaKodesh* 19.
13. *Zohar*, vol. 3, p. 28a; explained in *Tanya*, chaps. 18–19.
14. Note in *Tanya*, chap. 35.
15. Numbers 12:3.
16. *Likkutei Sichot*, vol. 23, p. 91.
17. *Tanya*, chap. 37.
18. See *Midrash Tanchuma, Nasso*, 16 cited and explained in *Tanya*, chap. 36.
19. As stated in the final paragraph of Maimonides' *Code*.
20. Deuteronomy 5:5.
21. Explained in *Likkutei Sichot*, vol. 24, p. 7.
22. Compare with *Avot* 2:4.
23. *Tikkunei Zohar, Tikkun* 69.
24. Note in *Tanya*, chap. 35.
25. See Rashi to Deuteronomy 27:8.
26. Joshua 8:31, 32; Malachi 3:22.
27. *Shir HaShirim Rabbah* 6:3.
28. Exodus 2:2.
29. Cited in Rashi's commentary to Exodus, ad loc.
30. *Tanchuma, Noach* 5.
31. *Tanya*, chap. 5.
32. Ibid., chap. 42.
33. An expression used by the *Zohar* in numerous places, denoting Moshe. See also *Sukkah*, 52b; *Tikkunim*, end; *Zohar Chadash* 104a; *Tanya*, ibid.

The Eighth Principle

> I believe with complete faith that the entire Torah that we now have is that which was given to Moses.

his principle declares our faith that the entire Torah given to us by Moses originated from God. More specifically, this principle teaches that it is a foundation of Jewish belief that everything in the Torah is the word of God. This means that the Torah is not merely a book of instructions communicated to Moses and then related to us in Moses' own words. If this were so, then only the inner content would be God's. But we believe that not only the contents are from God but every letter and every word is God's.[1] This same principle applies not only to the Written Torah (i.e., Scripture), but also to the Oral Torah, the body of work known as the Talmud, which was originally communicated orally from generation to generation. Although the Oral Torah was communicated to us via the great Jewish Sages, it too originated from God. This means that every word and every letter of the Talmud, the oral tradition, is also from God.[2]

GOD WITHIN THE TORAH, AND THE TORAH WITHIN GOD

There is a great difference between the belief that the Torah is from God Himself and the belief that it comes from a holy person who heard it from God. The difference, in fact, is immeasurable. For every prophet, even Moses, the greatest of all Prophets, is, after all, a human being. But we believe that the words uttered by the Prophets and Sages are God's words and not the words of the prophet or sage who transmitted them, and the prophecy as uttered by any of the Prophets, or the teaching delivered by a sage did not change either the form or the contents of God's words.

Moreover, this belief applies not only to the Prophets and the Sages mentioned in the Talmud, but to any Torah sage in any generation—as long as his teachings are based on the established rules prescribed by the Torah, his words are regarded as Torah. This means that his words are not only correct and legitimate but that they were taught at Sinai, when the Torah was given to the Jewish people, for they are the words of God.[3]

This is difficult to understand. Moses received the entire Torah on Mount Sinai in forty days and forty nights. How, then, is it possible that everything taught as Torah, including contemporary teachings, with thousands upon tens of thousands of details, could be taught to Moses by God in that period of time? One answer is that what was given at Sinai were the general rules and principles of the entire Torah.[4] All the details and particulars that come later are merely applications of the original general principles to specific cases. Moreover, some of those principles are rules that prescribe exactly how to apply the principles to specific cases. Therefore, as long as the principles are applied to the case in the proper way, the ruling that follows is Torah taught by God at Sinai.[5]

Some authorities answer the question of how later teachings could have originated at Sinai by explaining that since God is beyond time, any new teaching consistent with the laws of the Torah retroactively becomes something God said at Sinai: as far as God is concerned, the events at Sinai are not events that took place in the past but are taking place at this very moment, since He transcends time completely.

Chasidus[6] offers a profound explanation of this concept. Midrashic sources[7] state that although both the Torah and the souls of the Jewish people preceded everything else, nevertheless, the souls of the Jewish people preceded even the Torah! Accordingly, at a certain level, the soul has the ability to draw down into the Torah even more godliness than was originally revealed in the Torah. As the *Zohar* states[8] regarding King David —he bound the Torah to God, that is, he drew down an even more elevated revelation of godliness into the Torah than was there originally. This is also the meaning of the statement that the Sages attribute to God, "The words of the Sages are dearer to Me than the words of Torah itself."[9] This takes place on a plane beyond time, and therefore the events at Sinai are affected retroactively by the efforts of a soul in this world in this time span, as our Sages remarked, "Even that which an astute scholar will say before his master was already told to Moses at Sinai."[10]

When the Ten Commandments were given to the Jewish people on Mount Sinai, the event was accompanied by thunder and lightning, and the mountain was on fire with its smoke rising to heaven,[11] a truly awesome and terrifying experience. And as every command was uttered, as the words issued forth from God, the experience was more than the people could withstand and their souls left their bodies.[12] After each command, they all had to be resurrected. This would appear to be inconsistent with the nature of the laws given: straightforward commands that humans living in society could be expected to come up with on their own, such as refraining from murder and honoring parents.

Chasidus explains[13] that the reason for the foregoing is that when God gave us the Torah, He put Himself into it. In our discussion of the sixth principle we cited the Talmud's comment regarding the first of the Ten Commandments uttered on Mount Sinai: our Sages explain that the first word of the First Commandment, the word *Anochy* (אנכי—"I am . . .") is an acronym, that is, the letters of the word spell out an entire sentence, "*Ana nafshi chetavit yehavit,*" which *Chasidus* interprets as meaning, "I gave Myself in writing." That is, when I uttered the Ten Commandments, says God, I gave you Myself![14] This means that the Torah is, in effect, the Essence of God. And this is what was given to us when He gave us the Torah. The Torah is not a mere "handbook for proper living" or a comprehensive guide for conducting human affairs. It is the Essence of God Himself.

Moreover, the Essence of God is in every part of Torah equally—whether the subject in the Torah concerns the Oneness of God, or whether it concerns the signs of unclean (nonkosher) animals, or whether it mentions Moses or Pharaoh—God is equally within every part of the Torah.[15]

Because of the revelation at Sinai, we can take a physical object and perform a *mitzvah* with it and thus change the actual physical object into a holy object. This transformation could not be accomplished through our own power. As holy as Abraham, Isaac, and Jacob were, they would not transform the physical world into a holy world because, until the Torah was given, spirituality and physicality were two polar opposites.[16] Spirituality meant that a person had to raise himself above the world, transcending the boundaries and limitations of this world that merely conceal spirituality and godliness. Spirituality was purely an experience of the soul. For an object to remain physical and also be holy was impossible. Not even the Patriarchs could accomplish this transformation. Whatever the Patriarchs did through serving God remained between their souls and God. It did not transform the physical world into a vessel of divine revelation.

However, when the Torah was given on Mount Sinai, we were given the power to transform the physical world into holiness. The two states, physical and spiritual, were no longer antithetical. The reason for this is that God put Himself into the Torah, so that the Torah contains exactly the same power as the words God spoke at Mount Sinai. For this reason there were great and awesome miracles and thunder and lightning and the mountain was on fire. These great phenomena were the response to the incredible power that was being infused into the world.

The Torah then is not a merely means to an end, for the purpose, for example, of making the world a better place, or to refine and elevate us.[17] Although these are definitely consequences of God giving us the Torah, they are not the purpose of Torah. The Torah is not for the sake of the world; on the contrary, the world exists for the sake of the Torah, as the great sage Rashi (the most renowned commentator on the Five Books of Moses) points out in his commentary on the first word of Genesis.

From the foregoing, we can understand why it is essential to the faith of the Jew that we believe that the Torah was given by God. Were it merely given by Moses, who was inspired by God, the Torah would not have the power to take physical entity and transform it into a spirituality even while it remains a physical time-and-space-bound object.[18]

TORAH AND THE JEWISH PEOPLE

When the Torah was given, all the Jewish people were present. By this we do not mean that only the Jews who were redeemed from Egypt were present in their totality but that all the souls of all the Jews who ever lived or will live, and all the souls of the righteous converts to Judaism were present when God gave the Torah at Mount Sinai.[19] One might think that it would have been sufficient if the Torah were given to the leaders of the people, then handed down from one generation to the next generation until the present. But this would not have served God's purpose. *Chasidus* explains that when God uttered the Ten Commandments, it was not mere revelation. By speaking these words, God was creating.

God created the world through Ten Utterances:[20] "There shall be light . . ." created light; "There shall be a firmament . . ." created the sky, and so on, as we wrote at length in the discussion of the first and second principles. Similarly, when God uttered the Ten Commandments, which include the entire Torah, He also created. What did He create? He created the essential being of the Jewish people. They did not merely hear the Ten Commandments. They became the Ten Commandments. When God said the first of the Ten Commandments, "I am God, your Lord," as soon as He uttered these words, He become ours, so to speak, just as much as we became His.[21] Because everything God does is eternal, because He Himself is eternal, He became eternally ours, and we became eternally His.

Incidentally, this is why the Jewish people remain Jews forever and conversion to another religion has no meaning.[22] If a Jew becomes an apostate, heaven forbid, his "conversion" is considered of no account, except that he will be held accountable for his action. The reason for this is that a Jew has

God within him because of what God did at Mount Sinai, not because of their choice or their conduct or their commitment. At Mount Sinai, God created the makeup of the Jew as one with God. Therefore, conversion is impossible for the Jew. His actions can never undo the essential presence of God within him.[23]

Interestingly, the wording of the commandments in the imperative voice, "You shall not steal," "You shall not murder," or, "You shall honor your father and mother," and so on, can also be understood as a promise in Hebrew, "You *will* not . . ." or, "You *will* . . ." As soon as God commanded that we shall not, then it became our very nature, so that the command also functions as a promise. The nature of the Jew from Sinai onward is to desire to fulfill God's will as expressed in the Ten Commandments and thereby be close to God. Under no circumstances does the Jew want to be separated from God. (How a Jew can ever sin will be discussed later.) To accomplish this, it was necessary that all the Jews be present when the Torah was given at Mount Sinai. The Torah was not merely something the people heard and which could have been from a teacher at any time in history, but the Torah became one with the people because they heard it directly from God. The bonding had a permanent effect that is not subject to change.

Maimonides writes, in the laws of divorce,[24] that the essential nature of every Jew is to desire to do what God wants. Under no circumstances does the Jew want to be apart from God or rebel against the will of God. God accomplished this at Mount Sinai, where, by giving the Torah Himself, the spiritual and physical worlds were unified, and the Jew and the Will of God became one. This is not something that the Jewish people could have accomplished on their own. Only God Himself could cause the Jew to attain this level.

When a Jew, from time to time, transgresses the laws of the Torah, he is not only going against God's will but is violating his own nature. In effect, he is harming his own interests, for he is doing what he really does not want to do.

DIVERGENT TORAH VIEWS

We find innumerable arguments and controversies in the Torah. This may appear to be a contradiction to the concept that every word of the Torah comes from God Himself. If the entire Torah stems from God, then how is it possible that God would say one thing in one place and then contradict Himself in another place? If all opinions in the Oral Law are from God Himself, then all of them are correct, as indeed our Sages affirm: "Both views are the word of the living God."[25] And if all are correct, how can there be conflicting opinions or disagreements? Similarly, if the prophetic writings contained in the nineteen books written by the Prophets other than Moses all come from God Himself, then why should there be laws in the Five Books of Moses that take precedence over the words of the Prophets? And why should the Prophets take precedence over the *Mishnah* (the terse statement of laws that derive from Scripture), and the *Mishnah* over the *Gemara* (a vast body of commentary on the *Mishnah*)? Together the *Mishnah* and the *Gemara*, forming the Talmud, take precedence over the *Shulchan Arukh*, the Code of Jewish Law.[26] If every word is the word of God and all of them are regarded as one Torah, how can there be levels and conflicting teachings?

When two rabbis or rabbinical schools are in disagreement, such as was often the case with the schools of Hillel and Shammai in the Talmud, we compare and contrast the opinions, and based on the merits of the various opinions, we follow only one of them. This conclusion to a discussion or debate is called *halachah*. The word *halachah* means "going," or procedure. There must be a direction if one wants to travel. The *halachah* determines the direction. But since we maintain that both dissenting opinions are Torah and are therefore true, then *halachah* cannot be a determination of who is right and who is wrong. Right and wrong are not the issue in *halachah*. Procedure is the issue.

One way that the *halachah* is determined is by following the majority opinion. Even if the minority opinion would seem to have an equally logical basis, the Torah instructs us to follow the majority.[27] This is one of the rules of the Torah. But this does not mean to say that the minority view is false, or incorrect.

Every part of the Torah is Torah, all of one essence. There is no difference, in this sense, between the Written Torah and the Oral Torah. It all has one essence. This, however, is from God's perspective. There is also the perspective of revelation. With regard to the revelation of Torah, there are definitely levels. The Written Torah is higher than the Oral Torah, and within the Written Torah, the Five Books of Moses takes precedence over the other prophetic books, and so forth.[28] But this only exists in context of revelation, not in essence. This can be understood by way of an analogy: all parts of the orb of the sun are regarded as the sun itself. However, the sun's rays are not the sun itself but merely its radiance, which reveals the sun. When the rays of the sun shine in through different windows of a house, we do not say that there are different suns. There is only one sun but different rays.[29] Moreover, some rays might be brighter or hotter than others, depending on their distance from the sun, the angle at which they shine, and so on. The same is true of Torah. There is one Torah but different revelations. Some of the revelations are more intense, some are at one angle, others at another. But all have a single source and all reveal godliness.

In light of this, we can now understand that when two rabbis disagree over the same Torah matter (one sees it one way, and the other argues with him), it is because the two rabbis are experiencing the Torah on different levels. Both are having a true experience of Torah. But through their respective experiences, they have meditated and cogitated and studied and brought their way of seeing it into their own understanding, each convinced logically that his opinion is correct. And as long as both rabbis have followed the rules of applying the general principles to specific cases, *both* of them maintain **true** views. But only one opinion is the *halachah*. We do not follow both. We follow only one, for it is adduced as the proper direction for the Jewish people.

This brings us to the question of how the *halachah* is decided. We mentioned above that generally the majority view is followed. But this begs the question to a certain extent. What made the majority of rabbis decide in one way rather than the other? The answer is that although the essence of the Torah is the same everywhere, it is not revealed everywhere equally. The *halachah*, the final decision that we follow, is where the essence of the Torah is revealed.[30] And when the essence of the Torah is revealed in one opinion, the second opinion may not be followed. It is not the *halachah*. So the *halachah* does not mean that the opinion we follow is right and the other opinions are wrong. The *halachah* is the opinion that reveals the essence of the Torah. This is why only one level of Torah has the power to deal with the physical world and transmute it into a holy world. This level is the aspect of the Torah that pertains to the performance of the commandments, *halachah*.

However, if a person learns the theoretical side of the Torah in order to understand but not fulfill what the Torah teaches, he merely learns the logic of the Torah and does not have an effect upon the world. The world remains unchanged by his studies. Only when he learns *halachah* and actualizes the *halachah* does he bring the essence of the Torah into revelation and thus elevate and rectify the world. As long as the essence of the Torah remains hidden, it cannot affect the world.

THE TORAH OF MOSES

The Book of Deuteronomy, the fifth book of the *Chumash* (the Five Books of Moses), is also called *Mishneh Torah*, the repetition of the Torah. In the first four books, Moses recounts God's words to the Jewish people. In Deuteronomy, however, Moses speaks to the people in his own words.[31] That is to say, although the entire Torah comes from God, the Book of Deuteronomy was "processed" through Moses. He himself said it, not simply as teachings heard from *Hashem* but as teachings he related to with his own intellect. The first four books of the *Chumash* were transmitted to us by Moses but were not processed by him. Thus the first four books describe the communication of God's revelation of the Torah to Moses as follows: "And God spoke to Moses . . . ," in the third person, whereas Deuteronomy begins with the words, "These are the words that Moses spoke to all Israel. . . ." This is because the former teachings were not processed by Moses in any way; they were simply transmitted by him, whereas the latter were processed through Moses' intellect (although, as we stated earlier, all of the Torah is from God). And yet, all five volumes of the *Chumash* are regarded as having the same sanctity.

Chasidus explains[32] that God brought the Torah down to the level of Moses' intellectual comprehension in the Book of Deuteronomy so that the Torah could be understood by everybody. The Torah itself, being God's Will and Wisdom,[33] is utterly impossible for the human mind, even the greatest of minds, to understand. But because God gave us one of the Five Books of Moses through Moses' intellect, He thereby gave all Jews the ability to understand the otherwise incomprehensible essence of the Torah. Were it not for this fifth volume of the *Chumash*, the first four volumes would be incomprehensible. Nevertheless, Deuteronomy is exactly the same essence and precisely as holy as the other four books of the *Chumash*.

THE TORAH

But why was the Torah given to us in this way? Surely God could have given us the Torah in such a way that we would have been able to understand it without going through the process described above? In order to answer these questions, we must learn a bit more about what Torah is.

Torah, the *Midrash* says, existed before the world existed.[34] The word *before* means not merely in time but primarily in value or caliber, that is, in a spiritual sense rather than a temporal sense.[35] Torah, as the Will and Wisdom of God, entirely transcends the world. Therefore, for the Torah to relate to this world, it needs a mediator, a translator, who has within himself both aspects—being higher than the world and of the world. In talmudic times, a great master often had a translator (a *meturgeman*, as he was called) who listened to the words of the master and then conveyed them to the audience. This practice was introduced, not so that the master would not have to raise his voice but in order to convey the master's message in a language that the average individual could understand, for the master was on so lofty a level that he hardly shared a common language with the average individual. The translator therefore had to understand the master's language, as well as have the ability to relate to the students and know how to communicate in their language. The mediator, in this case Moses, had to be comparable on some level with both the teacher, God, and the students, the Jewish people.[36] And this is exactly what Moses was. He is referred to in Scripture as "the man of God"[37] (Psalm 90:1) and as being only "a little less than God."[38] Moses had no ego. His being was utterly nullified and subservient to God.[39] This level of self-nullification is higher than the nature of the world. Yet he was a human being living in this material world. With both these qualities, he was able to communicate God's Essence to the Jewish people. Thus, in order for the Torah to come down to this world, to allow this world to relate to it, it had to be given through Moses. Therefore one part of the Torah was communicated to us only after it had been processed by Moses.

NOTES

1. Maimonides, *Commentary to the Mishnah*, *Sanhedrin*, chap. 11, principle 8.
2. Ibid. See also Maimonides' introduction to his *Code*.
3. Maimonides *Code*, *Teshuvah* 3:8 and *Kessef Mishnah*, ad loc.
4. *Chagiga* 6b.
5. Regarding all of the above, see *Likkutei Sichot*, 12th *Tammuz* 5748.
6. *Likkutei Torah*, *Shir HaShirim* 19b, c; Discourses 5666, ד"ה וידבר וגו' במדבר סיני; Discourses 5605, ד"ה להבין ענין שמח"ת chap. 27; *Likkutei Sichot*, vol. 14, p. 169.
7. *Tanna d'Vei Eliyahu Rabbah* 14, 31; *Bereishit Rabbah* 1:4.
8. Vol 3, p. 222b; cited and explained in *Likkutei Torah Shelach* 51a.
9. *Shir HaShirim Rabbah*, 1:18.
10. *Vayikra Rabbah* 22:1.
11. Exodus 19:18 ff.
12. *Shir HaShirim Rabbah* 6:3.
13. *Likkutei Torah*, *Shelach* 48d ff. based on *Shabbat* 105a.
14. See also *Shemot Rabbah* 33:6; *Tanchuma Terumah* 3; *Tanya*, chap. 47.

15. Maimonides, *Commentary to the Mishnah, Sanhedrin*, chap. 11, principle 8.

16. As in the verse in Psalm 115:16: "The Heavens are God's, and the earth He gave to Man." This was prior to the giving of Torah, as stated in *Shemot Rabbah* 12:3.

17. See *Bereishit Rabbah*, chap. 44. Although Torah has the power to do this, it is not the ultimate purpose of Torah.

18. Regarding the above, see *Likkutei Torah, Bamidbar*, 15cff; *Likkutei Sichot*, vol. 8, p. 21ff.

19. See commentary of Nachmanides and *Daat Zekeinim* to Deuteronomy 29:9.

20. *Avot* 5:1.

21. See *Tanya*, chap. 47.

22. See *Sanhedrin* 44a.

23. See *Tanya*, chap. 18.

24. *Code, Gerushin* 2:20.

25. *Eruvin* 13b; *Gittin* 6b.

26. See Maimonides, *Code, Yesodei HaTorah* 7:6. Discussed at length in *Likkutei Sichot*, vol. 19, *Shoftim* 3.

27. Exodus 23:2.

28. See footnote 19.

29. See *Sanhedrin* 39a.

30. As in the talmudic expression: "God is with him, for the law follows his view" (*Sanhedrin* 93b).

31. Regarding the following, see *Likkutei Sichot*, vol. 4, p. 1087ff.; vol. 19, p. 9ff.

32. See *Likkutei Sichot*, vol. 4, p. 1087ff.; vol. 19, p. 9ff.

33. *Tanya*, chap. 23.

34. *Bereishit Rabbah* 8:2; *Vayikra Rabbah* 19:1.

35. *Likkutei Torah Emor* 32d.

36. See Deuteronomy 5:5: "And I stood between God and you, to tell you the word of God."

37. Psalm 90:1.

38. Psalm 8:6.

39. As he said regarding himself and Aron: "What are we?" (Exodus 16:7, 8).

The Ninth Principle

I believe with complete faith that this Torah will not be changed and that there never will be another given by God.

This principle describes our belief that the Torah is the eternal word of God and that it cannot be changed.[1] Nothing can be added to it or subtracted from it, as the verse states, "You shall not add to it, nor subtract from it" (Deuteronomy 13:1).

CAN GOD CHANGE THE TORAH?

Maimonides states that the Torah will not be changed. Why is this included among the thirteen principles of faith? Maimonides does not mean that man cannot change the Torah. This is obvious to all of us. Since we did not write it, and we are not its proprietors, it is clear that we cannot change it.[2] What Maimonides means here is that God will not change the Torah in any way, and even more than this, that even He cannot change the Torah![3]

There are authorities who disagree with Maimonides regarding this matter. Abarbanel,[4] for example, maintains that this principle should not be included among the thirteen principles of Jewish faith. He argues that prior to the giving of the Torah, God made changes in the commandments given to mankind in response to changing situations. For example, before the Flood man was forbidden to eat meat. After the Flood eating meat became permissible.[5] Abraham was given the commandment of circumcision,[6] and Jacob was given the prohibition of eating an animal's sciatic nerve,[7] and many others.

Moreover, if the purpose of the Torah is to purify and elevate man and the world, as the *Midrash* states explicitly,[8] then it seems logical to assume that the methods of purification will change from time to time as various stages of purification and elevation are achieved. This is common practice in education and in medicine. When a child begins learning, he is taught the alphabet and then taught to read words. Later, he is taught to analyze and evaluate critically, and so on. Similarly, in the medical field, when a person is seriously ill, he may require an operation. Subsequently, he is given antibiotics to prevent infection, and after this, he is given vitamins and other body-strengthening measures to return him to his former state of health. Accordingly, why should the Torah be any different? Therefore, the Abarbanel reasons that perhaps, in the future, the world will become greatly refined and holy. In that case, we may no longer need certain commandments to refine us or restrict us or to act as precautionary measures.

But Maimonides insists that we know that the Torah will not change, and cannot change, and that it is inconceivable to think that it is possible for it to change.[9] We know that this is so because the Torah itself tells us that this is so.[10] Therefore, this is a principle of faith, not a principle of logic. One who errs and imagines that the Torah can change, according to Maimonides, is missing one of the vital foundations of Judaism.

Chasidus explains[11] that here lies the secret of the very essence of the Torah. Many commentators try to understand what God's purpose was in giving the Torah at Mount Sinai amid thunder and lightning, while the mountain was on fire and the smoke rose to heaven. It seems like a great deal of unnecessary commotion for the giving of the Ten Commandments, which are all basically simple laws that we could have figured out on our own even if God had not given them to us.[12] After all, we find that Abraham, Isaac, and Jacob observed the entire Torah even before it was given.[13] And in order to observe the commandments of the Torah, they obviously knew the Torah. All the knowledge contained in the Ten Commandments was known and observed prior to being given at Mount Sinai. The Patriarchs handed down the knowledge of the Torah to their children and grandchildren.[14] In light of this, one must wonder why it was necessary to gather all the Jewish people and make such a commotion about something that they already knew.

The answer given in *Chasidus* is that the laws of the Torah prior to Mount Sinai were not comparable to the laws of Torah given at Mount Sinai.

God Himself did not command the Patriarchs to follow the laws of the Torah. Rather, through their meditation and service to God, the Patriarchs realized the truth of the Torah. But their understanding was finite, and despite their great holiness, they were limited human beings. The level of spirituality attainable before the Torah was given was limited to the spiritual capacity and sensitivity of each individual.[15]

The great innovation of Mount Sinai was that God placed His very Essence in the Torah, as explained previously. Although the commandments that the Patriarchs observed remained the same commandments and actions in outer form, their inner content was completely transformed. There was an infinite infusion of godliness into them. God put Himself into the commandments.[16]

The fact that God put Himself into the Torah and the commandments meant that the Torah and the commandments were not simply the means by which man and the world became purified and elevated. The Torah, in other words, was no longer simply a means to an end. Just as God is because He is—He does not exist for some purpose, because the world needed a Creator, and so on—so too the Torah is not a means to an end, for the Torah that was given on Mount Sinai is nothing other than God Himself (as we explained earlier regarding the meaning of *Anochy*, "I am . . . ," the first word of the Ten Commandments). This is why it is inconceivable that the commandments will ever change. Were the commandments given for a purpose or a reason, to refine the world and make it a better place, then one could argue that there is potential for change in the commandments. If the world becomes better, then the commandments could become diminished because their purpose is fulfilled. Once God put Himself into the commandments, they suddenly have a new character. They are none other than God Himself, and just as He will not, and cannot, change, so too the Torah will not, and cannot, change.[17]

To be sure, the commandments do refine and make the world a better place.[18] Their presence brings holiness to mundane existence. But their essence is not that they serve this purpose. Rather, they are a manifestation of God Himself. Even if the world were to become completely perfected, the commandments remain intact, for they are eternal.[19]

THE IMMUTABILITY OF TORAH

Maimonides regards the immutability of the Torah as a fundamental principle of faith because it lies at the heart of the nature of Torah and its commandments, the *mitzvahs*. Its immutability is not merely a technical point—will the Torah change or not? As far as Maimonides is concerned, the entire question is inappropriate, for the Torah is no less than God in words.[20] Just as God is eternal and immutable, as it says, "I am God, I do not change,"[21] so too, Torah and *mitzvahs* can never change. Their immutability stands at the very heart of what Torah is all about.

The Talmud,[22] however, points out that *mitzvahs* will be abrogated and will no longer be practiced in the World to Come! This seems to be a total contradiction to the thesis that the Torah is the eternal, unchanging word of God. *Chasidus* offers a solution to this apparent contradiction. The Talmud's intention is not that the *mitzvahs* will actually be abrogated but simply that in comparison with the tremendous revelation that will fill the world in the future, the light elicited by the *mitzvahs* will appear dim.[23] Another explanation is that only the laws (the *halachot*) of the Torah are eternal and will not be abrogated or annulled.[24]

We must thus understand the difference between *mitzvahs* and *halachot*. *Chasidus* explains that the word *mitzvah*, commandment, implies that there are two entities. There is God the Commander and there is the person who obeys the commandment. In the World to Come, the Torah and the world will not be experienced as two separate entities. The "I and Thou" relationship of the Commander and the commanded will be abrogated and replaced by a total unity of the two.[25] Therefore, the *mitzvahs* will cease to exist. The Commander and commanded will merge in the sense that the physical body will naturally act in complete harmony with the Torah. But this does not mean that the laws will change. They will not change. It merely means that the method of observance of the laws will change. We will not feel as if we are performing a commandment because we will do it as naturally as we breathe. Just as we do not have to make ourselves breathe, or instruct our heart to pump blood, or the stomach to digest food, for these are done automatically and involuntarily, so too we will become creatures who fulfill God's will instinctively, because of our very nature. Therefore, the idea of being commanded will no longer have any relevance. Our relationship to the law will change, not the law itself.[26]

Halachah does not necessarily mean a law that is practiced. Whether the situation to which the *halachah* applies will ever take place or not has no bearing on the essence of the *halachah*. There are several such situations, even within the Five Books of Moses, that never occurred, never will occur, and never could occur. Two examples of this are the idolatrous city that is condemned and destroyed[27] and the rebellious son who must be put to death.[28] The Talmud teaches that although these two *halachot* are described at length in the Torah, there will never be such a city or such a son.[29] Nevertheless, the *halachot* of both are eternal, for *halachah* itself is the word of God.

THE MESSIANIC ERA AND THE WORLD TO COME

Chasidus offers a further explanation of the two conflicting views mentioned above, regarding the status of the commandments: each view refers to two different eras. The view that maintains that the *mitzvahs* will not be abrogated in the future applies to the Messianic Era, and the opposing view, that they will be abrogated, refers to the World to Come.[30]

The era of *Mashiach* (the Messiah) is not the time of ultimate reward. That is reserved for the World to Come, the final period.[31] During the first period, the era of *Mashiach*, the *mitzvahs* will still be performed. Furthermore, we will observe them in their highest form. From the beginning of creation through all the periods of exile and redemption until the final redemption with the advent of *Mashiach*, we were not on the highest level and could not perform the *mitzvahs* perfectly. When *Mashiach* comes, we will be able to fulfill the *mitzvahs* on the highest level.[32] However, this will still indicate that we are exerting effort to fulfill God's will and that there is an apparent separation between the Commander and the ones He is commanding.

But in the World to Come, the final period, the Talmud teaches that there will no longer be *mitzvahs*. They will be nullified. Then we and the Torah will be intrinsically one existence and we will not perform *mitzvahs* as self-willed actions. We will simply do them as life's activities, like breathing, as mentioned above.

CONCLUSION

In light of the foregoing, we can understand why it is impossible for a prophet, or anyone else for that matter, to change anything stated in the Torah, even if he performs miracles. If the prophet tells us that he was told from heaven that there is to be a change in something in the Torah, we do not listen to him. His very words prove that he is a false prophet.[33] The prime function of the prophet is to awaken the people to correct their erring ways and to return to God. Therefore, when he announces a revelation that contradicts anything the Torah has established, in effect he is claiming to be changing God. And God does not change.

As explained above, the Torah states explicitly[34] that we are forbidden to add anything to any of the laws of the Torah. There are four sections in the *tefillin* worn on the head. We are forbidden to add a fifth. There are four corners on a garment onto which *tzitzis* are to be inserted. We are forbidden to add a fifth. Similarly, the Torah forbids any subtraction from any of the laws of the Torah. We may neither add nor subtract from any of the *mitzvahs*. And certainly we may not add a new *mitzvah*, making the total 614, or subtract one, making the number 612.

It is logical to wonder about what harm could there be in adding another *mitzvah*. But we are taught that there is harm in it, for the same reason mentioned above: the Torah and the *mitzvahs* that are in the Torah are not merely a code of ethics or a blueprint for moral behavior. The Torah is not merely a book of instructions that teach us how to live a spiritual life. The Torah is the way God handed Himself over to us within the Torah and *mitzvahs*.

Even the slightest change in the *mitzvahs* renders them invalid. For example, the *mitzvah* of *tefillin* (phylacteries worn on the arm and head) requires that four sections from Torah be written on parchment by a qualified scribe and inserted into the *tefillin* in a certain order, and so on. If one were to have only three sections of the *tefillin*, should he wear them? After all, three out of four is better than nothing. Again the Torah says, "No." By deviating from the *mitzvah* as expressly stated, one accomplished absolutely nothing at all. Similarly, three corners of a garment with *tzitzit* (threads tied in a certain pattern to the four corners of a four-cornered garment) and one corner without *tzitzit* accomplishes absolutely nothing.

Without the specifications exactly as stated in the Torah, there is no *mitzvah* at all in these cases and other cases like them. Because without the Torah's specifications, God is no longer present within the *mitzvah*, and the action done is worthless.

Based on the above, we can now understand that the actions required to fulfill the *mitzvah* have no intrinsic importance of their own. It is not because a specific action has the innate ability to produce a certain effect that that action was chosen by God as a *mitzvah*. If this were in fact the case, then why shouldn't a person wear *tefillin* containing three sections of Scripture instead of four, if this is all he has, or three *tzitzit* on his four-cornered garment? True, the effect would not be quite the same as if there were four sections or four *tzitzit*, but at least three-quarters of the effectiveness would be achieved.

The answer is, again, that nothing at all would be achieved. The ability of a *mitzvah* to elicit a revelation of godliness is only because God decided that that would be the case. There is no inherent relationship between the effect of the *mitzvah* on the one hand, and the actions and objects that elicit the effect on the other. Rabbi Shneur Zalman of Liadi once remarked that if we had been commanded to chop down trees instead of wearing *tefillin*, this is what we would do.

However, since God chose 613 specific channels through which His will is fulfilled, the actions and objects with which they are fulfilled (e.g., binding *tefillin* on the arm and head; eating *matzah* on Passover) are imbued with a special status, and a special level of sanctity (depending on the *mitzvah*).

The *Zohar*[35] explains that when Jacob set up peeled sticks in the watering troughs from which his flocks drank, on a spiritual level, he was performing what we perform when we don *tefillin*. Nevertheless, the spiritual flow he elicited from this act did nothing to change the status of the sticks he used for the job. After he completed whatever it is that he was doing, the sticks remained ordinary sticks that could be discarded. Once *tefillin* have been designated and used as *tefillin*, however, they remain objects of sanctity and must be treated with special respect and care.[36] The reason for this is that because God chose *tefillin* as the channel for a spiritual efflux, the objects and actions that fulfill the *mitzvah* become a vessel for His will and His essence.

NOTES

1. Maimonides, *Commentary to the Mishnah, Sanhedrin*, chap. 11, principle 9; *Code, Foundations of the Torah* 9:1.
2. Regarding all of this chapter see *Likkutei Sichot*, vol. 19, *Shoftim* 3; the Lubavitcher Rebbe's *Chiddushim u'Biurim b'Shas*, vol. 2, chap. 23.
3. See *Code, Foundations of the Torah* 9:1.
4. Don Yitzchak Abarbanel (1437–1508) a philosopher, statesman, and leader of Spanish Jewry at the time of the Expulsion in 1492. He was a prolific writer who is best known for his commentary on Scripture. He also commented on some of Maimonides' writings.
5. Genesis 9:3.
6. Genesis 17:10 ff.
7. Genesis 32:33.
8. *Bereishit Rabbah* 44:1; *Vayikra Rabbah* 13:3.
9. *Code, Foundations of the Torah* 9:1.
10. Deuteronomy 29:28; Leviticus 3:17, 10:9, 23:14; Numbers 10:8, 15:5, and so on.
11. *Likkutei Torah, Shelach* 48d ff; *Likkutei Sichot*, vol. 19, *Shoftim* 3; the Lubavitcher Rebbe's *Chiddushim u'Biurim b'Shas*, vol. 2, chap. 23.
12. *Eruvin* 100b.
13. *Kiddushin* 82a.
14. Ibid.
15. As explained in commentaries to the verse in Exodus 6:3.
16. *Shabbat* 105a; *Shemot Rabbah* 33:6; *Tanchuma Terumah* 3; *Likkutei Torah, Shelach* 48d ff.; *Tanya*, chap. 47.

17. *Likkutei Sichot*, vol. 19, *Shoftim* 3; the Lubavitcher Rebbe's *Chiddushim u'Biurim b'Shas*, vol. 2, chap. 23.
18. See *Bereishit Rabbah* 44:1.
19. As Maimonides rules in his *Code, Foundations of the Torah* 9:1.
20. *Tanya*, chap. 25 (p. 32a).
21. *Malachi* 3:6.
22. *Niddah* 61b.
23. Discourses 5672 by Rabbi Sholom Dovber of Lubavitch, chap. 193; see also *Torah Or*, 92a, 119b; *Likkutei Sichot*, vol. 19, *Shoftim* 3; the Lubavitcher Rebbe's *Chiddushim u'Biurim b'Shas*, vol. 2, chap. 23; *Hitvaaduyot* 5745, vol. 3, p. 1430 ff.
24. See *Torah Or*, 92a, 119b regarding the writings of the Prophets. See also Rashi, *Chullin* 137a.
25. See Maimonides, *Melachim* 12:5.
26. See *Tanya*, chap. 5, 25. Regarding all of the above, see *Likkutei Sichot*, vol. 5, p. 240 ff.
27. Called an עיר הנדחת: Deuteronomy 13:13 ff. See Maimonides, *Code, Avodat Kochavim*, chap. 4.
28. Deuteronomy 21:18 ff.; Maimonides, *Code, Mamrim*, chap. 7.
29. *Sanhedrin* 71a.
30. *Likkutei Sichot*, vol. 15, p. 417 ff.
31. *Tanya*, chap. 37.
32. *Likkutei Sichot*, vol. 15, p. 417 ff.
33. Maimonides, *Code, Yesodei HaTorah* 9:1.
34. Deuteronomy 13:1.
35. Vol. 1, p. 162a. Cited in Discourses 5562, p. 12.
36. See *Likkutei Sichot*, vol. 3, p. 888; vol. 5, p. 327.

The Tenth Principle

I believe with complete faith that God knows all of man's deeds and thoughts, as is written, "He has molded every heart alike. He knows all their deeds" (Psalm 33:15).

The tenth principle is that God knows all of man's deeds and thoughts. God never abandons man,[1] contrary to the view of those who say that God has forsaken the earth.[2]

A MATTER OF DIVINE PROVIDENCE

The belief that God watches everything that man (and particularly the Jewish people) does, and cares about what he does, is a fundamental principle in the Jewish religion, according to Maimonides. This doctrine is also known as individual Divine Providence (or *hashgacha pratit*). In his *Code*,[3] Maimonides explains further that because God knows Himself, He knows everything, and therefore, nothing is hidden from Him.

The Baal Shem Tov, the founder of *Chasidism*, also regarded the doctrine of Divine Providence as a fundamental principle of Jewish thought and belief. The Baal Shem Tov, however, explained that Divine Providence is not only that God watches over everything that man does, and over every detail of his life, but that every detail of the entire creation, even the way a leaf is blown about by the wind, is all by Divine Providence.[4] One of the ramifications of the Baal Shem Tov's explanation is that God Himself is involved in each and every detail of creation, not only in that which concerns man,[5] since everything partakes of His unity and nothing stands outside of it, as we explained in our commentary to the second principle.

The Baal Shem Tov explains further that not only is each and every detail of creation, and whatever events take place within all of creation meant to be, but each and every detail is also an integral part of God's total plan for all of creation. This is analogous to a puzzle, where even the smallest piece is still part of the puzzle and helps to complete the entire puzzle. If there is one little detail missing, then the whole puzzle is incomplete. The same is true of God's world. Each and every detail of every creature, and every event within creation, is a part of a master plan, and it performs its unique function in fulfilling the purpose of the entire creation, just as each limb and organ of the human body has its function and importance in the proper functioning of the whole body. Hence, each event is necessary, and there is a perfect order in which events occur. Of course, all this is not necessarily comprehensible to us or even accessible to human understanding.

One of the corollaries of this idea is that everything that goes on in life is of tremendous importance. No entity or event can be regarded as trivial, because every detail is a part of God's plan. (This makes coping with life's problems, however difficult they may be, much easier. Since everything is part of God's plan, even suffering has a purpose.)

We find a similar concept in reference to the Torah. Of

all the matters written in the Torah, we might assume that the commandments are the most important, and of the commandments, the Ten Commandments are surely the most important. Furthermore, of the Ten Commandments, the first two, which God Himself communicated directly to us, are of the greatest importance. In contrast, we might assume that the stories of the Torah are of lesser importance, and particularly the stories concerning wicked people, such as Esau and Bilaam. Yet, this is incorrect, for we find that each and every letter of each and every word in the Torah is equally holy. All of the Torah came from God, as explained previously. Therefore, all are equally holy. If one letter or word was missing from the Torah, then the entire Torah is regarded as blemished, and one may not recite the required blessing over it. For each and every letter and word is a part of the entire puzzle.

This concept, that every event is overseen by Divine Providence, and there are no random events throughout all of creation, leads to a further teaching of the Baal Shem Tov: that whatever a person sees or hears is presented to him by Divine Providence, so that he can benefit from what he saw or heard in his service of God.

Even when a person sees a fault in someone else, the Baal Shem Tov explained that this too is for a reason. Seeing a fault in someone else is the way in which God shows us a fault in ourselves. What we see in other people is simply a mirror image of ourselves.

REVEALED AND HIDDEN PROVIDENCE

The concept of Divine Providence as explained by the Baal Shem Tov (that there is individual Divine Providence for animals, plants, and inanimate matter as well as for man) does not necessarily contradict[6] the definition of Divine Providence as explained by Maimonides (that individual Divine Providence does not apply to animals, plants, and inanimate matter, but only to man). This is because there are, in a general sense, two types of Divine Providence:[7] (1) revealed individual Divine Providence, which is not concealed within what appear to be the logical result of natural events and the laws of nature. Maimonides maintains that this type of providence is dependent on the level to which a person's thoughts and understanding cleave to God, and it does not apply to animals, plants, and inanimate matter, or to the wicked who separate themselves from God; (2) providence that is hidden and concealed within the bounds of nature and natural law. This type of providence applies to all aspects of creation, including animals, plants, and inanimate matter. This is what the Baal Shem Tov was referring to.

Hence, also according to Maimonides, there is a form of Divine Providence that guides even the wicked. In this case, the Divine Providence is clothed in the garments of nature and therefore remains concealed, so that it is not clearly seen how each and every detail and event comes from the Holy One, blessed is He. This does not contradict Maimonides' view that a wicked person leaves himself at the mercy of "random" events, for it is part of God's plan that Divine Providence is concealed (although not removed) from the wicked, resulting in the apparent randomness of events. Nevertheless, revealed Divine Providence also operates, as regards the species but not the individual, as Maimonides maintains.[8]

It is possible that the view adhered to by the Baal Shem Tov was even acknowledged by Maimonides, although he did not propound it openly because it falls into the category of the secrets of Torah that must find the right time and climate to be revealed.[9]

LEVELS OF DIVINE PROVIDENCE

Let us return to our main theme, the workings of Divine Providence. From the Baal Shem Tov's explanation of Divine Providence—that not only is everything Divine Providence but the existence of everything in the world, and everything that happens in the world, is part of the divine plan—it follows that all things and all events in the world are interconnected. When a leaf shakes in the wind, when, how, and in which direction it shakes is part of the general puzzle. If this event did not take place, it would affect the whole world and everything that existed and everything that will exist. All of it is affected because everything is connected to the general purpose of creation.

However, also according to the Baal Shem Tov's explanation, there is a fundamental difference between the Divine Providence that oversees all of creation, including the minutest details of it, and the Divine Providence that guides the Jewish people, in even the minutest detail.

The explanation of this is that although all creations were brought into existence by God, He chose only the Jewish people from among all the nations.[10] This is also the meaning of the statement of our Sages[11] that the entire universe was created for the sake of Torah and the people of Israel. This implies that all the rest of creation is simply a means to an end: the fulfillment of God's purpose in creating the world, which is for the sake of Torah and the people of Israel. However, the Torah and the people of Israel are not a means to an end but the end in itself. They are the purpose of creation! This means that God chose them for themselves, not for the sake of fulfilling a task or purpose.

To explain this at greater length: Because each and every creation in the universe (other than the Torah and the Jewish people) has no purpose other than to serve God, each and every individual creation's importance is based on its purpose. To what extent does it participate in, and add to, the ultimate purpose of creation? This can be understood by way of an analogy to the body. Although each and every limb, sinew, bone, and organ is equally part of the body and makes up the entire body, there are nevertheless levels of importance among the limbs, organs, and so on. The brain is the most important organ, and then the heart, and then other limbs upon which a person's life depends. Although each and every organ and limb serves a purpose, the nails and hair, for example, are far less important than any other part of the body, for the life of the body does not depend on them at all. In the same way, different parts of creation are more or less important in fulfilling the divine plan, depending on the extent to which they serve the Torah and the Jewish people.

However, just as God Himself does not "serve a purpose" (i.e., He is not for the sake of something else, but is because He is), in the same way the Jewish people and the Torah are not here for some other purpose but are themselves the purpose, for this is what God chose. Accordingly, every single detail of the Torah, and every single individual and all the events that take place in the life of every individual Jew, are also ends in themselves, not means to an end. And therefore, every detail is of equal importance to God. Therefore, Divine Providence for the Jewish people is equal for *every* Jew (no matter his level of righteousness) because God chose the Jewish people in their entirety. The Divine Providence that guides the Jewish people applies to every single detail of each individual Jew's life, and each and every detail of his life is guided by His providence in equal measure (although this might not be evident in a revealed way).

This is not so with the details of the rest of creation, which gain importance only to the extent to which they serve the ultimate purpose. Just as we find that when a person wants something, and he has a definite picture of what he wants, then every little detail in that thing that he wants, he wants equally. He needs the whole thing in total. If one of those things is missing, then he does not have what he wants. The same principle applies to the Torah. If one single letter or word is defective, the entire Torah is defective and may not be read from in public, irrespective of whether the word or letter of the word is part of "I am the Lord your God," or part of the list of Esau's descendants, or part of a description of nonkosher animals, as we explained in our commentary to a previous principle. The same is true regarding the commandments of the Torah. On one hand we find that there are different levels of commandments. Some commandments are called minor and others major. Yet the Torah says that one should not weigh and count which commandments are more important than others, because they are all equal.[12] They are all God's will. Thus, if a convert to Judaism wishes to observe 612 of the 613 commandments, he is not accepted as a convert, until he accepts the Torah in its entirety.[13] The same principle applies to a person who says that although he believes in God and that God gave us the commandments, he does not believe that a certain detail of the Torah is from God. It is as if he denied the entire Torah. There is no difference if he denies the Ten Commandments or he denies any other word in the Torah.

PART OF GOD ABOVE

A deeper understanding of the Divine Providence overseeing the Jewish people relates to the verse[14] that states that the Jewish people are a part of God himself, just as a child derives from the essence of his father. This goes further than the statement that the children of Israel are the chosen people, for being chosen implies the existence of two entities. There is the one who chooses that which is chosen. However, the great Maggid of Mezritch writes[15] that the Jewish people were engraved in God's thought even before the world was created, even before the individual soul of a Jewish person was created as a separate entity.

As the Baal Shem Tov said,[16] "When you grasp a part of the Essence, you grasp the entire Essence." Because the essence is found totally in every part, when you are holding onto a part of the essence, you are really holding onto the essence in its totality.

We find an identical concept in Jewish Law. There is a law that states that if a person is involved in fulfilling a commandment, he is exempt from doing any other commandments.[17] *Chasidus* explains that the inner reason that he is exempt from doing any other commandments is that when he is observing one commandment, he is really observing all of them, for they are all, equally, the essential will of God. If he is fulfilling the will of God by observing one commandment, and "when you grasp a part of the essence, you grasp the entire essence," he therefore fulfills all the others as well.

In a similar sense, we find that the soul of a Jewish person is regarded as a whole world to the extent that we sometimes find that the soul of one person is regarded as just as important as an entire group of people.[18]

The law explains that if enemies attack a group of Jews and say, "Give us one Jew, and we will kill him, and if not, we will kill you all," the group may not give up the life of that individual to save the lives of the rest. *Chasidus* explains that the reason is that since every Jewish soul is of the essence of God, giving up one Jewish person is like giving up the entire

Jewish people. "When you grasp a part of the essence, you grasp the entire essence."

With this explanation we can understand that the Divine Providence that guides the Jewish people consists not only of the fact that God watches over every detail, and not only that all of the details are equally important in the fulfillment of the divine plan, but that when God watches over even a single detail, it is His Essence watching, and in His guidance of even the minutest detail, all of His Essence is expressed. This type of Divine Providence is unique to the Jewish people.

CONCEALED PROVIDENCE

One may ask, however, if the same principle applies to wicked people as well. Does Divine Providence guide them and guard them to the same extent as it guides and guards the righteous? *Chasidus* explains[19] that although the source of Divine Providence is exactly the same for every Jew, stemming from the ineffable four-letter Name of God, it is possible that on an individual basis the Divine Providence may be hidden, as a result of the individual's actions. This is the meaning of the verse, "I will hide my face on that day."[20] This is a metaphor for God's *concealed* providence, which still guides the erring Jew, albeit in a hidden way. This applies only on an individual basis but not to the people as a whole, who are always guided by *revealed* Divine Providence.

Now, it must be pointed out that even according to those views that maintain that individual Divine Providence applies only to mankind, and not to any other creatures, this is only in terms of God's guidance, but not in terms of God's knowledge, as the author of the *Ikkarim*[21] writes: it is absolutely unquestionable that His knowledge encompasses everything in existence, and every event in all of existence, and nothing whatsoever is hidden from Him. Nevertheless, His providence does not guide the animal world (and below the animal world) on an individual basis, to reward or punish them for their deeds. Rather, He oversees the species, not the individuals.[22]

HOW DOES GOD KNOW?

This brings us to a further statement contained in the tenth principle: that God knows all of man's deeds and thoughts. What does "knowing" mean as far as God is concerned? How does He know? Maimonides writes that everything that exists, besides the Creator Himself, exists only by virtue of the truth of His existence. By knowing Himself, God knows everything, and nothing is hidden from Him.[23] He adds that this knowledge is not something separate from Him; rather, the Creator and His existence and His knowledge are all totally one, unlike man, whose knowledge is not part of his essence but is acquired from outside of himself. We must therefore conclude that He is the Knower, the known, and the knowing, and all are one. This cannot be expressed in words, nor can it be clearly understood.

The Maharal of Prague,[24] among others, disagrees with Maimonides that God's knowledge is of His Essence, for this imposes a definition and limitation on His Essence, which is infinite and therefore cannot be defined or limited in any way. The Maharal explains this is why we call God "the Holy One, blessed is He," not "the intellect, blessed is He," because "holy" means removed and exalted from any definition or limitation. Therefore, the Maharal concludes that intellect or knowledge is only a creation of God, and whenever it says in the Torah that "God knows," it is equivalent to saying "God said," or

"God made," which means that God created the attribute of knowing, not that He Himself is the knowing. The exact details of their argument, however, need not concern us now.

In his seminal text of chasidic philosophy, *Tanya*,[25] Rabbi Shneur Zalman of Liadi explains that Jewish mysticism (the Kabbalah) agrees with Maimonides' view that God is the Knower, the known, and the knowing, all at once. Nevertheless the Maharal's view that He cannot be characterized in this way is also correct. Neither view is wrong in its proper context, for each view in fact refers to a different concept.

The explanation of this is as follows: There is God as He is in Himself, transcending any revelation or manifestation. And there is God's reflection, His "light," as the Kabbalah refers to it, that is, His revelation of Himself. Just as He is infinite, so is His revelation of Himself, His light, infinite. However, God then "condensed" His light through the ten attributes known as the ten *sefirot, chochmah, binah daat*, and so on (wisdom, understanding, knowledge, and the seven emotional attributes). Once the Infinite Light is revealed through the attributes, then we can refer to God as the Knower, the knowledge, and the knowing, because we are not speaking about God Himself but the way He reveals Himself in a limited creation, the attributes.

This may be compared to sunlight that shines through different colored windowpanes. Although the light is all the same, when it shines through green glass it appears as if the light is green, and through blue glass it appears as if the light is blue. In other words, as far as the way God is in Himself, before He condenses His revelation of Himself into the *sefirot*, the Maharal is correct. On that level you cannot call God knowledge, or knowing, or even the Knower. He does not have any definition or attribute whatsoever. You cannot say God and His knowledge are one. You cannot even say that God "knows" Himself! But after God condensed His light (i.e., His revelation of Himself) into the attributes, in the *sefirot*, then Maimonides is correct, since the attributes are really only a means through which God reveals and manifests Himself. The attributes are also God. They are God expressing or revealing Himself in a finite way. A true definition of infinity is that He has no limit, not even the limit that He has to be only limitless. God has the power of finitude as well.[26]

GOD'S FOREKNOWLEDGE AND MAN'S FREE CHOICE

Given all of the above, we may now raise a thorny question, one that Maimonides himself asks:[27] do we not find a paradox between God's knowledge of the future and man's freedom of choice? We must either say that God knows the future and therefore knows whether a person will be good or evil, or else we must say that He does not know. If we say that God knows that a person will be good, then it is impossible for that person to be otherwise, and he has no free choice. Alternatively, if we say that God knows that he will be good, but it is still possible for him to be evil (thus preserving man's free choice) then we must conclude that God's knowledge is incomplete.

Maimonides continues that the answer to this question is vast and involves a great number of important principles and lofty concepts. And, as explained above, God's knowing is part of His Essence[28] and is therefore beyond man's comprehension, just as His Essence is beyond comprehension, as the prophet states, "My thoughts are not your thoughts; My ways are not your ways" (Isaiah 55:8).

[It is interesting to note that Maimonides did not answer his question in the same way as other authorities and Sages[29] answered it—that just as our knowledge of an event is not its cause but its effect, so too the knowledge of the Holy One, blessed is He, except that in His case, He knows the future because as far as He is concerned it already exists because the limitations of time and sequence do not apply to Him. Hence, God's foreknowledge of a person's choice is because the person already made his choice, as far as God is concerned. According to this view, the question posed above does not even exist! Nevertheless, we can explain that Maimonides does not give this answer because his view is that God does not know in the same way we know—"My thoughts are not your thoughts; My ways are not your ways" (Isaiah 55:8), as explained above. Only as regards human thought does it make sense to speak of knowledge as the result of the event. God's knowing, however, is part of His Essence—by knowing Himself, He knows everything.[30] This is beyond man's comprehension, just as His essence is beyond man's comprehension. Accordingly, the question mentioned above still applies.]

Chasidus explains[31] that God's knowledge of future events is not a contradiction to man's free choice, because the opposite of free choice is not foreknowledge but coercion. That is, free choice means the ability to choose between alternatives without being forced to choose one of the alternatives. Accordingly, foreknowledge and free choice are not diametrically opposed. For example, if a person says that he knows with absolute certainty that if he throws a stone up in the air tomorrow, it will fall to the ground, no one will claim that the stone falls to the ground because that person said so or knew that it would happen. In fact, the contrary is true. The stone falls to the earth because God made gravity one of the laws of

His creation. And therefore a person can know with certainty that tomorrow too, the stone will fall to the earth if it is thrown into the air. From this we see that knowledge of an event is not the cause of the event but its result. The same is true of man's choice and God's foreknowledge. Since I will make my choices tomorrow without any coercion, therefore, God knowing what I will do does not force me to do it. His foreknowledge does not determine the future but merely knows the future. Because He is beyond time and space, it is as if my future actions are in the past. That is, His knowledge of the future is like our knowledge of the past. Just as our knowledge of past events, of history, does not determine those events, so too His knowledge of future events does not determine future events.

Of course, exactly how God knows the future as we know the past is difficult to explain. This is why Maimonides says that the matter is beyond human comprehension. God's knowledge is on an infinite level and therefore cannot be grasped by the finite human mind. This is not merely an elegant way of avoiding an answer. The answer is that since God's knowledge of future events is on a level that we cannot comprehend and that we are totally unaware of, it does not coerce us to act in any way. Hence, man does indeed have free choice.

KNOWLEDGE AND EXISTENCE

However, we can examine the question Maimonides posed regarding God's foreknowledge and man's free choice and examine his answer from an even deeper perspective. *Chasidus* explains[32] that God's thought and knowledge, which knows all created things, encompasses each and every created being from its beginning to its end and its inside and very core, all in actual reality (unlike man's thought, which merely visualizes and imagines an object without encompassing it in actuality).

For example, in the case of the orb of this earth, God's knowledge encompasses the entire diameter of the globe of the earth, together with all that is in it and its deepest interior to its lowest depths, all in actual reality. For this knowledge constitutes the vitality of the whole sphere of the Earth and its creation *ex nihilo*. Accordingly, since God's knowledge of any given object has such a profound effect upon it that it creates and enlivens it from moment to moment (as we explained at length in our commentary to the first four principles), we would think that there is no free choice at all. After all, a person cannot choose to be born, or even to continue living, if this is against the will of God, as stated explicitly in the *Mishnah*:[33] "against your will you were created, and against your will you were born; against your will you live; and against your will you die." Where then is free choice if we are totally dependent on God's knowledge and thought to even exist? According to this, it would seem that man is indeed forced to do what God knows he will do, for he cannot do anything other than what God knows he will do and still remain himself. In addition, how do we explain statements of our Sages such as, "Everything is in the hand of heaven other than the awe of heaven?"[34]

This is why Maimonides declares[35] that God's existence is totally incomprehensible.[36] *Chasidus* adds two explanations of this: (1) Since His knowledge is part of His Essence, we are talking about knowledge that is totally incomprehensible to man, just as His Essence is totally incomprehensible to man. Accordingly, it does not impinge on our consciousness at all, and therefore does not affect our free choice.[37] (2) Since He is totally Omnipotent, it is possible for Him to create and maintain existence by way of His thought, as explained above, and yet simultaneously ensure that His foreknowledge will not affect our free choice.[38]

TWO REALITIES

This needs clarification. We explained at the beginning of this chapter that each and every detail of creation, and whatever events take place within all of creation, is meant to be, and also that each and every detail is an integral part of God's total plan for all of creation and fulfills the purpose for which it was created—in the words of the verse, "God guides the steps of man." Therefore, how can we claim that man is free to choose whatever he wishes, that he has free choice (to the extent that he is rewarded or punished for his choices, as will be explained regarding the following principle)?

[It should be pointed out that as regards Torah and *mitzvahs*, free choice does not mean that one has an option to fulfill the *mitzvahs* or not, as one wishes, and this is an expression of man's free choice. This view is absolutely incorrect. We see throughout the Torah that we are cautioned to fulfill the *mitzvahs* and are liable to punishment if we transgress. Moreover, throughout the era of the *Sanhedrin* (the Jewish Court) punishment was meted out by the court and was administered by its officers for many types of transgressions. Accordingly, "free choice" does not mean that one has an option to do a *mitzvah*, or not do it—one is obligated by the Torah to do it, without any option in the matter.

Rather, as regards Torah and *mitzvahs*, free choice means that we are not driven by instinct or nature to fulfill Torah and *mitzvahs*. An animal does not have free choice because it is driven purely by instinct and its animal nature. An animal does not make choices because it simply reacts to circumstances. When it is hungry it looks for food, when it is frightened it runs away, and so on. A human being, by contrast, has the choice to *act* upon circumstances rather than simply *react* to circumstances.]

Chasidus explains that there are two types of knowing: the way God perceives everything and the way we perceive things. Both are real, for the latter type of knowing was created by God and is not an illusion. It is not to be understood that our knowledge of things is imaginary because we are on a lower level of awareness than God. Obviously, our knowing is incomparable to His. Nevertheless, it is still knowing.

The same principle applies to the creation itself. God's existence is the ultimate truth, as Maimonides points out at the beginning of his code. Nevertheless, we cannot say that creation is therefore a mere illusion. The Torah states explicitly that God created the world, and therefore it certainly exists. To understand this let us use the analogy of a teacher and a student. Not only does the teacher have more knowledge than his student but he understands things on a much higher level than the student, so that if the teacher were to talk to his student on the level of his own (the teacher's) understanding, the student would be totally lost. In order for the teacher to communicate what his student can understand, the teacher has to set aside his own understanding of the subject, the way that he understands things, and begin to think from the student's point of view, finding parables and examples to illustrate the concepts he wishes to communicate. Moreover, he does not explain all the ramifications of each concept and how each one is connected to the other. Rather, he clarifies the various subjects only briefly. When the student understands the subject thoroughly, he might eventually be able to understand things the way the teacher himself understands things. Now, as far as the teacher is concerned, even when he communicates an abbreviated and simplified version of the concepts he wants his student to understand, he himself understands the depth and breadth of the teachings he communicates and all the ramifications and interconnections his explanation has.

This is the way in which the *Mishnah* was written by Rabbi Yehudah the haNasi. The terse and to-the-point style of the *Mishnah* is expanded upon and amplified in the *Gemara*; but all the ideas mentioned in the *Gemara* are already contained in the *Mishnah*. The author of the *Mishnah* knew of all the ideas that would later be discussed in explaining the *Mishnah* and he included them within the *Mishnah*. But the students who read the same *Mishnah* did not see this. It took many years of effort and toil until they finally came to see the depth that lies in the *Mishnah*.

The same is true of the two forms of knowing mentioned above. Reality the way God sees it is that He is doing everything and directing everything. At the same time in our reality we are acting independently. As far as we are aware, we are not being led one way or another. We are the ones who are making the choice to do the right thing or stay away from the wrong thing. It is a strenuous process. Because of this strain, discipline, and effort that we expend, we deserve to be rewarded for what we do right. We, with our own effort, made the choice to do the right thing. This is because God created the world in such a way that we are unaware that everything is from God and that we are guided all the time.

NOTES

1. This follows the Kapoch translation.
2. See Ezekiel 8:12.
3. *Yesodei HaTorah* 2:10.

4. See *Keter Shem Tov*, addenda, para. 19ff.; Kehot Publication Society. *Likkutei Sichot*, vol. 8, p. 277ff.

5. In fact, although this doctrine was emphasized by the Baal Shem Tov, its roots can be found in the statements of talmudic Sages, as in the view of Rabbi Yochanan in *Chullin*, 63a. See Rashi, ad loc. Some authorities add that contrary to popular belief, this does not contradict Maimonides' view of personal Divine Providence. See Rabbi Dovber Schneuri's *Derech Chaim*, 13a–b, Kehot Publication Society; *Shaarei Emunah*, Kehot Publication Society, 5751 (1991), p. 91ff. See also *Shomer Emunim* close to the end; *Eilimah Rabbati*, Rabbi Moses Cordovero, *Ein Kol Tamar* 5:1.

6. *Derech Chaim, Shaar HaTeshuvah*, chap. 9. See also *Likkutei Sichot*, vol. 9, p. 181.

7. *Likkutei Sichot*, vol. 18, p. 199; *Hitvaaduyot* 5745, vol. 3, p. 1836.

8. See *Derech Chaim, Shaar HaTeshuvah*, chap. 9.

9. See *Likkutei Sichot*, vol. 30, *Sichat Yud Tet Kislev*.

10. Compare the blessing recited prior to the Torah reading ". . . Who chose us from among all the nations . . ."; see also Malachi 1:2.

11. Rashi, Genesis 1:1.

12. *Tanchuma, Eikev* 2. See *Avot*, chap. 2:1.

13. *Bechorot* 30b; Rambam, *Issurei Biya* 14:8.

14. Deuteronomy 32:9.

15. *Or Torah*, pt. 2, p. 3.

16. *Keter Shem Tov*, addenda, para. 116.

17. *Sukkah* 25a.

18. *Mishnah Sanhedrin*, 37a.

19. *Shaarei Emunah*, p. 94.

20. Deuteronomy 31:18.

21. Rabbi Yosef Albo (d. circa 1420). The *Sefer HaIkkarim* is a commentary to Maimonides' thirteen principles.

22. *Ikkarim* 4:7.

23. *Code, Yesodei HaTorah* 2:9–10; see also *Guide for the Perplexed*, pt. 3, chaps. 20, 21.

24. See, for example, the Maharal of Prague, Rabbi Yehudah Loewe, in his *Book of Divine Power*, Second Introduction.

25. Chap. 35.

26. See *Avodat HaKodesh*, Rabbi Meir ibn Gabbai, pt. 1, chap. 8.

27. *Code, Teshuvah* 5:5; *Guide* 3:20.

28. See *Code, Yesodei HaTorah* 2:9–10; *Guide* 3:20, 21.

29. *Midrash Shmuel* to *Pirkei Avot*, chap. 3, in the name of R' Moshe Almoshnino; also cited in *Tosafot Yom Tov*, *Avot*, ad loc.

30. *Code, Yesodei HaTorah* 2:9–10; *Guide* 3:20, 21.

31. The following sections are based on *Emunah u'Mada*, Rabbi M. M. Schneerson, pp. 19–26. Published by Machon Lubavitch, 5740 (1980); *Shaarei Emunah*, p. 225 ff.

32. *Tanya*, chap. 48; *Biurei HaZohar (Tzemach Tzedek)*, p. 266; Discourses 5672, chap. 58 ff.

33. *Avot* 4:22.

34. *Berachot* 33b; *Zohar*, vol. 1, p. 59a.

35. *Guide*, pt. 1, chap. 57.

36. An inadequate translation of מציאותו בלתי מציאות נמצא.

37. Discourses 5672, chap. 58.

38. *Biurei HaZohar (Tzemach Tzedek)*, p. 266.

The Eleventh Principle

> I believe with complete faith that God rewards those who keep His commandments and punishes those who transgress His commandments.

The eleventh principle involves belief in a system of reward and punishment that is conferred as a direct result of our actions.[1] In our discussion of the previous principle we explained that free choice is not an illusion. On the contrary, it is one of the foundations of the Torah. We concluded that since we expend great efforts in making the choice to do the right thing or stay away from the wrong thing we deserve to be rewarded for what we do right, or, conversely, to be punished for failing to make the effort to do the right thing or reject the wrong thing.[2]

On a simple level, we could explain that the reason that there must be a system of reward and punishment is that many people are not on the lofty ethical level to do what is right because it is right and stay away from wrong because it is wrong. Reward and punishment would then be merely a means of motivating people to do the right thing. In addition, with a system of reward and punishment, a person is aware that every action counts and must be accounted for, as the *Mishnah*[3] states, "Reflect upon three things, and you will never come to sin . . . and all your deeds are recorded in a Book." However, besides the fact that a person may not be motivated to do what is right either because the reward is not immediate, or not sufficiently attractive, or the punishment is not sufficiently threatening, our Sages state explicitly[4] that we should not serve God for the sake of reward. Moreover, Maimonides himself explains[5] that one should not fulfill the commandments of the Torah for the sake of reward, whether material or spiritual, nor should he refrain from transgressing simply to avoid punishment, whether material or spiritual. Ideally, one should serve God out of love,[6] without expectation of reward.[7] Accordingly, we may ask why it is that Maimonides rules that the principle of reward and punishment is one of the foundations of Jewish faith. From what we have said so far, it appears that reward and punishment are strictly matters of incentive or deterrent. However, a proper understanding of the concepts of reward and punishment will clarify why reward and punishment are indeed one of the foundational principles of Judaism.

MAN'S PLACE IN THE UNIVERSE

Chasidic philosophy explains that one of the axioms behind the concept of reward and punishment is that our actions have ramifications in both the physical and spiritual worlds. The world around us is affected by, and responds to, our deeds. The fact that we are rewarded for doing what is right, whether the reward is material or spiritual, and that we are punished for doing wrong, whether the punishment is material or spiritual, hinges on the fact that we are not islands unto ourselves.

On the contrary, our actions reverberate throughout the physical and spiritual universes because God created the world in this way.

The Torah teaches that when God created man, He said, "We shall make man. . . ."[8] Commentaries[9] ask who God was speaking to. Who is the "we" referred to here? Did God need any help or assistance in creating man?

Based on the verse, "The world too, He placed in his heart,"[10] *Chasidus* explains[11] that when God created man he created him from every level of this world, and every spiritual world, so that man comprises all levels and affects all levels. Accordingly, his actions have manifold ramifications and cannot be judged in isolation.

This also explains why biblical figures such as Abraham, Jacob,[12] and others sought rewards for their efforts and yet cannot be accused of self-seeking motives at all. *Chasidus* explains that these righteous men wanted others to see that when a person does what is right, he is rewarded. This is a sanctification of God's Name, for the world thereby sees how the physical and the spiritual are related: when a person acts in the right way, when his spiritual life is conducted properly, the physical world responds. When a person does what he should do, he fulfills the will of God and this affects his crops, his health, and so on. That the physical world should respond to his spiritual behavior is a sanctification of God's Name.

TWO TYPES OF REWARD

The *Shelah*[13] cites two opinions regarding reward and punishment.[14] One opinion is that reward and punishment are natural consequences of one's actions, like cause and effect. That is, they are a natural response to what we do, and the resulting reward is commensurate to the action. Another opinion he cites is that reward and punishment are really of a miraculous nature, for the infinite reward received is incomparable to the action that elicited it.

Chasidus offers a profound insight into the two opinions cited above. *Chasidus* explains that there is really no argument here between the two views. Rather, there are two different types of rewards. The first type of reward, the "natural response," is the effect that is produced directly and is commensurate to its cause. Then there is a higher, miraculous type of reward, transcending the limitations of nature. The first type of reward and punishment applies to all nations of the world, whereas the higher form of reward is unique to the Jewish people. Exactly the same is true of punishment.

Chasidic texts explain this in a deeper way by asking what the positive commandment to "serve" God[15] means. "Service" generally denotes attending to and assisting someone, such as a king, or a parent. What does this mean when we are talking about God, before Whom we are totally insignificant? What do we have to give or offer? The answer given is that because of His infinite love for us, God has bestowed the highest form of kindness upon us; the highest form of kindness is that which a person feels he earned. If you give someone something that he did not do anything to deserve, it probably does not sit well with the person because he knows that he is getting a free handout. On the other hand, when you give someone something, even though what you are giving him is much more than he deserved, but he knows in his heart that he did make some effort to earn it, then he feels much better about accepting it. Therefore, God gave us the *mitzvahs*. When we fulfill the *mitzvahs*, we have contributed something toward our own reward, even though the reward is infinitely greater than what we deserve on a purely cause-and-effect basis.

Thus, God designed a system in which this world, and all spiritual worlds, respond to what we do. Our ability to have an effect upon all the worlds is not because of our intrinsic importance but because God chose that this should be so.

Hence, the concept of reward and punishment is part of a much larger enterprise in the scheme of things, according to Maimonides' thinking. It involves the entire role of man in creation, the purpose of his existence and the creation of the world, and the nature of God's relationship toward us.

Let us clarify this on the basis of a *mishnaic* statement of our Sages regarding the performance of *mitzvahs*.[16] Rabbi Yehuda haNasi said, "Be as careful [in the performance of a seemingly] minor *mitzvah* as a major one, for you do not know the reward given for the *mitzvahs*." In his *Commentary to the Mishnah*, Maimonides explains that we were not informed of the size of the reward for any of the positive *mitzvahs* (unlike the prohibitions, whose punishment is stated explicitly in Torah) so that we will be careful to perform all of them equally.

The *Mishnah* continues, "Reflect on the loss incurred [in neglecting or transgressing] a *mitzvah* against the reward [gained by observing it]." Maimonides (ibid.) explains that although the Torah did not inform us of the reward due for the fulfillment of a positive commandment, we can nevertheless deduce it from the loss (punishment) incurred by neglecting to fulfill it.

However, this needs clarification; what difference would it make to a person if he was informed of the reward explicitly in the Torah or by comparing the punishments for failing to do them that are mentioned explicitly in the Torah, since the end point is ultimately the same? For one type of *mitzvah* one receives more reward, and for another type, less reward. Consequently, how can one be as careful in a *mitzvah* that offers less reward as in one that promises greater reward?

We must therefore conclude that there are two types of reward for fulfilling positive commandments. One type of reward is commensurate with the punishment that accrues for failing to fulfill it, and in this type of reward there are indeed differences between one *mitzvah* and another. However, there is also another type of reward, a much greater type of reward, in which there is no difference between one type of *mitzvah* and another—all *mitzvahs* are rewarded equally.[17] Regarding this type of reward the *Mishnah* states, "You do not know the reward given for the *mitzvahs*."

The foregoing is really based on the principle that the *mitzvahs* themselves comprise two aspects: (1) Each *mitzvah* fulfills God's will, and in this there is no difference between one *mitzvah* and another—all of the *mitzvahs* are equally the will of God, including rabbinical injunctions and decrees, for since the will of God is infinite, and each *mitzvah* is an expression of His infinite Will, we cannot say that God wants one *mitzvah* any more than another. In infinite terms, there is no "more" and "less"—all *mitzvahs* are equally the will of God and are equally infinite. This explains the statement of our Sages[18] that one should be as careful in the performance of a [seemingly] minor *mitzvah* as of a major one. (2) Each *mitzvah* achieves a purification of the person fulfilling it,[19] the objects with which he performs the *mitzvahs*, and the world in general.[20]

These two aspects of the *mitzvahs* are expressed in the two types of reward mentioned above. The reward given for a *mitzvah* that purifies the person and the world around him is limited, for the creation itself is limited, and therefore everything connected within creation is also limited. Accordingly, there are differences between the rewards given for one *mitzvah* and another: the greater the purification of the person and the world around him that the *mitzvah* achieves, the greater the reward that accrues for its performance. But as regards the reward due for fulfilling God's supernal will, where there is no difference between one *mitzvah* and another, since all *mitzvahs* are equally His will, this reward is unlimited.

The same principle applies to the punishments of the Torah. Although every transgression is ultimately a rebellion against the will of God (the factor common to all transgressions), each individual transgression causes its own blemish or stain. In order to remove different degrees of blemishes, different types of punishments are required. Accordingly, there are different types of punishments mentioned in the Torah, each one assigned to a different type of stain or blemish caused by the transgression.

This may also be explained in a slightly different way: there are two aspects of every *mitzvah*—the actual performance of the *mitzvah* and the *kavvanah*, the intention, the preparation and enthusiasm that a person has when he does a *mitzvah*. Here again, the reward for the *kavvanah* of the *mitzvah* is granted in *Gan Eden*, whereas the performance of the *mitzvah* itself is rewarded in the World to Come. Thus, as important as it is to have the right intentions and the right feeling when we do a *mitzvah*, it still does not match the actual performance of the *mitzvah*. If a person has the most beautiful thoughts and intentions but does not actually do the *mitzvah*, he has not fulfilled any *mitzvah* at all. On the other hand, when a person does a *mitzvah*, even without proper *kavvanah*, he still fulfilled a *mitzvah* because the essential aspect of a *mitzvah* is its performance in the physical world. The *kavvanah*, the human contribution that a person puts in while he does a *mitzvah*, as beautiful as it is, is still finite. Therefore, we are rewarded for the *kavvanah* of the *mitzvah* in *Gan Eden*. However, for the actual observance of the *mitzvah*, we could not be rewarded in *Gan Eden*. *Gan Eden* would be a limited level compared to what we deserve. Where do we get the infinite blessings, the infinite reward? This is mainly in the World to Come.

PARADISE AND THE WORLD TO COME

The two different levels of reward—the finite level of cause and effect and the infinite type of reward that transcends natural boundaries—are granted at different times, according to chasidic texts.[21] We find that there are two different periods of reward. There is the reward in Paradise, or *Gan Eden*, which is the reward that comes after we leave this world. When the soul leaves the body after living a righteous life in this world, it is given its due reward. Then there is the final and ultimate reward given on the level referred to as the World to Come, or *olam haba* in Hebrew. The reward in Paradise is of the cause-and-effect type, and is therefore limited, while the reward in the World to Come is of the transcendent, miraculous type, and is infinite.

Let us clarify these terms and the differences between them. *Gan Eden* actually comprises many different stages. Prior to its descent into a body, the soul is in *Gan Eden*. The soul descends into a body for a specific period of time and then returns (directly, if the person was righteous, or indirectly if he wasn't) to *Gan Eden*. But it is understood that the *Gan Eden* that the soul goes to after living a righteous life in this world is a much more lofty level of *Gan Eden* than it came from originally, for through the observance of the *mitzvahs* the soul reaches a much higher and closer relationship with God than it had before it left *Gan Eden*.

The World to Come refers to the era of the resurrection of the dead,[22] where the soul will also reside in a body. Now, regarding these two levels, there is a dispute between Maimonides and Nachmanides as to which level is regarded as the ultimate reward. According to Maimonides,[23] after the resurrection of the dead, there is going to be a period when the soul will return to *Gan Eden* without the body.[24]

However, according to Nachmanides,[25] the final and ultimate reward will be granted to the soul within the body. There will not be anything after that. The ultimate and final reward is given to the soul in a body. Chasidic texts[26] endorse Nachmanides' view, that the era of the resurrection of the dead will be the time when a person is granted his final and ultimate reward.

Nachmanides' view needs some explanation, for after all, the physical world and the physical body are finite entities, limited in time and space, whereas the soul is beyond time and beyond space. How could we conceive of the descent of the soul into the body once again as a reward? For a soul to be confined to the physical world would seem to be a constraint and a limitation. Moreover, this is described as the ultimate and greatest reward, with which no other reward compares. Why is this reward, given to the soul within the body, regarded as greater than the reward given to the soul without a body in *Gan Eden*?

Kabbalistic and chasidic teachings explain that the physical world that we are living in on one hand is the very lowest world (lowliness, in this context, meaning "base"). What makes this world the lowest? Not the fact that it is physical, or that it is limited in time and space, for that alone does not make it low. There are many examples of things that were limited to time and space and are extremely holy. Even Paradise,

Gan Eden, where Adam and Eve lived, was a physical place limited in space and time. And yet, it was a very holy place. Similarly, the most sanctified area in the Temple, the Holy of Holies, also had spatial dimensions—breadth, length, and height. Thus, the fact that something is limited in temporal and spatial dimensions does not necessarily make it of a spiritually low order. Rather, what makes this world the lowest of places is the fact that this world is totally unaware of its true existence, that God is really creating it every second. And not only are we unaware of this, but the natural tendency of this world is a denial of this fact. It appears to us that we are completely independent of God, to the extent that a person can even claim to be an atheist or agnostic and deny the existence of the Creator, which is the exact opposite of the truth.

GOD'S "HOME"

The *Midrash*[27] declares that God created this physical world for the purpose of making it His "home"—"God desired a dwelling place in the lowest world." Out of all worlds, out of all spiritual levels, God specifically chose this physical world as His "home." Thus, although from one point of view this physical world in which we live is the very lowest spiritual level, as we have explained previously, from another point of view, from the point of view of God's choice this physical world is the greatest world, the highest world—it is the place where He wants to be more than any other place. This is where the Essence of God is expressed.[28]

Chasidic texts[29] explain that although this world does not reveal God's Infinite Light (the *Or Ein Sof*, as it is referred to in kabbalistic texts), it is nevertheless a manifestation of His Essence, expressed in His innermost will. This far transcends

His revelation of Himself in the *Or Ein Sof*, for what can be revealed, even on the very highest of levels, is only a reflection of His Essence. Therefore, although this physical world exhibits less revelation of the Infinite Light than any other world, it also exhibits more revelation of essence than any other world. Every other level is superior in terms of its awareness of God. The higher the world, the greater the awareness of God. In this sense, this world is the lowest. However, as far as God Himself is concerned, His essence is manifested here more than on any other level because this is the place that He chose to be; this is His dwelling place.

For this very same reason the beings in this world tend to feel that they exist totally independently of God, to the extent that they can even deny that there is a Creator. In no other world, and on no other level, is it possible for a creature to feel independent of God. On the contrary, as explained above, every other plane of existence is aware of its spiritual source and on Whom it is dependent for its existence. The reason for this feeling of independence is that God's Being, which is truly of His Essence and is totally independent of any other existence (as explained in the first three principles), is manifested here. That is why we tend to feel that we have an independent existence! This means that this physical world has in itself something that only God Himself has and only from Him did we get this feeling. Just as God Himself feels that He exists upon His own, so do we, who come from the Essence of God, feel that we exist on our own.[30]

When the era of the World to Come dawns, and all concealment is removed so that the true being of everything will be visible to all, as will be explained in the following chapter, then it will be obvious that this physical world is an expression of God Himself. Therefore, the return of the soul to this physical world is not a restriction. On the contrary, the soul realizes that the body, the physical world and physical body, has an even higher source in God than the soul itself. For the soul is an expression of God's light and the body is an expression of His Essence. Therefore, when the soul is in the body, it will be in touch with the Essence of God, and this is the greatest reward that can possibly be given to the soul. Moreover, this is something that the soul cannot achieve without the body, for the soul can only comprehend spirituality, the radiance and reflection of God's Infinite Light. It is only through the body that it can experience God's Essence. That is why, in the era of the Resurrection of the Dead, the body will be the source of life for the soul, contrary to the way things are now, where the soul is the source of life to the body, as will be explained in the final chapter of this book.

TORAH AND *MITZVAHS*

Chasidic texts[31] also explain that the reward for learning Torah is given in Paradise, in *Gan Eden*, whereas the reward for the *mitzvahs* that we have observed is given mainly in the World to Come. The explanation of this is the same as we have given above, regarding the two aspects of *mitzvahs*. The reward based on our own spiritual achievements, each according to his abilities and efforts, is mainly in Torah study rather than in the practical observance of *mitzvahs* in which everyone is equal. Thus, we will be awarded the level of Paradise commensurate with the amount of Torah we have studied. *Gan Eden* is thus where we are granted a deeper spiritual understanding of what we studied here in this world. That is why the Talmud states, "Fortunate is one who comes here [to Paradise] and his Talmud [his learning] is in his hands."[32] Only what you have learned, and according to how you have learned it, will you be rewarded. If a person studied the tractate *Berachot*, then when he comes to *Gan Eden* he studies that same tractate, but on a much deeper level. But a tractate that he did not study, he will not study in *Gan Eden*. For *Gan Eden* is limited; it is based on a finite principle of cause and effect. Your reward is commensurate with your efforts.

However, the *mitzvahs*, which are physical, are connected to God Himself and are thus infinite, as explained above. Therefore, the reward for their fulfillment is in the World to Come, where the Essence of God will be revealed. This is why the *mitzvahs* are rewarded in a physical way, to the soul within a body, in the World to Come. This can be better understood according to Rabbi Shneur Zalman of Liadi's explanation of the statement of our Sages that "the reward of a *mitzvah* is a *mitzvah*" (*Avot* 4:2). He explains[33] that the cause of reward is the *mitzvah* itself, because by virtue of performing it, the person elicits a flow of Infinite Light from Above down into this world to be enclothed in the material world itself. Thus, when a person fulfills a *mitzvah*, the vitality that is in the objects with which he performs the *mitzvah* ascends and merges and is absorbed in the Infinite Light. Similarly, the physical energy of the person fulfilling the *mitzvah* is also elevated by this action, is absorbed into the holiness of the precept, and merges into the Infinite Light. Their reward is thus infinite.

PUNISHMENTS IN THE TORAH

Punishments in the Torah are not to be understood as revenge, God forbid. Punishment in hell, or *Gehinnom*, as it is referred to in Hebrew, is regarded as a process of cleansing in chasidic thought.[34] When a person gets a stain on his suit, he needs to give it to a dry cleaner to remove the stain. In a similar way, when we do something that we should not have done, we cause a stain on the soul, so it is for our benefit that this stain needs to be removed through a cleansing process. This is the idea of *Gehinnom*: there will come a time when those who have accumulated "stains" on their souls will undergo a purification process. God will remove the stains from their souls. Accordingly, the descent of the soul into *Gehinnom* is for the purpose of being cleansed in order to be able to enter *Gan Eden*. This cleansing process is, of course, temporary, just as the laundering of a suit is temporary; the intention is not to leave it in the machine but to clean it and then wear it. *Gehinnom* is thus an act of benevolence to those who did not remove the stains from their soul by themselves, through proper repentance, through *teshuvah*. Therefore, the issue that should concern a person who sins is not what will happen at some future date. The issue is what just happened, that he caused a stain on his soul! When a person accidentally spills something over an expensive suit, what concerns him most at present is not the fact that he will have to give his suit to a cleaner and that he will have to pay a lot to have it cleaned. What bothers him most is that his suit just got dirty. A person ought to react in the same way when he committed a sin. The problem is not that he is going to have to go to *Gehinnom*, the problem is the stain on his soul.

In addition, chasidic works[35] explain that *Gan Eden* and *Gehinnom* are not necessarily what take place to the soul *after* life in this world. Rather, "Your own evil will torment you"[36] in *this* world—how many people do we meet who are going through hell while alive? Conversely, a person may be in *Gan Eden* even now, in this world. This is hinted at in Rashi's commentary to the Pentateuch: when Jacob stands before Isaac, about to receive his blessings, the latter comments, "The scent of my son is like the fragrance of a field blessed by God" (Genesis 27:27). Rashi comments: "This teaches us that the fragrance of *Gan Eden* entered with him," for this was where Jacob's soul was to be found. In contrast, when Esau enters the tent, the verse states, "Isaac shuddered in great fear . . ." (ibid. 27:33). Rashi comments: "Isaac saw *Gehinnom* open beneath him."

Our Sages state that the reward for a *mitzvah* is a *mitzvah*.[37] Rabbi Shneur Zalman of Liadi explains that the word *mitzvah* derives from the word *tzavtah*, meaning connection or attachment.[38] Thus the reward for a *mitzvah* is the attachment to God one achieves by fulfilling a *mitzvah*. The same is true of a transgression; the punishment that accrues for transgressing a *mitzvah*, or failing to fulfill it, is that one becomes detached and alienated from God. This takes place at this very moment and not later. Therefore we have to worry about our state of attachment and closeness to God now and not later.

This is also one of the explanations for why people undergo suffering in this world. Suffering is not meaningless in Jewish thought.[39] On the contrary, it is regarded as the highest expression of God's love—"Happy is the man whom You, God, chasten" (Psalm 94:12). Moreover, suffering atones for sin,[40] for it purifies and cleanses the soul.[41] Moreover, suffering in this world can even be accepted with joy, for it is a substitute for suffering in the next world,[42] which according to all accounts is a lot more uncomfortable than minor suffering in this world.[43] (Of course, one should not seek suffering in this world, for only suffering brought upon a person from Above has this effect.[44]) This disproves the view of those who assume that God looks away, or turns His back, so to speak, on human suffering. On the contrary, it is specifically because God is so concerned with purifying the soul of the sinner that He brings suffering on the person. This is done out of love and not out of lack of concern. Moreover, temporary physical suffering in this world, when it is decreed from Above, must be evaluated in the context of the larger picture—the eternal life of the soul. This may be compared to a doctor who amputates a limb in order to save the person's life. An observer who is unaware that the limb was ill might view the doctor's life-saving actions as cruelty.

This is also one of the explanations of the doctrine of reincarnation, which is discussed at length in kabbalistic literature.[45] It is explained that one of the reasons and intentions of the reincarnation and transmigration of the soul is in order to rectify past transgressions that were not corrected during the person's lifetime, and in this way the soul is able to make amends for its previous actions and receive its due reward. Thus, suffering in this world can often be understood within this framework—as a rectification of a past incarnation or incarnations. Kabbalistic literature[46] cites examples of people who died in early childhood, and even in infancy, as being simply because the soul is sometimes removed from the body as soon as the required rectification has been done. This might even be accomplished by the trauma of birth. Alternatively, reincarnation is viewed as an opportunity to fulfill *mitzvahs* that for some reason the person was unable to fulfill in a previous incarnation and in this way achieve its reward.

THE PHYSICAL WORLD

In this context, we may ask a profound question regarding the entire idea of reward and punishment. Why is it that we do not find in the Torah, the Bible, any mention of spiritual rewards?[47] The only rewards mentioned in the Torah are material—if we listen to God our crop will grow, our cattle will be healthy, the rain will come on time, and so on.[48] Maimonides[49] maintains that these material rewards are not really the true or final reward and punishment for Torah and *mitzvahs*. Rather, if we fulfill the *mitzvahs* happily, and always act wisely, the things that prevent us from fulfilling the *mitzvahs*, such as illness, war, and hunger, will be withheld from us, and the things that enable us to fulfill the Torah and *mitzvahs*, such as wealth, plenty, and peace, will be given in abundance, so that we will be able to spend all of our days in Torah study and be free to perform the *mitzvahs* in the best possible way. However, the essential reward for keeping the Torah and *mitzvahs* is not mentioned in the Torah, so that a person will serve his Creator without thought of reward (i.e., for its own sake) and not because of fear of punishment. Other commentaries explain simply that these physical rewards are not the main reward that will be given for the *mitzvahs*. The main reward will be spiritual.[50] And the reason that the Torah does not mention the spiritual rewards for fulfilling Torah and *mitzvahs* is so that we will serve God altruistically and not for the sake of reward.[51]

Ibn Ezra answers that the Torah intends to relate to everyone, even the simple people, even people who do not appreciate spiritual rewards. The Torah wants to talk on a level that everyone can relate to. This is why the Torah speaks about the physical and not about the spiritual.[52]

Nachmanides[53] and Rabbeinu Bechaya[54] have a different approach. They explain that our observance of Torah and *mitzvahs* has a direct effect on the physical world, evidenced in the rewards that accrue for our fulfillment of them. Had the Torah not mentioned that our serving God has an effect upon the physical world, we would never have known it. And that is why the Torah mentions it. However, as regards spiritual rewards, this goes without saying. There is no need for the Torah to write about spiritual rewards because it is self-understood.

Another approach to this question is found in the Cuzari and in the writings of Rabbeinu Nissim.[55] They maintain that the reason the Torah speaks about physical rewards is to make us understand that the source of every event in the world is only God. For there are those who believe that things happen by themselves and that God does not involve Himself, that God is not the one who makes things happen.[56] So, if stating that when a person does a *mitzvah* it affects the physical world demonstrates that everything that happens in the world happens because God makes it happen. If you do what He wants you to do, He gives you what you need in this physical world.

Another approach to this question is that there are those who maintain that to dwell in this world is beneath God's dignity.[57] According to this view, spirituality and physicality are polar opposites and can never meet. By giving physical reward for spiritual *mitzvahs*, God shows us that spirituality also permeates this physical world.

All the views mentioned above have one common denominator—that the question we are asking is why the Torah mentions only material rewards and does not mention spiritual rewards as well. The *Shelah*,[58] however, approaches this question from a completely different point of view. The aforementioned views are all based on the premise that the main reality dealt with in the Torah is *this* material world. The *Shelah*, however, bases his view on the statement of our Sages that the Torah speaks primarily of the upper worlds (i.e., about godliness and spiritual matters) and merely hints to the lower worlds (the physical).[59] He explains that when we read the Torah, we first understand it on a simple level, and when we go deeper and deeper into the teachings of the Torah we see that there is more in it than what meets the eye. But the Torah is in reality a book of spirituality and it addresses a spiritual world while merely hinting to the physical world. Therefore, says the *Shelah*, you cannot ask why we do not find spirituality in the Torah. Not only is there spirituality in the Torah and spiritual rewards and spiritual punishments, but this is primarily what the Torah is talking about. The fact that we read about physical rewards in the Torah is because we only see the tip of the iceberg, the lowest level of the Torah, which hints to physicality. We find also in the *Midrash*[60] that every word in the Torah is really a Name of God. One of the explanations of this is that every word in the Torah is really a spiritual concept and a spiritual attribute.[61] It is only to us, who read the Torah on our level, that it appears to be talking about a physical world.

REVEALING THE ESSENCE

Chasidus[62] gives a different answer to the question of why only physical rewards are mentioned in the Torah. In the view of the *Shelah* and of all the other authorities mentioned above, the material world is strictly inferior to the spiritual worlds. According to *Chasidus*, however, it is precisely in this material world that the Essence of God is revealed,[63] or, in other words, that the material world has its root in the Essence of God, as we explained above and at length in our commentary to the first principle (and will also be elaborated concerning the resurrection of the dead). Briefly, this idea is expressed as follows: although[64] this world does not reveal God's Infinite Light (the *Or Ein Sof*), it is nevertheless a manifestation of His Essence, expressed in His innermost will. This far transcends His revelation of Himself in the *Or Ein Sof*, for what can be revealed, even on the very highest of levels, is only a reflection of His Essence. Therefore, although this physical world exhibits less revelation of the Infinite Light than any other world, it also exhibits more revelation of the essence than any other world. Every other level is superior in terms of its awareness of God. The higher the world, the greater the awareness of God. In this sense, this world is the lowest. However, as far as God Himself is concerned, His Essence is manifested here more than on any other level because this is the place that He chose to be; this is His dwelling place, as explained above. It is for this reason that the Torah expressly mentions material rewards, for they are the highest form of reward in that they reveal God's Essence!

Chasidus offers another explanation as well. Regarding the Torah, the verse states that "it is your life, and your longevity."[65] This means that not only does the Torah bring life in this world, and in the World to Come, but it is actually the life force of every Jew. The Torah is not something additional to a Jew; it is his essence and his life force![66]

Now, the life force of a person is found in all of his body equally, from head to toe. The reason for this is that since a person's life force is his essence, it is therefore found in every part of him equally. Moreover, the proof that something is of the essence of a person is that it is revealed not only in the more-elevated aspects of the person but also in the less-elevated aspects, and even in the very lowest aspects of himself—to the heels of his feet!

This can be understood by way of an analogy. When a person is joyful, the test of whether the joy is merely superficial or permeates his entire being is whether it is expressed in only part of him, such as in his thoughts, or in his power of speech, or in all of him, to the extent that he even dances and claps his hands.

The very same is true of the Torah as our life force. The clearest proof of the Torah being totally united with us is that this is expressed not only in the person's elevated spiritual aspects but also in his physical aspects. Thus, if the reward for learning Torah for its own sake were only the great spiritual achievements mentioned by our Sages,[67] this would be no proof that the Torah had totally permeated a person's being, for they might be merely the natural result of his spiritual efforts. However, when the rewards are manifested on even the physical plane, "Rain in its time, and so on," then it is a proof that Torah and *mitzvahs* are not merely something additional to his being but are of his very essence.

The reason that the Torah is a Jew's life force is that the Torah and the Holy One, blessed is He, are absolutely One.[68] Therefore, just as God is the ultimate and absolute existence, from Whom all of existence derives,[69] so too as regards Torah —all of existence benefits from it, in every way, including the physical.

Accordingly, we see that the contrary thesis is true: it is precisely through physical rewards that we are aware that the Torah has permeated all of a person's being and all of creation!

NOTES

1. Maimonides, *Commentary to the Mishnah Sanhedrin*, chap. 11, tenth principle.
2. *Code, Teshuvah* 6:1. In ibid. 6:2, Maimonides adds that this is only true when one does not repent.
3. *Avot* 2:1.
4. See *Avot* 1:3.
5. *Code, Teshuvah* 10:1.
6. Ibid., 10:2.
7. See *Avot*, ad loc.

8. Genesis 1:26. Or, "Let us make man," according to some translations.

9. See Rashi, Ramban, *Or HaChaim*, *Kli Yakar*, who all offer explanations of this puzzling statement.

10. *Kohelet* (Ecclesiastes) 3:11.

11. See *Sefer HaLikkutim*, s.v. אדם, chap. 1; *Maamarim* 5666, Discourses 3, 5. See also *Zohar*, vol. 1, p. 55a.

12. See Genesis 15:1 ff, 28:20 ff.

13. The acronym of *Shnei Luchot HaBrit*, a semikabbalistic work written by Rabbi Isaiah Hurwitz (1560–1630), rabbi in Poland, Frankfurt, and Jerusalem, and a leading scholar of the early seventeenth century. This work is of great importance in Jewish mystical philosophy.

14. *Bayit Acharon* 12a–b.

15. See Deuteronomy 11:13.

16. *Avot* 2:1. Explained in *Likkutei Sichot*, vol. 4, p. 1191 ff.

17. See *Yalkut Shimoni Yitro, Remez* 298; *Mishlei Remez* 937; *Yerushalmi Peah*, 1:1.

18. *Avot* 2:1.

19. See *Bereishit Rabbah*, chap. 44; *Tanya, Iggeret HaKodesh*, chap. 29.

20. *Tanya*, chap. 37.

21. See *Likkutei Sichot*, vol. 17, p. 344 ff.

22. *Mishnah Sanhedrin* 11:1, Bartenura; *Midrash Shmuel* on *Pirkei Avot* introductory *Mishnah*.

23. *Code, Teshuvah* 8:2; see also ibid., 9:1.

24. See *Sefer HaIkkarim* 4:31.

25. Shaar Hagemul, end. See also Raavad's comments to Rambam's *Code, Teshuvah*, 8:2.

26. See *Likkutei Torah, Tzav* 15c; *Shir HaShirim* 65d; *Derech Mitzvotecha, Tzitzit.*

27. *Tanchuma, Nasso*, chap. 16.

28. See *Tanya*, chaps. 36, 37.

29. For example, *Tanya*, ibid.; Discourses 5666, Discourse 1.

30. See *Biurei HaZohar, Beshallach*, p. 43a by Rabbi DovBer, the son of Rabbi Shneur Zalman, and the second Rebbe of the *Chabad* dynasty.

31. *Likkutei Sichot*, vol. 17, p. 344, and notes, ad loc.

32. *Pesachim* 50a.

33. *Tanya*, chap. 37.

34. *Likkutei Sichot*, vol. 22, p. 335, vol. 5, p. 135; *Tanya*, note in chap. 24; *Likkutei Torah Bamidbar*, pp. 25b, 66b.
35. See the Mitteler Rebbe's יפה שעה אחת.
36. Jeremiah 2:19.
37. *Avot* 4:2.
38. *Likkutei Torah, Bechukotai* 45c.
39. See *Tanya*, chap. 26.
40. *Beraita Yoma* 86a.
41. As explained at length in *Iggeret HaTeshuvah*, chaps. 1, 2.
42. *Iggeret HaTeshuvah*, chap. 12.
43. Ibid., in the name of Ramban in the Introduction to his commentary on the Book of Job.
44. *Iggeret HaTeshuvah*, chap. 1.
45. See *Zohar*, vol. 2, *Mishpatim, Shaar HaGilgulim* and *Sefer HaGilgulim* among the works of the Arizal.
46. Ibid.
47. Abarbanel to Leviticus 26:3 ff. See also the Lubavitcher Rebbe's *Likkut to Behar-Bechukotai* 5751.
48. Leviticus 26:3 ff.
49. *Code, Teshuvah* 9:1.
50. See Abarbanel, ad loc.; *Kli Yakar* to Leviticus 26:12, following Maimonides, *Teshuvah* 9:1.
51. Abarbanel and *Kli Yakar*, ibid.
52. Ibn Ezra to Deuteronomy 32:39.
53. Deuteronomy, ad loc. See also his *Shaar HaGemul*.
54. Deuteronomy, ad loc.
55. Cited in *Shelah, Bayit Acharon* 10a.
56. *Tanchuma, Noach* 4:4; *Tanna d'Bei Eliyahu Rabbah* 18.
57. Ibid.
58. See *Shnei Luchot HaBrit* 13b ff.; 161a ff.
59. Rabbi Menachem deFano in *Asarah Maamarot, Chikur HaDin*, pt. 3, chap. 22.
60. *Otzar HaMidrashim* (Eisenstein), p. 181 ד"ה שבעים שמות יש.
61. See Arizal's *Likkutei Torah, Bereishit*; *Shelah* 13b ff., 161a ff.; *Asarah Maamarot, Chikur HaDin*, pt. 3, chap. 22.
62. *Shaarei Emunah*, p. 277 ff.
63. See *Tanya*, chaps. 36–37; *Iggeret HaKodesh*, chap. 20.
64. For example, *Tanya*, ibid.; *Discourses 5666*, Discourse 1.

65. Deuteronomy 30:2.
66. See *Avodah Zarah*, end of 3b.
67. *Avot* 6:1.
68. *Zohar*, cited in *Tanya*, chap. 5, beginning of chap. 23. See *Zohar*, vol. 1, 24a; vol. 2, 60a.
69. Maimonides, *Code*, *Yesodei HaTorah*, chap. 1.

The Twelfth Principle

I believe with complete faith in the coming of the Messiah. Even though he tarry, I will eagerly await his coming every day.

he twelfth principle is that we believe with perfect faith in the coming of the Messiah (*Mashiach*), and we also eagerly await his coming. We are certain that *Mashiach* will come and "although he tarries, we await him."[1]

There are commentaries that question why Maimonides regards belief in the coming of *Mashiach* as a foundation of Jewish belief. Why does he maintain that if a person doesn't believe in *Mashiach* he is lacking a foundation of Judaism, even if he still believes in the entire Torah and follows its commandments? In addition, the Rambam writes[2] that not only one who doesn't believe in the coming of *Mashiach* denies a fundamental principle of Jewish belief, but even one who doesn't look forward to and eagerly anticipate his coming denies the words of the other Prophets and of the Torah and Moses our teacher. This requires some clarification.

THE ULTIMATE GOAL

First of all, we have explained all along that Maimonides did not intend his principles to be understood as thirteen individual tenets of Jewish belief, some of which are about God, others of which are about Torah, prophecy, reward and punishment, and so on. Rather, all the principles are essentially about God Himself, His relationship to the world, to the Jewish people, and to His purpose in creating the world. That is to say, the thirteen principles are not about the Torah or about the Prophets, about reward and punishment, or about *Mashiach* per se but about the way God reveals Himself in the Torah, the way He reveals Himself through the Prophets, through the advent of *Mashiach* and through the resurrection of the dead. Each successive principle builds upon the previous one and adds a new dimension to our understanding of God's essential existence, His Oneness, and so on.

Accordingly, *Chasidus* understands that when Maimonides discusses the twelfth principle, he does not discuss *Mashiach* merely as a great human being, a statesman and scholar descended from King David, who will lead the Jewish people to independence from the world's nations, to freedom, peace, and prosperity. Rather, he discusses *Mashiach* in the context of a further revelation (in fact, the ultimate revelation) of God in the world.

We explained previously, chiefly in our discussion of the first principle, that God had a specific purpose in creating the world—that it must become (primarily through the efforts of the Jewish people) a place where godliness is totally revealed. This is the ultimate goal of creation: that God should dwell in this world in a fully revealed way, by virtue of the world preparing and refining itself for such a revelation.

However, until *Mashiach* comes, this purpose is not fully realized.³ This is comparable to a building that is under construction for thousands of years, but the owner still didn't move in. With the advent of *Mashiach*, the time when God finally "moves in to His home" will arrive. This means that the physical world will achieve its spiritual peak.

At present, we tend to view the Torah as a means to an end, a very noble end—how to serve God—but nevertheless a means to an end rather than an end in itself. In this sense, we view the Torah as having been given for our sake so that we can become righteous, holy, and God-fearing, or for the sake of the world's purification and ultimate perfection. When *Mashiach* comes, however, we will see how the world was created for the sake of Torah.⁴ It will be obvious then that the world is for God. This is why Maimonides insists that one who doesn't believe in *Mashiach* is missing a fundamental foundation of the whole religion—because he misunderstands the entire purpose of creation, of the giving of the Torah, and of the descent of man's soul into this world!⁵

The advent of *Mashiach* will bring many things. There will be peace. We will be filled with knowledge of God. There will not be any wars. However, all the different predictions of what the world will be like when *Mashiach* comes are merely a result of what *Mashiach* represents: the revelation of the ultimate purpose of the world's creation, of the giving of the Torah, and of the descent of the soul into this world. And so, if a person doesn't have this in mind, then he is lacking something—awareness of the purpose of his (and the world's) creation and what his task and function ought to be in this world.

Similarly, Maimonides maintains that if a person doesn't wait for *Mashiach*'s coming and hope for his coming, he is again lacking in this fundamental belief. Even if a person knows intellectually that the world was created in order to become a dwelling for God but does not long to achieve this and strive to realize this goal, then he is missing the entire purpose of his being in the world. He is, in a sense, like a body without a soul; since the purpose of the descent of the soul into this world is to reveal godliness in the world, if this is **not** what he has in mind constantly, he cannot be fulfilling his purpose. Accordingly, it is as if his soul were not even present!

Moreover, if a person's intention is to fulfill the purpose for which God created the world, that is, he wants *Mashiach* to come sooner, then he will work harder and with more enthusiasm, because he knows that his observance of Torah and the *mitzvahs* will hasten the advent of *Mashiach*.

The fifth Lubavitcher Rebbe, the saintly Rabbi Sholom Dovber, once remarked that the difference between Maimonides and Aristotle was that Maimonides first laid down the center point and then he drew the circumference around it, whereas Aristotle first drew a circle and then tried to find the center. The coming of *Mashiach* ought to be the focal point of our lives in this world. This is not merely a detail that will be fulfilled sooner or later, and meanwhile we can continue living without it. The advent of *Mashiach* is the ultimate purpose of our lives and of all creation.

This should not be misunderstood to imply some kind of hero worship. According to the Torah, a Jewish king was not an object of worship but a role model, a person who was totally dedicated to God.[6] A Jewish king such as Moses or King David was the epitome of humility and self-effacement. They saw their roles as the servants of God, and their greatness was a product of their humility; the greatness of a holy person is that he is totally subservient to God and has no ego. He sees his role as actualizing God's will on earth. The same is true of

Mashiach. Although he will be a very great king, the greatest king of all time, nevertheless, he shall meditate constantly on the Torah[7] and be preoccupied with *mitzvahs*. He shall teach the entire Jewish people and instruct them in the ways of God. Moreover, he will prevail upon the Jewish people to follow and observe the entire Torah.[8]

Thus, *Mashiach* is not only a human being who has reached the peak of human perfection as defined by the Torah but he also represents the perfecting of the Jewish people. That is, *Mashiach* does not fulfill our duties by proxy, fulfilling our own religious obligations or acting as some kind of godly mascot. On the contrary, the Rambam writes that one of the identifying characteristics of *Mashiach* is that he succeeds in bringing the Jewish world and the world as a whole to the proper service of God.[9] In this sense, *Mashiach* also represents an age: the era of universal awareness, perception, and knowledge of God. In the Messianic Age, the world will finally become what it ought to be—a receptacle for the revelation of godliness through the Torah and its commandments.

CONCEALMENT AND REVELATION OF GODLINESS

Before we can fully understand this extraordinary vision of the future and what it means for us practically in our own daily lives, we must first understand some world history. *Chasidus* explains that the word for "world" in Hebrew is *olam*. *Olam* derives from the word *he'elem*, meaning concealment. In the process of creating the world, God concealed His infinite revelation so that a finite creation could come into being. For this reason, this world is referred to as the "world of untruth"—for deceit and darkness predominate to such an extent that not only are godliness and truth invisible, they are even concealed—the difference being that in the former case the truth is simply not seen, whereas in the latter case, the opposite of the truth is taken to be the truth.

There were, in fact, several stages of concealment, so that several planes of reality, or worlds, came into being. The greater the revelation of God, the loftier the world, and conversely, the greater the concealment of God, the lower the world. This physical world (i.e., the entire physical universe) exhibits the lowest degree of revelation and the highest degree of concealment. Nevertheless, the concealment is only a garment, a cover that can be removed, so that the Essence of godliness can be revealed. Everything that we are doing now until the coming of *Mashiach* is working to remove that cover, so that the godliness inherent, but hidden, in the world can be revealed. At the moment, the world appears to exist independently, and events appear to be random, without purpose or direction. In fact, as we pointed out earlier, the entire world is constantly being created every moment by God and is totally dependent on God's energy for its continued existence. The same is true of an event that takes place in the universe. So the coming of *Mashiach* means the concealment of godliness will be removed, and we will see the truth as it really is. Therefore, to believe in the coming of *Mashiach* means to believe that there will be an end to the concealment of godliness and that we will finally attain knowledge of the true existence of God. And this must be not only a belief but an ardent hope, for this is the purpose of our existence and of all creation.

There is a story told about Rabbi Levi Yitzchak of Berditchev, the famous defender of the Jewish people, who once complained to God, saying, "God, You put temptations in front of our eyes and spirituality in the books. Why don't You try the reverse? If You put all the temptations in books and Yourself in front of our eyes, no one will sin!" And this is exactly what we should be striving for: that what we learn in the books, in the holy books of the Torah that speak about the unity of God, should be finally felt and seen. This is the aim and ambition of a Jew throughout exile, to be uncomfortable with the falseness of the world and to strive for the truth. And the only way to get to that is through observance of Torah and *mitzvahs*.

ACHIEVING PERFECTION

There is another explanation of why the advent of *Mashiach* is fundamental in Judaism. We mentioned earlier that there are two levels of Torah and *mitzvahs*. There is the level of Torah and *mitzvahs* that makes the world a holy place, a place fit for the revelation of God. And then there is the level of Torah as it is the manifestation of God's Essence. God's Essence is what He put into Torah and *mitzvahs*, and just as God Himself is not a means to an end, but He simply *is*, so too His Torah and *mitzvahs* are not a means to an end but are an end in themselves. Throughout the time of exile and even in the era of the First and Second Temples, the *mitzvahs* were not done in the fullest, most complete way. (In addition, there are *mitzvahs* that have not been done at all, such as separating six refuge cities.) This is because in order to do a *mitzvah* perfectly, the person doing the *mitzvah* would also have to be perfect, so that his intentions and actions would do justice to the sanctity of the *mitzvah*, and there was never yet a period of time where we were on this level. The same is true of all the four levels of created beings in this world, inanimate things, plants, animals, and humans. None of these four ever existed in a state of perfection. And the same is true of Torah—to understand the

Torah on every level, not just on the simplest level, is presently beyond human capacity. Similarly, God was never revealed totally in the world, in such a way that all creatures would recognize Him. But since the Torah and *mitzvahs* were given to us, God surely intended that we fulfill them perfectly. Similarly, since God's intention was that the world should be made into a fitting place for the revelation of His Essence.[10] When *Mashiach* comes, this will be possible. Therefore, the belief in the advent of *Mashiach* is, in different words, the belief that God is perfect and Torah is perfect and His *mitzvahs* are perfect, and there will be a time that this perfection will actually be manifested.

Maimonides therefore explains that when *Mashiach* will come, he will not introduce new *mitzvahs* or discard any of the 613 *mitzvahs*. But what he will do is strengthen the same 613 *mitzvahs* and help all Jews to fulfill the 613 *mitzvahs* in the most perfect way. As we explained earlier, in our commentary to the ninth principle, the Torah can never be changed, for the Torah itself is the Essence of God and just as He does not change, the Torah does not change. That is why even *Mashiach* cannot add or subtract even one *mitzvah*. Therefore, even if someone who purports to be the Messiah performs a miracle but he deviates from the Torah, failing to fulfill the 613 *mitzvahs* as the Torah itself prescribes, then we know automatically that he is a false messiah.

THE SOUL OF *MASHIACH* (THE MESSIAH)

Chasidus explains[11] that the soul of every Jew comprises five levels, each one higher than the other. The lowest level of the soul is called *nefesh*. This corresponds to the level of action.

Then there is a higher level called *ruach*, which is the source of the emotions: love, fear, compassion, and so on. The third level of the soul is called the *neshamah* and is manifested particularly in the area of intelligence, in understanding the greatness of God. After this comes the level called *chaya*. This level of soul is manifested in the willpower of the divine soul, that is, its will to fulfill Torah and *mitzvahs*. Finally, the fifth level of the soul is called *yechidah*, that level of the soul that is always united with God and is regarded as the essence of the soul.

Of these five levels of soul, only the first three are connected to the physical body. But the two most elevated levels of the soul are generally hidden to most people and produce their effects in a subconscious or subliminal way. It is possible for a person to live a morally proper life and be fully observant, following all the laws in the Torah, and yet never consciously experience the two higher levels of his soul. At times, however, in order to overcome a great test, a person may have to tap inner energies that transcend his intellectual and emotional faculties. In chasidic terminology, this is called connecting oneself to the higher parts of the soul. A classic example of this is a situation in which a person becomes a martyr. Although his intellect may not be able to explain why this is beneficial, and his emotions might find it very difficult to accept, so that he feels a paralyzing fear of death, or an overwhelming love of life, these are nevertheless subdued by the soul's willingness to martyr itself out of devotion to God and/or His Torah. This is a result of the functioning of the highest levels of soul. As such, a person's education, knowledge, talents, and abilities are irrelevant. The essence of his soul in its completeness and absolute devotion to God takes over and guides him through the steps that he must take. It is a manifestation of his superconscious.

The Talmud states that every day a voice calls out from heaven[12]—God is calling us to return to him. The Baal Shem Tov asks to whom God is talking. Obviously we don't hear it. And if we don't hear it, then what purpose does it serve? He answers that the soul above does hear it, and from time to time it signals down to the soul below. That is why we find that many times a person suddenly feels inspired without knowing what the source of his inspiration is. The answer is that it his soul above, his *chaya* or *yechidah*, that impinges on his consciousness and guides, directs, or informs him in hidden ways.

These five levels of the soul are not five separate souls that somehow communicate from time to time. Rather, they are five levels of the same soul, the essence of which is the level called *yechidah*. The essence of the soul, *yechidah*, remains pure and unsullied and is always together with God. Even when a person sins to the extent that his soul suffers excision and is "cut off" from its source, this applies only to the lower levels of the soul. But the essence can never become detached from God. It never left so it need not repent to go back. It is always one with God.

Just as the physical world came into being through a process of concealment, so too the soul descended into the physical body through various stages of concealment. As a result our regular everyday consciousness is out of touch with our own essence, our *yechidah*. This is true of most people throughout the period of exile. When *Mashiach* comes, however, the essence of the soul will be manifested in our ordinary everyday consciousness, and we will become totally aware of our intrinsic connection with God. This is also the explanation of a remark made by Rabbi Shneur Zalman of Liadi that when *Mashiach* comes, there will be no necessity for anyone to be informed of this by others. The *yechidah* of each person's soul will immediately impinge on his consciousness and every person will become aware that *Mashiach* has arrived.

Chasidic teachings explain that the reason for this is that the soul of *Mashiach* himself is on the level of *yechidah*,[13] and since a spark of *Mashiach* resides within every Jew,[14] the advent of *Mashiach* will reveal the yechidah inherent in every Jewish soul. Thus, when *Mashiach* comes, we are going to get to know ourselves as we really are, and we will live with the constant awareness of the essence of our own soul.

It is interesting to note that of the five types of divine inspiration (*Ruach HaKodesh*) listed and explained by the Arizal,[15] the revelation of the essence of a person's soul is one of the most elevated, far surpassing the revelation of Elijah the Prophet, who may reveal himself for special reasons to those who are worthy.

"SELF-REALIZATION"

This gives us a deeper understanding of the importance of *Mashiach* to every individual. Until the coming of *Mashiach* we have a very powerful, holy, pure part of us that we don't even know about. This situation is comparable to a person who is in a jail and cannot express his intellect, or his emotions, or his talents in art and music. There is nothing more distressing and frustrating than being unable to express one's talents and abilities. How filled with joy a person will be when finally released. He can be himself and express himself. The same is true on a spiritual level. Until the advent of *Mashiach* no human being ever has the opportunity to express his own self, his real self, to his fullest capacity. True, from time to time, once in a lifetime perhaps, one's *yechidah* may be revealed in overcoming an obstacle where self-sacrifice is demanded, but in most cases, most of the time, that part of a person remains hidden. When *Mashiach* comes, we will live on a completely different plane of awareness.

This is one of the explanations of how *Mashiach* will teach all the righteous men and women of all generations, including Abraham, Isaac, Jacob, and Moses. One may ask how one person will be able to teach so many people of so many different levels, from the ordinary man in the street to Abraham and Moses. Second, what will he teach Moses, Abraham, Isaac, and Jacob that they don't know already? The answer is that whatever the Patriarchs, and even Moses, learned was all in the way of intellectual grasp and understanding. However, *Mashiach* will not teach by way of the intellect but by way of direct experience or "seeing"—"and the glory of God will be revealed and all flesh will *see* . . ." (Isaiah 40:5, emphasis added).[16] This is how is he will teach so many people, at so many different levels, all at the same time. When one has to explain something, one cannot explain to everyone at the same time because every person is on a different level of understanding. But if something is shown, everyone can see it at the same time.

Until the coming of *Mashiach*, the essence of things is hidden, for the world is in a state of *he'elem*, as we explained earlier. We can nevertheless understand something about them, much as we can understand how electricity works from observing its effects, even though we cannot actually see a stream of electrons passing down the wire. Our understanding is limited to what we can deduce from the effects that we observe. The same is true of Torah. We can understand that the *mitzvahs* we fulfill are directly connected to He who commanded them and we can understand the concept of His unity and oneness, but we do not see this. *Mashiach* will teach us Torah in a way of seeing and experiencing firsthand so that we will see godliness: "The glory of God shall be revealed, and all flesh shall see together that the mouth of God has spoken" (Isaiah 40:5). Similarly, "The earth shall be full of knowledge of God as the waters cover the seabed" (Isaiah 11:9); "They shall no longer teach one another, and a man his brother, saying, 'Know God,' for they shall all know Me—from the least of them to the greatest of them" (Jeremiah 31:33).

Accordingly, when *Mashiach* comes, it not only means he comes in this world, the final stage of concealment in the process of creation, but that he is revealed in all worlds, all spiritual planes, for this was the purpose of their creation. The Essence of godliness will be revealed in the world. Moreover, the real nature of Torah and *mitzvahs* will be revealed so that everything achieved through the fulfillment of all of the Torah and *mitzvahs* accumulated throughout the generations will then become revealed.

We can now understand the importance of the principle of faith in the advent of *Mashiach* and the fervent hope that his arrival is imminent. The advent of *Mashiach* is not a subsidiary or marginal matter in Torah. It is the purpose of Torah and the purpose of creation, so that if a person does not place sufficient emphasis on this principle, he is lacking the essential point of his existence—that for which he was created and for which his soul descended into this world. Furthermore, he is lacking in his relationship toward God's creation, toward Torah and *mitzvahs*, and toward God Himself.

NOTES

1. *Habakkuk* 2:3.
2. *Code, Melachim*, 11:1.
3. *Sanhedrin*, 98b; *Tanya*, Rabbi Shneur Zalman of Liadi, chap. 36.
4. See Rashi's commentary to Genesis 1:1.
5. See *Tanya*, chap. 36.

6. See *Derech Mitzevotecha, Minui Melech* p. 108a ff.
7. See *Midrash Tehillim* 2:9, 110:4.
8. *Code, Teshuvah* 9:2; *Melachim* 11:4.
9. *Code Melachim*, ibid.
10. *Midrash Tanchuma, Nasso*, para. 16. See *Tanya*, chaps. 36, 37; Chasidic Discourses 5666, Discourse 1.
11. See *Bereishit Rabbah* 14:9; *Devarim Rabbah* 2:37, endorsed and explained by Rabbi Yitzchak Luria (the Arizal), in *Etz Chaim, Shaar* 42; *Shaar HaGilgulim*. See at length *Inyana Shel Toras HaChasidus*, chap. 5.
12. See *Berachot* 3a.
13. *Inyana Shel Toras HaChasidus*, chaps. 5, 6. See *Vayedaber Elokim* 5699 (second discourse), chap. 4. See also *Shaar HaGilgulim*.
14. *Me'or Einayim, Pinchas* by Rabbi Nachum of Tchernobyl in the name of the Baal Shem Tov.
15. *Shaarei Kedusha*, sec. 3.
16. See *Torat Chaim, Tetzaveh*, p. 482bff.; *Shaar HaEmunah*, chap. 25.

The Thirteenth Principle

I believe with complete faith that the dead will be brought back to life when God wills it to happen.

he thirteenth and last principle is the belief in the resurrection of the dead. That the dead will be resurrected is one of the foundations of Jewish belief handed down by Moses. It is fundamental to the extent that one who does not believe in the resurrection of the dead is regarded as a heretic[1] and will be excluded from the resurrection when it takes place.[2] Moreover, the resurrection of the dead is meant literally and is not to be interpreted allegorically, as is stated explicitly in the Prophetic Writings (Daniel 12:12): "Many who sleep in the dust shall awaken, some to everlasting life, and some to shame and reproach."[3]

This subject requires clarification. Two major questions need to be answered: (1) Why is it so important to believe in the resurrection of the dead, to the extent that this is regarded as on of the fundamental principles of Judaism? (2) Why is it necessary for souls to descend once again from *Gan Eden* (Paradise) into a physical body in this world? The souls of the righteous, such as those of Moshe Rabbeinu (Moses), Abraham, Isaac, and Jacob, have been in *Gan Eden* for thousands of years. Nor have they been sitting there idly. Our Sages affirm[4] that "the righteous do not have any rest, neither in this world, nor in the World to Come [i.e., *Gan Eden*]" for they are in a constant state of ascent, level after level, day after day for thousands of years now. What benefit will they gain by descending once again into a physical body in this world?

A MATTER OF LIFE AND DEATH

Before we can answer these questions, we must first understand why there is death in the first place. From where does it originate? We find in the Torah[5] that because Adam and Eve ate from the Tree of Knowledge, one of their punishments was that they would die. Had they not eaten from the Tree of Knowledge, they (and we) would have lived forever. This would not have been a miracle, or something supernatural, but a natural phenomenon.[6] Thus, death is a direct result of the sin of the Tree of Knowledge. What is the connection between the two?

Based on the verses, "You, who cleave to God your Lord, are all alive today" (Deuteronomy 4:4); and, "For He is your life" (Deuteronomy 30:20), *Chasidus* explains that only when one is attached to God and godliness is one regarded as alive.[7] The source of all life, and in fact of all existence, is from God.[8] If God removed the life force with which He imbues creation, it would not be a dead creation, it would simply not be period,[9] as we explained in our commentary to the first principle. Accordingly, by sinning in the way that they did, Adam and Eve rejected their innate connection to God, the Source of all life and existence, and thus incurred their own death.

A similar idea applies regarding anything impure or evil, which is the opposite of life[10] and is explicitly referred to as death.[11] When Adam and Eve sinned by eating from the Tree of Knowledge, they incurred spiritual impurity, which leads naturally to physical death,[12] since they are essentially the same, except that spiritual death is becoming separated from the Source of life,[13] while physical death is becoming separated from the body's source of life, which is the soul.

This is one of the reasons why there will not be any death in the World to Come. Since all sin will have been rectified and purified, including the sin of the Tree of Knowledge, there will be no place for death, and life will therefore be eternal.[14] Not only will there be no death, there will be resurrection of the dead,[15] as we will explain.

Another explanation of why the sin of the Tree of Knowledge incurred death is that in eating from the Tree of Knowledge, Adam and Eve became impure. If Adam and Eve had lived forever, then impurity would also have remained forever. And for this reason alone death had to be introduced, for impurity is contrary to the whole purpose of creation.[16] In this sense, death is a process of purification.

A third explanation of why there had to be death as a result of the Tree of Knowledge is because Adam and Eve's bodies were affected by their sin and became mixed with good and evil. Knowledge, or *da'at* in Hebrew, means much more than simply knowing. It implies attachment and bonding to the point that the person and the idea become one. This is what happened when Adam and Eve ate from the Tree of Knowledge. Until that moment, evil was only a potential state, removed from the person. But when Adam and Eve ate from the Tree of Knowledge, evil became an integral part of their physical being. This evil or impurity had to be removed, and this was achieved through death. The body was recycled and cleansed of its admixture of evil, the impurity that they acquired through the sin of the Tree of Knowledge.

All punishments in the Torah are a means of rectifying and purifying and are not intended as revenge or retaliation, God forbid. All punishments are for our benefit, to cleanse us and to remove the stains that we have acquired (as we explained in our commentary to the eleventh principle). Similarly, death is not a punishment or retribution but a method of cleansing ourselves of the sin of the Tree of Knowledge. By way of an analogy, when you put clothes in a washing machine, the purpose is not to keep them in the washing machine but to wear and enjoy them. So too every punishment, including death, is intended to lead to the next step—resurrection of the dead. Through death the body becomes purified and ready for the incredible revelations that will take place at that time.

The body would have lived forever had it not been for Adam and Eve's sin. However, once the problem of sin is dealt with in the proper way, the body will revert to its original state of being. Just as the soul is eternal, the body too will be eternal, because it will become a perfect vessel for the revelation of godliness.[17] This, in fact, was the original plan; if the body had remained subservient to the soul, there would have been no reason for the body to die, and Adam would have lived forever.

THE PURPOSE OF CREATION

Nevertheless, it is only the physical body that was, and is, affected by sin. The soul itself remains pure and unsullied and does not require rectification.[18] Thus, the descent of the soul from *Gan Eden* (Paradise) into a physical body was not for its own sake. There too, the soul was aware of godliness. Rather, its descent was for the sake of elevating and purifying the physical body, and in fact, the entire physical world. This is what Adam was supposed to do in the first place.[19]

As we explained in our commentary to the first principle, our Sages inform us that the entire purpose of the creation of the world is that this world should become a dwelling place for God,[20] and all of the *mitzvahs* that we do are intended to bring this about.[21] This is why the Torah was given in this physical world[22] and why the *mitzvahs* are performed with physical objects, by a soul in a physical body. The soul descends and becomes imbued in a physical body in order to rectify the body and the world through Torah and *mitzvahs*, and reveal godliness in the world. Each *mitzvah* corresponds to a different part of the body and thus rectifies a different aspect of the body,[23] and correspondingly, a different aspect of creation.[24] The cumulative effect of all the Torah and *mitzvahs* of all the generations, past and present, has purified and elevated the world to unprecedented levels. (Since the very lowest levels are presently being rectified and elevated, the progress achieved so far is not readily visible.)[25]

We can now understand the importance of the resurrection of the dead and why it is so fundamental to Jewish belief. In the Messianic Era, the Jewish people will achieve the highest level of perfection of which man is capable, attaining the level of Adam prior to the sin of the Tree of Knowledge[26] (see our commentary to the previous principle). At this stage, the world will become a perfect medium for the Torah. However, this will take place only in the first stage of the Messianic Era. But, since the world in general will not yet have reached this level, therefore, in a sense, even the perfection of the Jewish people will not be complete. Consequently, all those who live during the Messianic Era will die prior to the resurrection of the dead and only be resurrected afterward.[27]

At a later stage, an even higher level will be reached, when the world will be connected to the Torah the way the Torah transcends the world. Torah itself existed before the world was created[28] and, being the will and wisdom of God,[29] is eternal, transcending time and space. Torah itself is not for the sake of the world. On the contrary, the world is for the sake of the Torah.[30] There is an aspect of Torah that refines the world,[31] and then there is Torah the way it is in itself. The ultimate goal, however, is that the world will not only be the way the Torah wants it to be, a perfect world, but the world will be a part of a reality that is connected to Torah as Torah transcends the world.

This will take place in the era of the resurrection, when the spirit of impurity (which includes death), will have been completely removed from the earth.[32] Then mankind as a whole will reach perfection, and the purpose of creation will be completely realized, and the Essence of God will be revealed.[33]

REWARD AND THE ULTIMATE PURPOSE

All of the above does not answer our second question, posed at the beginning of this section: Why is it necessary for the souls of the righteous, such as those of Moshe Rabbeinu (Moses), Abraham, Isaac, and Jacob, which have been in *Gan Eden* for thousands of years, to descend once again into a physical body in this world? This clearly seems to imply that this world is actually superior to the spiritual realm known as *Gan Eden*! How is it possible that a soul within a physical body in this physical world will be worthy of a level of divine revelation that by far supersedes that which is revealed to the soul devoid of a physical body?

This matter is, in fact, the basis of a disagreement between Maimonides and Nachmanides, which we have touched on previously, in our discussion of the eleventh principle. Both authorities ask where the final reward will be given: is resurrection of the dead the final period, the final reward? Or is there resurrection of the dead, but afterward there will be death again and the soul will leave the body and be given the final reward as a soul without a body? Maimonides argues that the ultimate reward is spiritual[34] and will be bestowed upon the soul without a body. After the resurrection of the dead, there will be a period when the soul will return to *Gan Eden* without the body, and there it will reside forever.[35] Nevertheless, the body is also given reward for its part in fulfilling the *mitzvahs*. According to this view, since the reward granted is a product of the type of service that the person did in this world, therefore the reward granted must also be of the same type. Hence, since the soul fulfilled Torah and *mitzvahs* while clothed in a physical body in this physical world, it must receive its reward in a like manner—in a physical body—and this is the purpose of the resurrection of the dead[36] and why the soul must descend once again into a physical body in this world.

Nachmanides, however, maintains[37] that the final and ultimate reward will be granted to the soul within the body, which will no longer experience death. This will take place during the era of the resurrection of the dead. Chasidic texts[38] endorse Nachmanides' view that the era of the resurrection of the dead will be the time when the final and ultimate reward will be granted.

The question of where the final reward will be granted is not just a question of priority, which comes first and which last. Rather, the argument is really which reward is the highest. Is the highest form of reward spiritual, given to a soul without a body (as Maimonides argues), or is the highest form of reward physical, granted to a soul in a body (as proposed by Nachmanides and endorsed by *Chasidus*)? At first glance, it seems that Maimonides' opinion is the more logical, because, after all, this world is finite, limited in time and space. For a soul to be confined to a physical world, stuck in a physical body forever, should be torture, not a reward. Therefore, Maimonides argues that the final reward is given to the soul without a body (i.e., in *Gan Eden*).

What, then, is the explanation of Nachmanides' view? Although the question as to why the soul descends once again into a body poses no difficulty for this view (for in this case we can also answer as above, that the reward given to the soul for fulfilling the *mitzvahs* in a physical body is granted to the soul in a physical body), nevertheless, it is difficult to understand why this is the ultimate reward and not a comedown and a setback for the soul—to have to leave its state of spiritual bliss in *Gan Eden* and descend once again into a physical body. Wouldn't the soul rather forego such reward and remain in its spiritual paradise? We must therefore conclude that according to Nachmanides and *Chasidus*, the benefits of this physical world must surpass those of the spiritual world, and for this reason the final and greatest reward is granted precisely in this world and not in the spiritual worlds.

Chasidus explains[39] that the physical body of a Jew is actually superior to the soul in a certain way. True, the body is apparently a lowly and even despicable entity when compared with the holiness and spirituality of the godly soul. Nevertheless, it has something that even the soul does not have. Therefore, for the soul to receive the level of revelation that will be attained during the era of the resurrection of the dead, it must descend into a physical body in this physical world.

The explanation of this idea can be understood by way of an analogy. When a river is allowed to flow without any obstruction, it flows tranquilly on without any great force.

When the water is dammed up and the flow of water is stopped, it appears, at first glance, that the river has dried up. However, when the weight of the dammed up water is so great that it bursts the dam walls, the water gushes forth with tremendous power, sweeping along everything in its path, including the dam walls. What appears to be a barrier and disturbance to the flow of the river is precisely what causes the water to flow immeasurably more powerfully than before.

The same is true as regards the soul. Through the descent of the soul into this world its power is increased immeasurably. The opposition, conflict and resistance, and the concealment of godliness that the soul must face and overcome in this world, awaken its latent powers and capacities. These are revealed and expressed precisely through its descent into this world.

THE EQUALITY OF SPIRITUAL AND PHYSICAL

The foregoing, however, merely explains what convinces the soul to descend to this world and be clothed in a physical body. It does not explain wherein lies the superiority of this physical world over the spiritual realms. In fact it emphasizes the deficiency of this world in that it conceals and even opposes godliness!

Moreover, the idea that this material world is superior to spiritual realms appears to contradict our common sense and our everyday experience regarding the spiritual and the material. We naturally regard the spiritual as infinitely superior to the material because the latter, by definition, is a tremendous limitation and concealment of godliness. And yet here we are informed that precisely in this material world, when souls are clothed in physical bodies, they are able to attain a revelation of godliness that is infinitely higher than the revelations attained by the disembodied soul in *Gan Eden*!

In fact, there are two parts to this question: (1) How is it possible at all to make a comparison between this material world and the spiritual world of *Gan Eden*? (2) Even if we can explain how it is possible for the loftiest levels of godliness to be revealed in this world, we must still explain why they are revealed precisely in this world, and not in *Gan Eden*. To put these questions slightly differently: (1) How can material existence reveal godliness? (2) And even if it can also reveal godliness, in what sense is it superior to spiritual existence?

In fact, these questions are not only relevant as regards the resurrection of the dead, they involve the entire concept of the descent of the soul into the physical body in this material world.

Chasidus explains that from one point of view, this physical world is indeed the lowest world that there could be.[40] In our commentary to the first principle we explained that there are various planes of reality, called the four worlds. Each world comes about through the progressive concealment of godliness. In this physical world, godliness is almost completely concealed. In this sense it is the lowest of all worlds.[41]

However, the differences between higher worlds and lower worlds are only as regards godliness that is revealed (or concealed) in the process of creation. What was revealed in the process of creation was only a reflection and radiance of God's Infinite Light.[42] In this sense, the higher spiritual worlds are appropriate "vessels" for a greater level of revelation than this material world, which is not an appropriate "vessel" for such revelation. However, as regards the Infinite Essence of God, there is no difference between the higher worlds and the lower worlds. To use an analogy,[43] it is obvious to all that the number 10 is larger than the number 1. Correspondingly, the number 100 is much larger than both 10 and 1. However, in relation to an infinite number, 1 and 10 and 100 are all equal, for an infinite number is infinitely bigger than 1 and infinitely bigger than 10 and equally infinitely bigger than 100! This is the definition of infinity. When limited numbers are compared with one another, there are degrees and differences between large numbers and small numbers. But any number, large or small, is equally incomparable to infinity. The same is true as regards the finite revelation of godliness that is revealed within creation. Here there are degrees and levels—one world is regarded as higher, and another, lower. However, as regards the infinite and uncontracted light of godliness, which completely transcends all of creation and which will be revealed during the era of the resurrection of the dead, there is absolutely **no** difference between this material world and the supernal spiritual worlds, for none of them are appropriate "vessels" for this light. From this point of view, the spiritual worlds have no superiority over the physical world; all are equally inappropriate for this essential revelation.

In other words, the way that a higher world surpasses a lower world in qualitative and quantitative terms is not comparable to the way in which the Holy One, blessed is He, surpasses even the highest worlds. It is incorrect to say that the Holy One, blessed is He, surpasses the very highest of all worlds in all qualitative and quantitative terms, since He is the epitome of perfection and completeness and is totally unlimited, whereas all the worlds are, in some way, limited and imperfect. According to this view, God is simply at the top of the pyramid, because He possesses all positive qualities to the greatest degree possible. This implies that God is quantifiable, or at least qualifiable, and if He is not, this is merely due to our human inability to comprehend His greatness and superiority over us!

In contrast, *Chasidus* explains that the entire pyramid of values, attributes, and qualities that we could possibly ascribe to God, even if we had the ability to do so in infinite measure, do not really apply to Him at all, since they are all created, limited terms. On the contrary, any quality or attribute that we posit constitutes a limitation of His Essence. Therefore, in comparison with His Essence, all things are equally "distant," and the spiritual has no advantage over the physical. All levels are equal.

THE SUPERIORITY OF THE MATERIAL WORLD

Although we have shown that in relation to the Essence of God, spiritual and physical are equal, we still have not answered the question why material existence is superior to spiritual existence in terms of revealing the infinite, the Essence of godliness?

Chasidus explains that precisely because this world is the lowest of all worlds, and the end point of all creation, it is superior to the highest of worlds.[44] Our Sages observed that "the beginning is wedged in the end,"[45] meaning that there is an intrinsic connection between the very highest of levels and the very lowest. Since this world is the very lowest of worlds, only this world, and not any of the higher worlds, is able to reveal the very highest of levels, that which is absolutely unlimited and infinite, the very Essence of God.

One of the explanations of this is that only God Himself could have created a physical world, for it could never have come about by a gradual process of contraction and descent.[46]

A contraction and reduction of spirituality would merely produce something less spiritual but never something physical. *Chasidus* explains that only God Himself has the power and ability to create *ex nihilo*,[47] and this supernal godly energy is imbued specifically within this material world. At present this aspect is concealed, but in the future, in the World to Come, that is, in the era of the resurrection of the dead, it will be revealed.[48]

It is because this world and all the creatures in it were created by God alone that the creatures of this world feel themselves to be independent, self-sufficient entities who are even able to declare, "I made myself!"[49] On every other plane of existence (i.e., in all the spiritual worlds) there is an awareness that the existence of that world, and all the creatures on that plane of existence, come from a higher source, that there is a Creator. The creatures of our world, by contrast, are not only *not* aware that they are constantly being created by God, they feel just the opposite! *Chasidus* explains[50] that God's existence being of His Essence and His total independence of any other creature or existence (as we explained in our commentary to the first principle) is manifested in this physical world more than any other world and any other level.[51]

By way of analogy, Scripture declares that King Solomon was so wise that he was able to give 3,000 parables for every concept.[52] Why does this describe his wisdom even more than the fact that he could understand the language of birds and animals? The 3,000 parables are not to be understood as simply 3,000 ways of explaining the same thing, using different analogies and terminology. Rather, with any concept, King Solomon was able to discern 3,000 levels, one lower than the other, and was able to find the appropriate analogies and terms to communicate the idea on 3,000 different levels of understanding. This means that King Solomon was 3,000 levels greater than the average person, and yet someone 3,000 levels lower than him could also understand King Solomon's wisdom. The greatness of his wisdom was that he was able to bring it down 3,000 levels. In a similar sense, the greatness of God is nowhere more evident than in the very lowest of levels. Thus, on the verse "Great is God in the city of our Lord,"[53] the *Zohar*[54] comments that the greatness of God is manifested specifically in "the city of our Lord"—referring to this world of limitation and multiplicity.[55]

Furthermore, the final and ultimate purpose of creation is revealed specifically in this world.[56] This can be understood by way of another analogy. When a person builds a home he makes a plan of exactly what he wants the building to have, what kind of windows, what kind of fixtures, and so on. Each step along the way—laying the foundation, putting up the walls and roof, etc.—although virtually important to the final product, is only a step and does not constitute the final purpose. Each room in the house and each fixture has its function and importance, but all of them are only a means to an end. Although the construction of the foundations, the walls, and the roof are far more important than painting and decorating the house and furnishing it, nevertheless, the job is regarded as complete only when the house needs no further work. Only then is the person's original intention in building the house in the first place finally achieved. In the same way, although this world is the last and the final world God created (and is therefore the lowest in terms of revelation), it is nevertheless the completion and consummation of the entire building process, the icing on the cake, so to speak. This physical world is therefore the culmination of the purpose of the entire creation.[57]

BODY AND SOUL

We explained above that prior to the soul's descent into this world, it resided in the spiritual realms referred to as *Gan Eden*. There it was filled with love and awe for God, and in the absence of any evil inclination, it naturally cleaved to God, and delighted in the spiritual radiance of the Divine Presence.

It is therefore self-understood that the descent of the soul into a physical body in this world is a tremendous downfall and even degradation for the soul. Accordingly, we asked, what is the purpose of this descent with all the difficulties and suffering it will surely experience? We answered that this descent is for the purpose of an even greater ascent afterward, which comes about by virtue of its association with the physical body in this world, after fulfilling the purpose for which it descended —to rectify this material world and the physical body by making a "dwelling place" for God in the world through Torah and *mitzvahs* and revealing the godliness hidden within materiality.

The reward for this service will be given to the body in the era of the resurrection of the dead. Regarding the World to Come, a verse in Isaiah (11:9) states, ". . . the earth shall be full of the knowledge of God as the waters cover the sea." Chasidic texts[58] explain that this is meant to be understood literally; this physical earth, and all its inhabitants, the very lowest levels of creation, will become purified and refined and elevated to the extent that they will achieve the very highest of levels of knowledge of God. Not only will this knowledge of God equal the knowledge of God attained at the highest of spiritual levels, it will even surpass it, for there will be an awareness of the Essence of God, which is the source of physical being, and not merely an awareness of spiritual levels, however elevated they may be, which is the source of spiritual being, as explained above.

Then the body will no longer need to receive its sustenance from the food that it consumes. It will receive its life force and energy directly from the Essence, whence it was created, and its Source will no longer be concealed, as it is at present. This is the meaning of our Sages' declaration that there will be no eating or drinking in the World to Come,[59] for the body will not require recourse to food and drink to stay alive. It will be nourished directly from Above.

Moreover, in the era of the resurrection of the dead, the body will be even greater than the soul, and instead of the soul conferring spirituality on the body, the body will confer spirituality on the soul![60] This is also understood from several verses that refer to the revelation of godliness that will take place in the World to Come: Isaiah (40:5) states, "The glory of God shall be revealed, and all flesh shall see together that the mouth of God has spoken." Similarly, a verse in Joel (3:1) states, "I shall pour out My spirit upon all flesh. . . ." Chasidic texts[61] explain that when these levels of divinity will be revealed, the "vessel" that will be able to receive these revelations will be the physical body and not the soul, since the source of the former is from the Essence of God, whereas the source of the soul is only associated with the radiance and reflection of godliness.

Accordingly, even those souls that have been in *Gan Eden* for thousands of years will once again descend into a physical body, in order to receive this revelation. This is why Nachmanides maintains that the ultimate reward will be given to the soul within the body, for the revelation will transcend the source of the soul itself.[62]

Chasidus explains that all of this is by virtue of the *mitzvahs*, which constitute the practical fulfillment of the Will of God. The *mitzvahs* are associated with physical objects in the physical world,[63] while the Torah remains abstract and spiritual, even though it applies to cases and situations in this world.[64]

One can ask how it is that God, Who is beyond time and space, should be totally concerned about the physical world and the dimensions of a *Sukkah*, for example, so that only if that *Sukkah* is made with the right dimensions does it fulfill the *mitzvah*, but if it is smaller than the minimum size, or higher than the maximum height, it is not a *mitzvah*. Similarly, only when one has consumed a minimum amount of *matzah* on Passover has one fulfilled the *mitzvah*. One would think that since a *mitzvah* comes from God, the main thing would be the spiritual aspect of the *mitzvah*, with the physical aspect either having no role or being of secondary importance. Yet we find that the exact opposite is true. If a person did the actions required, even if he didn't have the right intent, he has nevertheless fulfilled the *mitzvah*. But if a person has the most beautiful, most mystical thoughts but he doesn't actually do the *mitzvah* in a physical way, he has no *mitzvah* to his credit.

The answer is as mentioned above, that in the physical world lies even the ultimate purpose of creation and of the descent of the soul into this world. In other words, before the soul descended to this earth, when it resided in *Gan Eden*, it meditated upon God, attained understanding God, and felt the beauty of God. Here in this world, however, through observance of the *mitzvahs*, the soul becomes one with God's Essence.

THE ULTIMATE REWARD

In our commentary to the eleventh principle, we explained that *mitzvah* comes from the word *tzavtah*, meaning attachment or bonding.[65] The greatest reward of the *mitzvah* is the connection to the Essence of God. Although this will only be revealed in the World to Come, the actual connection takes place now, in this physical world,[66] as our Sages interpret the verse "Do them today" (Deuteronomy 7:11)—today, in this world, but not tomorrow;[67] "and receive their reward tomorrow"—in the World to Come.[68]

This is also why everyone has a share in the World to Come, as the *Mishnah*[69] states explicitly: "All Israel have a share in the World to Come." As regards *Gan Eden*, there are restrictions and limitations as to who can enter and what level they achieve,[70] since *Gan Eden* is the reward given primarily for learning Torah.[71] Since this is chiefly a spiritual activity, the reward is given to the soul without a body. As regards the reward in the World to Come, which is the reward given primarily for the fulfillment of *mitzvahs*, as explained above, even a person who was wicked for his entire life has hope and will eventually be purified and rise up to cleave to his Source, God Himself,[72] since "all Jews, even deliberate sinners, are filled with *mitzvahs* like a pomegranate."[73]

BEYOND THE TORAH?

Regarding the relationship of the Jewish people to the Torah, our Sages state that a Jew is even more elevated than the Torah itself.[74] *Chasidus* explains[75] that after the reward for the fulfillment of Torah and *mitzvahs* has been given, and the godliness that was drawn down by their fulfillment has been revealed in this physical world, there will be an even further stage, when the Jewish people will ascend to an even higher level, transcending that which was elicited by the fulfillment of Torah and *mitzvahs*. We could say that this is the revelation of the inherent superiority of the Jewish people over the Torah! In fact, we may even say that this is the primary aspect of the World to Come, for the revelations elicited by the *mitzvahs* will be manifested in the Messianic Era as well. The unique revelation that will take place in the World to Come, the world of resurrection, is the revelation of the intrinsic connection between the Jewish people and the Essence of God.[76]

CONCLUSION

Perhaps the reason that Maimonides' final principle is about the resurrection of the dead is in accordance with the maxim that "the beginning is wedged in the end, and the end in the beginning."[77] Right in the beginning we explained that belief in God comes from God himself, that God Himself is revealed to the soul. We conclude with the idea that the relationship of God to the Jewish person as a whole, comprising both soul and body, will ultimately be revealed in the era of the resurrection of the dead. Thus we see that the Essence of God is connected in every way to the life of a Jew in this world. As explained by *Chasidus*, the final principle emphasizes that this intrinsic connection is everlasting and will ultimately be revealed forever. In this sense, there is no end. The final principle thus explains how there is no end.

NOTES

1. Maimonides' commentary to *Mishnah Sanhedrin* 11, thirteenth principle.
2. *Mishnah Sanhedrin* 10:1. (This *mishnah* appears in the tenth chapter of the *Mishnah* and the Jerusalem Talmud, but in the eleventh chapter of the Babylonian Talmud; Maimonides' *Code*, *Teshuvah* 3:6.

3. Maimonides' *Essay on Techiyat HaMeitim*.
4. *Pesikta Zuta* 7.
5. Genesis 3:19.
6. The reason for this is explained in *Or HaChaim*'s commentary on the verse.
7. *Tanya*, chap. 17; *Likkutei Torah, Va'etchanan* 11b; *Kuntreis HaHitpaalut*, chap. 1. See also *Berachot* 18b; *Midrash Bereishit* 39:7.
8. *Tanya*, chap. 48.
9. *Shaar HaYichud v'HaEmunah*, chap. 1.
10. As clearly understood from the verse in Deuteronomy 30:15: ". . . I have placed before you life and good, and death and evil."
11. Ibid. See also Rashi's commentary, ad loc.
12. See *Or HaChaim*'s commentary, Genesis 3:19.
13. Isaiah 59:2.
14. See *Bereishit Rabbah* 12:6; at length in *Avodat Hakodesh*, pt. 2, chap. 38. See *Igrot Kodesh* of the Lubavitcher Rebbe, vol. 2, p. 65 ff; the Lubavitcher Rebbe's *Teshuvot u'Biurim* (Kehot, 5734) p. 47 ff.
15. See *Sanhedrin* 92b; *Zohar*, vol. 1, p. 114a.
16. *Tanya*, chap. 37.
17. Ibid.
18. Ibid., chaps. 24, 37, 38.
19. *Pirkei d'R. Elazar* 11:1
20. *Midrash Tanchuma, Nasso* 16; quoted and explained in *Tanya*, chap. 36.
21. Ibid.
22. See *Shabbat* 88b ff.
23. *Tanya*, chap. 37. See also *Sefer HaChareidim* for some of the practical implications of this idea.
24. As is understood from the midrashic statement (*Kohelet Rabbah* 3:16) that "the world too, he placed in (man's) heart," meaning that man is a microcosm and affects the macrocosm.
25. *Igrot Kodesh* of the Lubavitcher Rebbe, vol. 2, p. 68.
26. See *Bereishit Rabbah* 12:6; *Avodat HaKodesh*, pt. 2, chap. 38.
27. *Igrot Kodesh* of the Lubavitcher Rebbe, vol. 2, p. 69.
28. *Tanna d'Vai Eliyahu*, chap. 12; *Midrash Tehillim* 90:12.
29. See *Tanya*, chap. 5.
30. Rashi Genesis 1:1.
31. See *Bereishit Rabbah* 44:1.

The Thirteenth Principle

32. See Zechariah 13:2.
33. *Igrot Kodesh* of the Lubavitcher Rebbe, vol. 2, p. 71. See also *Tanya*, chap. 37.
34. *Code, Teshuvah* 8:2; see also ibid., 9:1; beginning of "Preface to Chapter *Chelek*."
35. See *Sefer HaIkkarim* 4:31.
36. See *Sanhedrin* 91a–b, regarding punishment of the soul and body together. The same rule applies as regards reward.
37. *Shaar Hagemul*, end. See also Raavad's comments to Rambam's *Code, Teshuvah*, 8:2.
38. See *Likkutei Torah, Tzav*, 15c; *Shir HaShirim* 65d; *Derech Mitzvotecha, Tzitzit*.
39. *Igrot Kodesh* of the Lubavitcher Rebbe, vol. 2, p. 65 ff; the Lubavitcher Rebbe's *Teshuvot u'Biurim* (Kehot, 5734) p. 47 ff.
40. This matter is dealt with at length in several places, among them the Tzemach Tzedek's *Derech Mitzevotecha, Mitzvat Tsitzit*. See also the references given in the footnotes following.
41. See *Tanya*, chap. 36.
42. Ibid., chap. 20.
43. See ibid., chap. 48.
44. See ibid., chaps. 36, 37.
45. *Sefer Yetzirah* 1:7.
46. *Tanya, Iggeret HaKodesh*, chap. 20.
47. Ibid.
48. *Tanya*, chap. 37.
49. Ezekiel 29:3.
50. Rabbi Dovber of Lubavitch in *Biurei HaZohar, Beshallach*, 43c.
51. See *Tanya*, chap. 36; *Iggeret HaKodesh*, chap. 20.
52. 1 Kings 5:12
53. Psalm 48:1.
54. Vol. 3, 5a; *Zohar Chadash* 44a.
55. Explained at length in the discourses כבוד מלכותך and ולקחתם לכם of the year 5661.
56. *Tanya*, chap. 36.
57. Ibid.
58. Ibid.
59. *Berachot* 17b; *Kallah Rabbati*, chap. 2; *Zohar Chadash Yitro* 33b; *Tikkunei Zohar Tikkun* 8. Note that Maimonides (*Code, Teshuvah* 8:2)

concludes that therefore the World to Come is the world of disembodied souls.

60. See the series of discourses titled וככה 5637, chap. 91; *Maamarim Kuntreisim*, vol. 2, p. 413b.

61. Ibid.

62. וככה 5637, chap. 92.

63. See *Tanya*, chap. 35.

64. See *Torah Or, Yitro* 73b; the Tzemach Tzedek's *Derech Mitzevotecha* 15b; Discourse כי ישאלך 5679, chap. 2.

65. *Likkutei Torah, Bechukotai* 45c.

66. *Tanya*, chap. 37.

67. *Eruvin* 22a; *Avodah Zarah* 50a.

68. As explained in *Tanya*, chap. 17.

69. *Sanhedrin* 10:1 (or 11:1).

70. Discourse כי ישאלך בנך 5700, chap. 1; *Igrot Kodesh* of the Lubavitcher Rebbe, vol. 1, p. 141; *Teshuvot u'Biurim*, p. 28.

71. See *Torah Or, Yitro* 73b; the Tzemach Tzedek's *Derech Mitzevotecha* 15b; Discourse כי ישאלך 5679, chap. 2.

72. *Igrot Kodesh* and *Teshuvot u'Biurim*, ad loc. The rebbe explains this at length in several ways, citing numerous sources.

73. *Eruvin* 19a; *Chagiga* 27a. This explanation is given in *Maamarim Melukat*, vol. 3, p. 34.

74. *Tanna d'Vei Eliyahu*, chaps. 14, 31; *Bereishit Rabbah* 1:4.

75. *Maamarim Melukat*, vol. 3, p. 34 ff.

76. Ibid.; *Discourses 5666*, p. 507.

77. *Sefer Yetzirah* 1:7.

Index

Abarbanel, Don Yitzchak
  on belief in God, 27–28
  on immutability of Torah, 146
Adam and Eve, sin of, as cause of death, 216–218
Alter Rebbe. *See* Zalman, Rabbi Shneur
Animal soul, 7, 108–109
Anthropomorphism. *See* Third principle (God has no physical form)
Arizal. *See* Luria, Rabbi Yitzchak (Arizal)
Ark of the Covenant, 51
Ashkenazi, Rabbi Isaac Luria. *See* Luria, Rabbi Yitzchak (Arizal)
Attributes, system of
  Infinite Light and, 73–76
  knowledge of God and, 167–168
  prayer and, 99–100
  prophecy and, 124–125

Baal Shem Tov
  on creation, 30
  on Divine Providence, 157–161
  on Essence of God, 116, 164
  on oneness of God, 54, 55
  on trust in God, 20–21
Bechaya, Rabbeinu, on rewards in Torah, 193–194
Book of Deuteronomy, 141–142

Chochmah, highest attribute, 124–125, 127
Conversion
  of Jew, 136–137
  to Judaism, 163

Creation
- concealment of God and, 39, 205–207
- continuousness of, 29–34
- Divine Providence and, 158
- emanation theory, 48
- finite from the infinite, 47–50
- God as first and last and, 87–89
- God's foreknowledge and, 171
- immutability of God and, 86–87
- of man, 179
- oneness of God and, 55–58
- planes of reality and, 38–40
- purpose of, 40–43, 218–220, 227
  - *Mashiach* and, 202–203, 213
- role of man and, 42
- *Shabbat* and, 33–36
- ten utterances and, 38–39
- time and, 36–37, 80
- true existence and, 58–61
- *tzimtzum* doctrine, 38, 49–50, 84–85

Creation *ex nihilo*, 29, 32, 47–50, 227

Death, sin of Tree of Knowledge as cause of, 216–218
Divine Providence (tenth principle), 33, 157–174
- concealed providence, 165–166
- differences in definitions, 159
- God as Knower, views on, 166–168
- and Jewish people, 161–165
- levels of, 161–163
- and man's free choice, 168–174
- revealed and hidden providence, 159–160

Dovber, Rabbi (Maggid of Mezritch), 127, 204

Ego
- holiness and, 39, 118
- oneness of God and, 60–61
- planes of reality and, 38–39

Eighth principle (Torah as word of God), 131–143; *see also* Torah

Eleventh principle (system of rewards and punishments), 177–197; *see also* Rewards and punishments

Emanationism, 48

Essence of God
- expression in physical world, 186–188, 195–197, 224
- God's foreknowledge and, 168–169
- prayer to, 99–100
- received by prophets, 115–117

revealed to Moses, 122–124
soul's experience of, in era of resurrection of the dead, 188, 229, 232; *see also* Soul
Torah as, 134–135, 147–148
Eternity of God, 72, 79–89
concept of above and below, 83–85
God as first cause, 85–87
meaning of first and last, 87–89
time and space and, 80–83
tzimtzum and, 84–85
Evil/wickedness
as concealing godliness, 64–65
Divine Providence and, 160, 165
Existence of God
incomprehensibility of, 171–172
nature of, 27–29
proving, 10–14
Existence of world, human awareness of, 59–61, 187, 227
Ezra, Ibn, on Torah, 193

Faith
applying to daily life, 8–9
experience of soul and, 1–4, 5
as *mitzvah*, 10–14
reason and, 9–10

self-sacrifice and, 5–6
trust compared to, 18–21
Fifth principle (praying only to God), 93–110; *see also* Prayer
First cause, God as, 85–87
First principle (belief in existence of God), 27–43; *see also* Creation; Existence of God
Four-letter Name of God, 18
Fourth principle (eternity of God), 79–89; *see also* Eternity of God
Free choice, of man
and God's foreknowledge, 168–174
mitzvahs and, 172–173

Gan Eden
mitzvahs and, 183–184
rewards and, 183–186, 188–189
soul and, 184–186, 215–216, 220–222, 229–232
Gehinnom (hell), 189–192
Godly soul, 6–7, 108–110

Habakkuk, Prophet, 22
Halachah
compared to *mitzvah*, 149–150
determination of, 138–141
Holiness, defined, 39

Honoring parents, reasons for, 51–52

Idols, worshiping of, 62–63
Infinite Light *(Or Ein Sof)*
  concept of first and last and, 83–85
  God as Knower and, 166–168
  planes of reality and, 38, 41–42
  prayer and, 103
  system of attributes and, 73–76
  tzimtzum doctrine and, 49–50
Infinite system (transcendent revelation of God), 75–76
Intellect
  involvement with faith, 9–10, 12–14, 17, 23–24
  objectivity of, 23–24
  prophetic experience and, 115–117
Intermediate agency, theory of creation, 48

Jacob, 153–154
Jewish people
  conversion of, 136–137
  Divine Providence and, 161–165
  Moses as mediator between God and, 126–129
  as part of God, 163–166
  resurrection of the dead (era of World to Come) and, 232–233
  Torah and, 136–138
Judgments, type of *mitzvah*, 15

Knowledge of God. *See* Divine Providence (tenth principle)

Laws of nature, God not bound by, 51
Luria, Rabbi Yitzchak (Arizal), 117
  on creation, 40
  on divine inspiration, 211
  on dreaming, 34
  tzimtzum doctrine of, 38, 49–50, 84–85

Maggid of Mezritch (Rabbi Dovber), 127, 164, 204
Maharal of Prague, on God's knowledge, 166–167
Martyrs, and *yechidah* of soul, 209–210
Mashiach (Messiah); *see also* Messianic Era
  belief in coming of, 201–213
  purpose of creation and, 202–205, 213
  revelation of godliness and, 206, 211–213
  self-realization and, 211–213
  soul of, 208–211

Index

Meditation, versus prayer, 96–98

Messiah. *See Mashiach;* Messianic Era

Messianic Era, 203–205; *see also Mashiach*
  mitzvahs in, 150–151, 207–208, 213
  perfection of Jewish people in, 219

Mishnah, content and style of, 174

Mitzvah of belief, 10–14

Mitzvahs (commandments)
  categories of, 15
  compared to *halachahot,* 149–150
  equality of, 163, 181–182
  free choice and, 172–173
  Gan Eden and, 183–184
  immutability of, 152–154, 208
  kavvanah compared to performance of, 183–184, 231
  logic of, 15–17
  in Messianic Era, 150–151, 207–208, 213
  need for, and true existence, 58–60
  observing one at a time, 164
  performance of
    compared to *kavvanah* of, 183–184, 231
    compared to Torah study, 129
  prayer as, 104–105
  reason for 613, 104–105
  resurrection of the dead (era of the World to Come) and, 149–151, 183–184, 232
  role of, 4
  time and place limitations of, 54–55
  transgression of, types of punishment for, 183, 189–192
  types of rewards for, 179–186, 193–195

Moses
  chochmah level of prophecy of, 124–126, 127
  faith of, 14
  as mediator between God and Jewish people, 126–129
  prophetic experience of, 122–124
  as superior prophet (seventh principle), 121–129
  Torah and, 128–129, 132–135, 141–143

Nachmanides
  on belief in God, 27–28
  on final reward for soul, 185, 220–222
  on rewards in Torah, 193–194

Name of God, 18, 72, 83

Ninth principle (immutability of Torah), 145–154; *see also* Torah
Nissim, Rabbeinu, on rewards in Torah, 194

Oneness of God
   Baal Shem Tov on, 55
   being and nothingness and, 54–58
   classical view, 50–52
   creation and, 47–50, 55–58
   existence of world and, 58–61
   human ego and, 61–62
   infinite and finite duality of, 52–55
   self-sacrifice and, 62–64

Pain/suffering, reasons for, 19, 191–192
Physical world; *see also* Creation
   concealment of God in, 205–207, 223
   Essence of God revealed in, 186–188, 195–197, 224
   lowliness of, 185–186, 224–226
   spiritual source for, 70–71
   superiority of, 223–228
   ultimate and final reward for soul in, 184–188, 215–216, 220–223, 229–232

Planes of reality, creation and, 38–40
Positive thinking, and trust in God, 20–21
Prayer
   as blessing God, 106–107
   as bonding to God, 100–101
   as commandment versus rabbinical ordinance, 104–105
   to God alone, 93, 98–100
   human needs and, 93–95
   praising of God, reasons for, 101–104
   as service of the heart, 95–96
   as substitute for sacrifices, 108–110
   in vain, 95
   verbally, 96–98
Precepts, type of *mitzvah*, 15
Principles of faith; *see also individual principles*
   connections among, 202
   reasoning behind order of, 125
Prophecy, levels of, 124–126
Prophets; *see also* Moses
   belief in words of (sixth principle), 113–118
      belief in God and, 113–115
   as Torah, 132
   compared to sages, 117
   false prophets, 151–152

as *meshugga*, 115
preconditions for prophecy, 117–118
prophetic experience of, 115–117
Punishments. *See* Rewards and punishments

Rashi, 135
  on *Gan Eden* and *Gehinnom*, 190–191
Rebbe, functions of, 8
Reincarnation, 192
Resurrection of the dead (era of World to Come)
  belief in, 215–233
  concealment removed in, 187–188
  Jewish people and, 232–233
  lack of death in, 217
  mitzvahs and, 149–151, 183–184, 188–189
  perfection of mankind in, 220
  Torah and, 149–150
  ultimate and final reward for soul in, 220–223, 229–232
Rewards and punishments, 177–197
  Gan Eden and, 183–186, 188–189
  man's place in universe and, 178–179
  physical (material) rewards, 192–195
  punishments in the Torah, 183, 189–192, 218
  reward for *mitzvahs*, 188–189
  reward for Torah study, 188–189
  rewards in the Torah, 192–195
  spiritual rewards, 192–195
  types of rewards, 179–184, 192–195
Rosh Hashanah, 107

Sacrifices, prayer as substitute for, 108–109
Sages
  compared to prophets, 117
  words of, as words of God, 132
Schneerson, Rabbi M. M., on *mitzvahs*, 106
Second principle (oneness of God), 47–65; *see also* Oneness of God
Self-sacrifice
  meaning of, 5–6
  oneness of God and, 62
Seventh principle (belief that Moses is chief prophet), 121–129; *see also* Moses
Shabbat, 16
  creation and, 33–36
Shelah (Shnei Luchot HaBrit)
  on reward and punishment, 179–180
  on Torah, 194–195

Sixth principle (belief in words of prophets), 113–118; *see also* Prophets
Solomon, 227–228
Soul
  animal soul, 7, 108–109
  descent of, and godliness, 1–4, 218–219, 229
  divine revelation and, 1–5
  five levels of, 209–211
  Gan Eden and, 184–186, 215–216, 220–222, 229–232
  godly soul, 6, 108–110
  of Jewish person, 2–4, 164–165
  of *Mashiach*, 208–211
  prayer and, 100–101
  purification of, 189–191
  reincarnation and, 192
  on *Shabbat*, 35
  Torah and, 133
  ultimate and final reward for, 184–188, 215–216, 220–223, 229–232
Speech of God, compared to man's speech, 55–56
Spiritual source, for physical world, 70–71
Study
  role of, in faith, 9, 14
  of Torah
    compared to performing *mitzvah*, 129
    compared to prayer, 101, 110
    reward for, 188–189
Suffering, as purification of soul, 191–192

Talmud
  on creation, 37
  on inconsistency in belief in God, 7–8
  as word of God, 131
Tefillin, 152–154
Ten Commandments; *see also Mitzvahs;* Torah
  equal to rest of Torah, 159
  first word of *(Anochy)*, 116
  giving of, 128, 133–134, 147
  Jewish people and, 136–137
  wording of, 137
Ten utterances, 38–39, 55, 136
Tenth principle (individual Divine Providence), 157–174; *see also* Divine Providence (tenth principle)
Testimonies, type of *mitzvah*, 15
Tetragrammaton, 17
Third principle (God has no physical form), 69–76
  human terms for God, reasons for, 69–72
  system of attributes and, 73–76
  time and change and, 72–74

Index

Thirteenth principle (belief in resurrection of the dead), 215–233; *see also* Resurrection of the dead (era of World to Come)
Time
  creation and, 36–37
  eternity of God and, 79–91
  mitzvahs bound to specific time, 54–55
  and space, 80–82
  in the spiritual worlds, 82–83
  Torah and, 132–133
Timeliness of God. *See* Eternity of God
Torah
  Book of Deuteronomy of, 141–142
  coming of *Mashiach* and, 207–208, 213
  on creation, 33–34, 80
  divergent views on, 138–141
  as Essence of God, 134–135, 147–148
  giving of, 132–135, 142–143, 147, 218
  halachah and, 138–141
  holiness of each letter, 159, 163
  human terms describing God in, 69–73
  immutability of (ninth principle), 145–154
    divergent views on, 145–148

Jewish people and, 136–138
  levels (revelations) of, 139–141
  as life force, 196–197
  Moses and, 121, 128–129, 132–135, 141–143
  punishments in, 183, 189–192, 218
  on rewards for *mitzvahs*, 192–195
  study of
    compared to performing *mitzvah*, 129
    compared to prayer, 101, 110
    reward for, 188–189
  timelessness of, 132–133
  translations of, 128
  as word of God, 131–143
Tree of Knowledge, sin of, as cause of death, 216–218
Trust
  compared to faith, 18–20, 21
  positive thinking and, 20–21
Twelfth principle (belief in coming of Messiah), 201–213; *see also Mashiach*; Messianic Era
Tzaddik, 118
  faith of, 22–23
Tzedek, Tzemach, on prayer, 105

Tzimtzum doctrine, 38, 49–50, 84–85
Tzitzit, 152–153

Unity of God. *See* Oneness of God

World to Come. *See* Resurrection of the dead (era of World to Come)

Yechidah of soul, 209–211
Yehudah the Prince, Rabbi, 174
Yitzchak, Rabbi Levi, 206–207

Zalman, Rabbi Shneur
   on attachment to God, 3, 4
   on creation, 30–31, 49, 56–58
   on God as Knower, 166
   on Infinite Light and *chochmah,* 127
   on oneness of God, 62
   on praying to God, 98
   on reward for *mitzvahs,* 189
   on soul, 110
Zohar
   on oneness of God, 52–53
   on reasons for creation, 40–42

ABOUT THE AUTHOR

Noson Gurary is an ordained rabbi and Jewish judge. He received his rabbinical ordination at the United Lubavitcher Yeshiva in Brooklyn, New York. He recently received his doctorate in Jewish philosophy from the Moscow Lomonosov University in Russia. Rabbi Gurary is currently the executive director of the *Chabad* Houses in upstate New York and has taught in the Judaic Studies Department at State University of New York, Buffalo, for the past twenty-four years. He has published numerous articles in rabbinical publications and has lectured on campuses all over the United States. Rabbi Gurary lives in Buffalo, New York, with his wife and seven children.